A SURGEON'S STORY

From a kid in a Cyprus Village to
Top Surgeon in New York

GEORGE C. CHRISTOUDIAS MD

To my parents

I dedicate this book to my parents Christos and
Maritsa Christoudias, who made me what I am, and my wife and
children for supporting me in this journey.

Christos C. Christoudias, 1907–1961, and
Maritsa Hadjiloukas–Christoudias, 1911–1976

I also dedicate this book to the many colleagues, nurses, surgical
technicians, and ancillary personnel of the hospitals for helping me
take care of my patients.

What is Cancer?

"Doctor, what is cancer? Where does cancer come from?"

I heard these questions countless times in my practice as a cancer surgeon.

The scientific answer is actually too complicated for people to understand. I thought about it long and hard and came up with a simple explanation of this difficult and complex subject, which helped me answer my patients' questions.

Think of the human body as a country. Then think of the trillions of cells of the human body as equivalent to the citizens of the country. Just like a country has laws, rules and regulations, which every citizen has to abide by and live with, the normal cells of the body obey the laws and follow the rules that control their function and their behavior.

At some point, some cells decide not to follow the laws, rules and regulations of the body and disregard their obligations to the rest of the normal cells, just as lawless criminals and rebels of a country may conspire to destroy its very existence. The cancer cells grow independently and at the expense of the rest of the law-abiding citizen-cells, and if they are left unchecked, they will spread to other areas leading to the demise of the person. If, on the other hand, the abnormal rebel cancerous cells, are identified at their very early stages, they can be neutralized and exterminated, and the body saved. The challenge for medical science is to identify the cluster of these abnormal cells at an early stage, when removal and/or destruction of these cells is possible.

What does "stage" mean and how is it determined?

Just like a revolution which starts at one point, then spreads locally, then to a wider area, then to a region and finally all over the country, the cancer cells start and are localized at a certain point only, what we call carcinoma In Situ, a stage at which the cancer can be eliminated and the patient cured.

Cancer then grows and accumulates locally in Stage 1, at which the cancer can be contained and eliminated.

It then expands by growing directly to the surrounding region, becoming Stage 2, at which complete eradication of the cancerous tumor and cure of the patient, is possible but diminished.

In Stage 3, the cancer spreads further away from the point of origin to the lymph nodes, which are the "check points" of the body. The lymph nodes identify the cancer cells as rebels and try to contain them. The more lymph nodes that contain cancer, the more likely it is that cancer cells have spread to more remote areas of the body, substantially decreasing the probability of a cure.

Stage 4 indicates that the cancer has spread in multiple areas of the body far away from the place where it first originated. This stage is associated with almost certain demise of the patient from the disease.

How cancer develops:

- Certain forms of cancer are caused by inherited genes, such as some breast and colon cancers.

- Continuous irritation, inflammation and infection over many years can cause cancerous tumors. Examples of this category are smoking and ulcerative colitis.

- Radiation and Electro Magnetic Fields (EMF) could cause cancers of the blood and lymphatic systems.

- Chemical substances such as pesticides.

Treatment Modalities For Cancer

- **Surgery**. Surgical excision of the cancerous tumors can result in cure in the early stages. In advanced stages surgery may be used to improve the quality of life and/or life expectancy.

- **Radiotherapy**. X-Ray treatment is used in certain radiosensitive tumors, either alone or in combination with surgery and / or chemotherapy.

- **Chemotherapy**. Chemotherapy is used either alone or in combination with surgery and/or radiotherapy, in the treatment of cancers that are sensitive to one or more chemotherapeutic agents.

- **Immunotherapy**. This modality uses ways and methods to stimulate the body's own defense mechanisms to fight the cancer cells.

Looking Back Instead Of Forward

This is just some very general information of the vast science of oncology. It is not meant to offer any scientific knowledge, but rather a very basic understanding of the disease.

I decided to look back at my life's journey after retiring from surgery at the age of 73. For the first time in my life, I did not have to look ahead and instead, I could look back and turn my attention to the past. All my experiences, good and bad, all the lessons I learned and my development from a little kid in a small Cyprus village to a successful surgeon in the New York-New Jersey Metropolitan area, appeared in my memory, ready to be explored and examined. Looking back, I know and recognize that my parents had the greatest impact on my development, my life and any achievements I accomplished.

My story starts at a beautiful, idyllic village of Cyprus, Karavas. It is located by the Mediterranean Sea and expands from the shore through the valley to the adjacent hills. It actually is the extension of a town, Lapithos, which was founded 3,000 years ago by one of the Trojan warriors, King Praxandros of Sparta.

This is where my roots began, and it all started from my parents.

Part 1: My Parents Maritsa and Christos

Maritsa Hadjiloukas Christoudias

Maritsa & Eleni Hadjiloucas

Maritsa Hadjiloukas Christoudias, was the youngest of seven children. She was born to Constantinos Hadjiloukas and Eleni Spanoudis Hadjiloukas on July 7, 1911 in Karavas, Cyprus and died December 16, 1976. She had four brothers, Stavros, Christodoulos, Loucas and John, and two sisters, Orthodoxia and Evgenia.

She grew up in a loving family, wealthy and possesing a lot of land. Her family members were farmers and also dealt with commerce. She was trained to pull her weight in the family and when she turned 10 and completed the fourth grade, she was pulled out of the elementary school. She was then assigned to a number of household chores. During those times, girls were supposed to learn how to be good housekeepers, since education was not considered to be of primary importance. Her own mother did not even go to school at all.

My mother was a devout Christian and played an important role in guiding each and every one of her children in religion, civic duties and the code of behavior that was deemed appropriate in the society. She taught us to respect each other's rights, know and demand whatever is ours and recognize and fulfill our responsibilities.

Christos Constantinou Christoudias

Growing up and going to America

Christos was the youngest of five children. He was born to Constantinos Christoudias and Maria Xenophontos on July 9, 1907 and died on April 28, 1961.

His father Constantinos worked as a carpenter and farmer and their family had limited resources. My father often spoke of the financial difficulties the family suffered at times when he was a child, and also about the mischief he got into.

My grandfather's twin sister Yallourou had an obsession with neatness and cleanliness. Every fall, she spent a lot of time sweeping the almond tree leaves that fell all over the yard around the house. Little Christos liked having some fun and used to climb the almond trees right after she swept everything clean. He would shake the tree, covering the yard with a lot more leaves. Yallourou would then start sweeping all over again, cursing the "wind" that covered the yard with more leaves. Christos would try not to laugh out loud and reveal his mischief.

Christos dropped out of school after finishing the fourth grade so he could work and help with the family's finances. At the age of 10, he would load his family's donkey with merchandise to sell around the island of Cyprus. He sold knives made by Lapithos craftsmen and pottery jugs full of carob molasses produced in Karavas and Lapithos. He sold olives and olive oil from his family farm, and almonds, walnuts and citrus fruit produced at the region of his base.

He did not get rich with his entrepreneurial activities, but he made enough to relieve his family's financial squeeze. Every sales trip took several days, so he would sleep outside on a canvas sack or blanket. The weather was (and still is) very mild, and it hardly ever rained in the summer, spring or autumn. He was a smart, kind and likable boy. Not only did he always sell out his entire stock of merchandise, but he made additional income, singing at weddings. If there was a wedding while he was on the road, he would show up and start singing traditional Cyprus and wedding songs, walking around to collect the tips.

He continued working as a wandering merchant, and at times as a carpenter apprentice, until he was 20 years old. By that time, he heard a lot about America as a country full of promise and unlimited opportunity. Many young men from Karavas and Lapithos had already left in search of a better life in the New World of America. Self-confident and ambitious, Christos, too, wanted that chance for prosperity and loved that his success would depend on his hard work and enterprising abilities.

He set sail for Ellis Island aboard the Andros SS, traveling through Port Said, Egypt, and Marseille, France. He arrived at Ellis Island in November 1929, and after the standard processing, he went ashore to look for a job. America was in the midst of the Great Depression, and he didn't speak English. Although the odds of finding work were against him, he eventually got a job washing dishes at a diner. He took his job very seriously, not bothered by the menial tasks. He strived to excel in everything he did and always aimed to be the best of the best.

He knew the language barrier was a handicap blocking his pathway to success, and he had to eliminate it in order to reach his goals. He went to night school and quickly learned to proficiently speak, read and write English. To save money, he cut his rental expenses in half by renting a room for 12 hours a day; the other 12 hours were sublet by someone else. I know that he mentioned many times that he worked and lived in Long Island City, and at times in Port Jefferson, Long Island, both in New York. The 1930 U.S. Census records indicate he was a roomer at 156 Main Street in Port Jefferson, Suffolk County, New York. The landlords, living at the same dwelling, were Albert Winter from Germany and his wife Mary from Ireland.

Christos Christoudias in Port Jefferson

Christos was determined to succeed and continued to work hard and save money. He did not spend much. He told a story about buying a jacket at a bargain price. He was happy about his purchase until it fell apart after he got caught in the rain. That taught him a valuable lesson: "you get what you pay for."

Saving money was an important goal for my father, but it never affected his love and passion for justice and humanity. One day the diner where he worked got robbed and as a result, people stopped coming in. Times were already hard because of the ongoing depression and the robbery caused a substantial drop in business. The owner called his employees together and explained that he couldn't afford to keep everyone and had to let one of them go, and chose an employee named Steve. Steve had a wife and small children; the job loss would bring hard times for his family.

Christos realized this and turned to the boss and said, "Sir, this man has a wife and children. He has a family to support while I am alone. He needs this job more than I do. Please keep him and I will go!" The owner of the diner was surprised to hear my father giving up his job for his coworker because "he needed it more."

But the owner accepted the suggestion and let my father walk away from his job. It did not take my father long to find another job. His hard work and a keen interest in whatever job he was doing, earned him a promotion to a short order cook.

Everyone in the entire country found themselves in hard economic times following the stock market crash of 1929. People who were wealthy one day, found themselves financially ruined the next. I was amazed to hear my father describe what was going on at the time. "There were people so desperate, that they were jumping out of the windows from high floors, killing themselves," he used to tell us. It appeared that the opportunities in his new country were suddenly lost or taken away by the circumstances, replaced by unemployment, misery and financial difficulties.

My father had worked hard for four years and had managed to save about $500, a small fortune at the time. The economic destruction of the country was the catalyst that caused my father's return to Cyprus in 1932. He left open the possibility of "someday" returning to the United States, but that "someday" never happened.

Return to Cyprus, Settling Down

He returned to his hometown of Lapithos and started looking for a bride, realizing it was time to settle down. As was customary in Cyprus at the time, he sent a matchmaker on his behalf to propose to a girl in the neighborhood he had always liked. The proposal was declined by the girl's father because he considered my father's family too poor. It was disheartening to my father, but he took it in stride.

George Hadjigregoriou (Karkaoutchis), my father's friend and my mother's first cousin, was sure he knew the right girl and decided he should be the matchmaker. He arranged for an acquaintance meeting and lunch with his beautiful cousin Maritsa Hadjilouca and the family. Of course, Christos had not even seen Maritsa, and he did not even know if he would be interested in making her his bride. They agreed that during lunch, my father would step on George's foot to indicate his interest in proceeding with the proposal and associated dowry negotiations.

George and Christos showed up at the home of Costas Hadjiloucas, AKA Yennadios. George made the introductions among Christos and Maritsa, and her parents Costas and Eleni. Maritsa's mother Eleni, AKA Yennadiena, was not impressed. Her four sons were tall and strong, and my father was short and skinny. Maritsa was even taller than Christos! Yennadiena likely wondered how he could possibly carry out the necessary heavy work needed by the man of the house. By the time the introductions were done Yennadiena had devised a way to test Christos's physical fitness and see if he was strong enough to be her daughter Maritsa's husband.

"Christo, come with me," she said, taking him to the back of the house to the orchard. "Can you chop this wood? Costas (her husband Yennadios) is too old to do it. Here is the ax!"

Christos took the ax and quickly chopped the wood, proving himself worthy. With the introductions completed and the physical fitness test fulfilled to his future mother-in-law's satisfaction, everyone sat around the table for lunch. Christos studied the girl and liked what he saw. Maritsa was beautiful, tall and presentable, perfectly fit to be the mother of his kids. Maritsa, however, wasn't thrilled by the freckles on Christos's face. She thought he was good looking, but those freckles! Otherwise she thought he seemed pleasant and smart.

Since Christos liked the girl, he stepped on George's foot, maybe a little too hard, to start the conversation of "closing the deal." George's reaction: "Christos, why are you stepping on my foot?" He was trying to embarrass my father, but he got the message and initiated the discussion.

"Christos likes Maritsa and wants your permission and blessing to marry her," he said to his uncle Costas (Yennadios) and aunt Eleni (Yennadiena). "He also wants to know what you are going to give for her dowry."

The parents consented, allowing Maritsa to marry Christos; the dowry would be their house.

Maritsa's parents' house was built in 1869 by her mother's father— her grandfather—Stavros Spanoudis, the date carved on the front door. The house was her mother's dowry when she got married to Yennadios, having been built by her own father when he married her mother. It was a big house with three bedrooms on the top floor and a large balcony overlooking the lemon and fruit orchard. They had a magnificent view of the village spreading down the hill, all the way to the ruins of the ancient port city of Lampousa and the Mediterranean Sea.

Aside from a dining room and storage room, the first floor had a central room with a front entrance and a rear door leading to the orchard. The backdoor opened to a covered patio with three arches serving as the boundaries to the fruit orchard. The ground floor's storage area was large and had a separate access from the patio, and was situated next to a huge, woodburning oven. Under the storage room was a stable that had access from the street, going up the hill along the side of the house and meeting the street in the front. This house was certainly "Archontiko," a rich man's house, and definitely much bigger than any of the houses Christos had lived in.

It was customary in Cyprus that brides get a dowry from their parents that could include money, land, a house, and other items of value that would help the new couple get a head start. The dowry depended on the financial strength of the parents. Maritsa was the last of the three daughters to get married, so her mother offered her own house and orchard as the dowry. The stipulation was that Costas and Eleni could also live there for the rest of their lives. Eleni also offered "six finger breaths" of village spring water for the orchard's irrigation. The written dowry contract, dated Oct. 29, 1932, was in my father's handwriting.

The Dowry Agreement

The translation of the text of the dowry contract is as follows:

Sales Contract

By the present document, I declare, the undersigned Eleni K. Hadjilouca, from the Village of Karavas, that today I gave to my daughter as dowry, Maria K. Hadjilouca, one house in Karavas village, consisting of three upstairs rooms, a store, 4 downstairs rooms, 3 prostathia (10,000 sq. ft) orchard, 6 finger breaths water on Sundays, and all the trees within the orchard, but she is obligated to leave one of the rooms downstairs under my command so I can live there, and after my death will become hers, borders are street on 3 sides and (the property of) Olympiada Papapetrou.

Therefor as of today I declare my daughter owner of the house and the orchard without interference and without any demand, I am obligated, at her request, to provide her with a title of said house. In the event that I want to cancel this contract, I am obligated to pay her (100. 0. 0) one hundred sterling pounds and (50. 0. 0) fifty sterling pounds punitive compensation.

Therefore for her security I gave her this document in her hands so she can use it where deemed necessary.

In Karavas 29. 10. 1932

Witnesses	*Signature of the former owner Georgios Themistocleous*
	Eleni K. Hadjilouca at her directions as illiterate.
	Signing and witnessing Georgios Hadjigregoriou.

My father composed the dowry contract on the day of his wedding, witnessed by Georgios Hadjigregoriou and Georgios Themistocleous. Eleni, my future grandmother, was illiterate. During the time she was growing up at the end of the 19th century, education for girls was not a consideration. Girls were expected to stay home and take care of the house, their husband and their children.

The contract stipulations are mostly easy to understand, but no one knows what "6 finger breaths of water on Sundays" means except for someone who lived in Karavas before the 1974 Turkish invasion.

The Lapithos/Karavas area was inhabited from the ancient times. It was founded by a Trojan war hero, King Praxandros of Sparta, after Troy's fall, about 1000 years BC. The lifeline of the area was provided by two springs, high up on the adjacent hills, which provided water for the whole region. The water was of substantial quantity and used for crop and tree irrigation as well as drinking. It was the most precious commodity of the region and it was treated and traded as such.

A neroforos (water-bearer) was assigned to oversee water distribution to the rightful owners. An elaborate system of water channels was in place, allowing water distribution to everybody's property. The way the time allotment was measured was by the shadow movement of a pole of a certain height, which was placed in a perpendicular position on a level surface. When the water flow was diverted to the owner's property the point of the end of the pole's shadow was marked. If the owner had four finger breaths of water, for example, the water was allowed to flow to his property until the shadow of the pole moved the distance of four finger breaths. At that time the water would be cut off and directed to the next owner's property. The dowry contract indicates the water assigned to the orchard mentioned was distributed every Sunday.

During the acquaintance meeting the discussions about the dowry led to an agreement. An engagement was then agreed and carried out, and the wedding was arranged for Oct. 29, 1932.

The Wedding

There were no invitations "mailed out" and no RSVP requested or received. Everybody was invited to the Oct. 29, 1932 event by the standard village method of walking to people's houses and extending a verbal invitation to the relatives and friends, and by word of mouth, for the rest of the village. Everybody was invited!

The celebration started with the preparation of the bride at her home and the groom at his.

The bride was attended by her friends and her mother. She was helped with the wedding gown and her hair. She wore high heeled shoes, which were custom made by the village shoemaker, her Uncle Pieris. She walked to Saint Irene's Church for the ceremony, the same place that her parents and grandparents got married and where she was Christened.

Walking to St. Irene's Church was a festive event with two musicians leading, one with a violin and another with a lute. The bride followed with her parents, maids of honor, friends, neighbors and relatives, all forming a big procession. They walked all the way up on the hill, about 10 minutes west from her house. Maritsa wasn't used to walking in high heels, but she endured for her Big Day, climbing up the hill to the church plateau with her entourage.

Meanwhile, preparation for Christos was also in the works. A violin was accompanied by traditional songs handed down through generations, and specifically composed for the groom's preparation. He was shaved, combed, dressed and ready for the church. He took the 10-minute walk east from his house, accompanied by his mother Maria, brothers, sisters, nephews, nieces and the other relatives, friends and neighbors. When he arrived at the church, the air was filled with the melody of the traditional violin and lute sounds of the approaching bridal procession.

The bride arrived and joined her groom. They entered the church and walked to the altar to begin the one-hour ceremony. As part of the ceremony, bible verses were read about the miracle of Jesus converting water to wine at a wedding celebration in Canaan. The priest preached about the relationship between the couple, something that stayed with Christos and Maritsa for the rest of their lives.

Constantinos and Eleni Hadjiloucas Family

"The man is the head of the family, like Jesus is the head of the Church. He will love the woman like Jesus loves the church," preached the priest. After the ceremony, the couple walked out of the church hand in hand, back to their house, with the violin and lute musicians leading the way. The entourage of the bride and groom joined together and followed the couple to their house given to them by Maritsa's mother, Eleni.

Christos and Maritsa 's Wedding Picture

The Wedding Entourage

It was traditional in the village to have a three-day celebration and everyone helped with preparation. There were hundreds of guests who were mainly relatives and members of the bride's and groom's families. Other than the feast that continued every night with the violin and lute music, the highlight of the first night's celebration was the "decoration of the bride." This tradition called for a dance by the bright during which the guests pinned money to the bride's wedding dress, as a gift to the new couple.

A New Life for a New Couple

After recovering from the joyous wedding celebration, planning began for the new family. Maritsa was in good hands as Christos knew where he wanted to take the family. She trusted him, though her family had their doubts. It appeared that they doubted his abilities and resolve to accomplish whatever he put his mind to.

Taking into consideration the available assets at his disposal, he decided to open a grocery store. He had the large store as part of Maritsa's dowry, as well as $500, a large sum of money for that time. He had experience selling and trading merchandise when he traveled around Cyprus as a child. Above all, he had the strong desire to succeed and the track record to prove it. He went to America penniless during the Great Depression, the worst possible time, and returned to Cyprus four years later with $500, a small fortune by his and anybody's standards.

He opened the store, using some of his money to build inventory. Although most of his time was spent taking care of the grocery store, he also looked after the orchard, which included about twenty lemon trees. He would sell the lemons and make enough money to contribute to the family's income. There were also fruit trees like orange, tangerine, plum, prune, fig trees, pomegranate, apricot, apple and pear trees and grape vines. He sold whatever fruit wasn't needed by his family. He also proceeded to buy an acre of land in the valley and planted more lemon trees, a move that showed long range planning and his ability to see an opportunity to secure future income for the family.

By October 1933 a year had passed, and the grocery store was operational. He planted small bitter orange trees on the newly acquired land, which were later grafted to hardy lemon trees. Transportation was secured in the form of a female donkey. Everything appeared to go according to plan but the gossip started that there may be something wrong with Christos because after a year of marriage there was no offspring yet!

Like every new couple, Christos and Maritsa were watched very closely, and everybody had something to say about everything, concerning the life and activities of the new couple. In the village of Karavas, anybody's business was everybody's business! This subject however was appropriately addressed, and the gossip died down seven months later with the birth of their first son on Wednesday, May 23, 1934 at 4 p.m., as Christos registered in the "children page" of his ledger.

It was a boy! According to custom, the first son is named after the paternal grandfather, Constantinos in this case. The fact that the maternal grandfather's name was also Constantinos should have made things easier, but it didn't matter. The baby was born in the house built in 1869 by Stavros Spanoudis, Eleni's father. Maritsa's mother Eleni decided the baby boy should be named Stavros to honor his great grandfather. And so it was. Little Stavros was Christened after his great grandfather a few months later.

Maritsa had four brothers, and all of them had immigrated to the United States. The older brother, Stavros, had a hotel in Nyack, Rockland County, New York. Christodoulos, the second son, trimmed his name, from Christodoulos Hadjiloucas, to Christ Loucas and had a shoe repair store in the Bronx. The third son, Loucas, was hit by a car and killed when he was 37 years old. The youngest of the brothers, John, also ran a shoe repair store in the Bronx, though he was really not a shoemaker. John would take in shoes that needed to be repaired and take them to his brother who did the repairing.

Uncle Christ told me a story about someone who brought him a totally worn-out pair of shoes for repair. He saw the terrible condition of the shoes, and told him that they could not be repaired, because there was too much work involved.

The guy left and took that pair of shoes to Uncle John. "Can you repair these shoes?" he asked. "Yes I can!" Uncle John replied and accepted the shoes. He then went to his brother, my Uncle Christ, and handed him the shoes. "I got you more business!" John boasted.

Uncle Christ looked at the worn-out pair, smiled and told John that he had just sent the guy with those shoes out of the store because the shoes were so worn out, it did not pay to have them repaired.

"Oh no!" Uncle John exclaimed. "You have to fix them, because I promised the guy, and I always keep my word!"

So, Uncle Christ spent a lot of time to repair them and gave them back to John. The customer came back a few days later, picked them up, paid, and headed straight to Uncle Christ's shoe repair store.

He got in the store, and showed the repaired shoes looking like new. "I don't think you are going to make it, because there is another shoe-maker, a few minutes from here, who does a great job. Look at these shoes, which you could not fix! You may do better at a different job, so start looking!"

Uncle Christ looked at him, smiled and replied, "I will give it serious consideration!" and continued his work.

The only one of my uncles who stayed permanently in America was Uncle Christ. Uncle John first, and then uncle Stavros, returned to their roots in Karavas, Cyprus, in 1935. Uncle Stavros saw the enterprise my father had founded and liked what he saw. There was the store, the arrangement with the textile merchants to have their yarn made into cloth by some village workers, and then the bakery, baking bread and other products in the huge wood oven behind the house. Uncle Stavros wanted to be a partner in my father's business, and my father needed the help, so he agreed to sell half the business to him.

A detailed inventory of the store was taken and recorded on Oct. 21, 1935, the day of the partnership agreement. The inventory was entered in Christos's ledger, and was accompanied with the value of each of the over 200 items, for a total value of 139 Cyprus pounds, 10 shillings and one-half piaster. At the time, the amount of 139 pounds was definitely enough to buy somebody a building lot in a prime area of Nicosia, the capital of Cyprus. One pound had 20 shillings and one shilling had nine piasters. The list included wheat, rice, barley, sugar, sesame seeds, candles, soap, brooms, buckets, shovels, yarn, textiles, lamps and accessories, coffee, tea, brushes, candy, carobs, pens and writing paper, just to mention a few. Stavros paid half that amount as per my father's notes and became a partner.

On a Monday, Nov. 25, 1935, their second child arrived, a girl. She was named Eleni, the maternal grandmother's name, as was customary. The paternal grandmother's name, Maria, could not be used anyway, because the mother of the baby, Maritsa = Maria, had the same name.

Eleni was a beautiful baby with long, slender fingers and made everybody happy. Things were going well. The grocery's business was good, keeping the family's finances steady. Then, tragedy struck suddenly. Eleni, just shy of three months old, was found dead in her crib on the morning of Feb. 18, 1936. Maritsa and Christos were heart broken, as were Maritsa's parents and Christos's mother. His father had already died in 1930 at a very advanced age while Christos was in America.

Sad and heartbroken though they were, life still had to go on. They managed to continue with the daily routine until they were blessed with a new arrival, on Thursday, Jan. 28, 1937 at 10 a.m. It was a baby girl.

They could have named her Eleni, but Maritsa's mother had her way again. Eleni wanted the baby named after her own mother, Irini, who died young, when Eleni was just nine years old. And so it was. Irini was baptized a few months later.

The third child, Constantinos (costas) was born Friday, Oct. 28, 1938 at 9 p.m. In the meantime, Stavros was growing up. From the age of two onward, Eleni and her husband Yennadios were using him to irk and aggravate each other. Yennadios would direct him to go play with Eleni's loom and have him mess up the threads! She would retaliate by sending him to play with Yennadios's garden tools. Yennadios was a character. He always liked to joke around and tease people, especially those close to him, just like his wife.

The Second World War

The 1930s saw some serious changes in Europe that caused a lot of concern. Germany came under an extremist group, the Nazis, that posed serious threat to their European neighbors and as it turned out, the whole wide world.

Dark clouds started showing up on the world horizon. Hitler, the Fuhrer, leader of Nazi Germany, was a racist and white supremacist whose desires and plans were to achieve world domination. On Sept. 3, 1939 Great Britain and France declared war on Germany, two days after the invasion of Poland by the Nazis. The Second World War had started in earnest. A pact between Germany, Italy and Japan was reached, called the axis, that looked to attack and subdue the entire world. On Oct. 28, 1940, Mussolini sent an ultimatum to the Greek dictator Ioannis Metaxas to surrender Greece to the Italian forces or be attacked by Italy.

Metaxas's answer was a resounding "OXI" (pronounced OHI), which means NO. The Italian forces immediately started marching from Albania, which was under Italian control, through the Greek border, in North western Greece. This invasion, however, did not end well for Mussolini and his forces. Not only did they fail to gain any ground, but the Greek forces pushed back and gained substantial ground in Albania. Eventually Hitler sent the Nazi forces to subdue the Greek army and occupy Greece in the Spring of 1941. All the Greek Islands also came under German occupation.

Cyprus was a British colony at the time (1878-1960) and did not come under attack or occupation by the axis. Preparations for defense were in place. Christos joined the "air defense" department but thankfully never saw action.

With the entire continent of Europe under occupation and the British Isles under continuous attack, European clothing mills and factories were out of commission. There was a great need to manufacture cloth for the Cyprus market since the European sources had dried up. My mother, Maritsa, had a loom, which she used for weaving clothes for the family needs. The loom came down to her through generations. She knew how to use it and produce cloth. Of course, you may say, one weaving machine would not make any difference, and you are right. But like my mother, there were many households in Karavas that had looms. So now we are talking about quite a lot of weaving machines in Karavas that could manufacture cloth.

There were several other villages in the area, within a few miles radius. They were small communities of a few hundred people each, located high up on the hills or down the valley by the sea. Collectively, there were many looms and experienced workers that could produce a substantial amount of cloth, enough to have an impact on the shortage. What was needed was somebody to organize and coordinate the distribution of the yarn, collection of the finished product and compensation of the weavers. Christos stepped in and filled the position of that" somebody."

He was already connected to the textile merchants of Nicosia, buying yarn from them, which he was selling in his store long before the war started. He already had the connections in place, so he organized the manufacturing enterprise, by expanding and doing what he was already practicing, but on a much bigger scale. The cloth merchants from Nicosia provided the weaving yarn in adequate quantities and delivered it to Christos's store in Karavas.

Once Christos got the yarn, he spread the word that he would provide it to women with weaving machines so they could produce cloth for a fee. The women would have somebody pick up the yarn from the store and deliver it to them and they then weaved it into cloth and returned it to the store. They were paid for their work and given a new lot of yarn for processing. Christos kept a detailed account of the transactions in his ledger. Once enough cloth was manufactured, the merchant from Nicosia would come to collect the finished product, pay for it and deliver a new lot of yarn for the manufacturing process to continue.

This enterprise was running like a well-oiled machine and proved very profitable for the family. Maritsa was involved in the business, helping out with the process. In the meantime, she also gave birth to two new additions to the family.

A girl was born on Wednesday, Jan. 29, 1941, at 4 a.m. She was named Anastasia, which means "resurrection" in Greek, to represent the hope for the resurrection of Greece and Europe, which were still under Nazi occupation. She was a totally blond, blue eyed girl, with a stunning similarity to Christos's aunt, the twin sister of his father. Now there was a balance in the family, two boys and two girls.

The next baby was born Jan. 15, 1943. Maritsa had gone to the spring to bring water for bread making as part of their bakery operation. She loaded the water containers on the family donkey and headed home, about 10 minutes away. As soon as she arrived, she unloaded the water containers from the donkey and told Christos to call the midwife because she was in labor. Christos rushed to fetch the midwife as Eleni, Maritsa's mother, placed a pot of water on the fire to sterilize the midwife's tools. Everything went very smoothly. The midwife arrived and the delivery went well, without any problems.

A healthy boy arrived that night and because it was late for Christos to go to the village registrar to report the birth, he did not do it until the next day, Jan. 16, 1943. That is why my official date of birth is Jan. 16, as that was the day I was registered. The entry in Christos's ledger states: Born, at 8:20 p.m., on Friday, Georgios Christoudias. Yes, that boy was me. They named me George, after the Protector of the Family, Saint George. The routine guessing game was again in play as mother was laboring, with my two brothers hoping for a boy and my two sisters for a girl. I tipped the scale towards the boys' side, three boys two girls.

After me, there was another pregnancy of twins which ended in miscarriage in 1944.

The family was growing, and everyone contributed to their abilities. Stavros, since the age of six, was tasked with transferring wheat to the mill for grinding into flour. Irene helped my mother with the house chores and taking care of the younger ones. Our house was always involved in some kind of useful, productive activity, and everybody able to contribute, did. That was the trademark of the family, as it was structured by Christos and Maritsa. There were a lot of activities keeping the family going: Cloth manufacturing enterprise, grocery store, bakery breadmaking, orchard care and farming. The family raised chicken for food and eggs, and goats for milk and meat. One of my first memories, at three years old, was the birth of three baby goats. The goat gave birth in the stable, on a cold, rainy day. I remember my father holding the newborn goats close to the fire to warm them up.

We had our own transportation: A female donkey, which was used as a passenger transport, with the kids sitting in the pouches of a double sac on the back of the donkey and the parents walking alongside.

Every day my mother would go to the spring, by St. Irene Church, to fill the jugs with water and bring them back to the house for drinking, baking and cooking. I remember being carried by my sister or brother to the spring and a lot of women there would ask me, "What are you going to be when you grow up? and I would answer, "a doctor." I must have been about two or three years old, and little did I know that I was destined to keep my promise, for reasons that I could have not imagined.

Rainwater for bathing and laundry was collected in large barrels placed under the spouts of the roof gutters. There was no plumbing or running water inside the house. The toilet was outside the house, a small structure with a thick flat stone with a hole in its center over a pit.

Life continued to be interesting all the time. WWII ended in 1945, and so did the need for cloth manufacturing. A new member of the family arrived on Sept. 7, 1945, tipping the scale heavily to the boys' side: four to two! His name was picked as "Loucas." As the family was on its way to the church for the Christening, they passed by the nearby house of my grandfather's first cousin, Hadjikostas Papapetrou. Maritsa's brother John, the godfather, carried the baby. Hadjikostas' wife saw them passing by and popped the question: "Oh! You are going to church to Christen John?" Uncle John, the godfather, liked the idea and when asked by the priest what the name of the baby would be, he did not hesitate: "John," he said, and so it was. My parent's sixth child was named John instead of Loucas.

Life was good for the family and Christos had proven himself to be worthy of respect, but Maritsa's family was not about to accept him as equal. Christos did not pay much attention to them. He had much more important problems and concerns to attend to.

He was successful and happy in the village, but he also realized that the opportunities for the education and achievements of his children would be better in the capital of Cyprus, Nicosia. He knew that his decision, whether to stay in Karavas or move to Nicosia, would affect the chances of success for his six children. He discussed it with his wife, Maritsa, before a final decision was made. He had to balance the future of the family, against the village's easy life, for a new direction for the children's future, with potential difficulties in a new environment, and a new place away from the comfort of his and her greater family and acquaintances.

They had six children ranging from one to 12 years old, and if there was a time for a bold move this would be it! Both Christos and Maritsa agreed that for the future of the children and the family, they should move. They had faith in their abilities, work ethic and Christos's entrepreneurial qualities. The decision to move to the capital was made, despite the objection and negative reception of the idea by Maritsa's family.

Planning for the Family's Move to Nicosia

Both Christos and Maritsa were aware of how important and serious the move to Nicosia was going to be. Serious planning was necessary, with strict adherence to a detailed plan and perfect execution of every detail. They wanted to avoid bad results and the possibility of total failure.

The plan called for building a house with an attached store, this way they had shelter and the opportunity to open a rent-free grocery store. An additional advantage of having the business at the same location as the residence of the family, was that, any and all the members of the family could lend a hand at the store when needed without having to travel to a different location. The cost of the construction of the building would be reduced to the bear minimum by using the expertise present in Christos' family. His brother in law, Achilleas Pantechis, and his son

Costas were masons. His sister's Polyxenis's son, Kyriacos, was a carpenter, and more men of his family could work as laborers. They would all be paid their regular fees, which would be less expensive than having a contractor build it. Christos served as both, contractor and laborer.

He drew the plans with the help of his group. The plans called for a three-bedroom home with a kitchen, living and dining room, a 12- by 16-foot basement with separate entrance, and a 20- by 30-foot store. The plan specifications were drawn out by an architect.

All they needed was a building lot in a good area at an affordable price. In 1946, Christos went to Nicosia and looked around. He asked the people he knew and was directed towards an up and coming area in west Nicosia, Ayios Andreas where a new elementary school was being built. He asked around and found a lot for sale for 150 pounds, approximately $450. The area and location were good and the price reasonable. He proceeded with the purchase as the building drawings and plans were drawn.

A letter from Mr. Kilaras confirmed that the plans were submitted for approval to the Nicosia Municipality on Nov. 10, 1946. A bid by a construction company, dated January 12, 1947, was for 850 pounds, including material and labor. If Christos provided the material, the labor would be 640 pounds. The amount appeared excessive to Christos, who then decided to undertake the project as his own contractor.

The construction started in January of 1947. The basement was built first to offer shelter for the workers so they wouldn't have to commute 16 miles back and forth every day, from Karavas to Nicosia. My oldest brother Stavros had enrolled in Terra Santa High School in Nicosia, so he also stayed in the basement with the workers, avoiding the daily long commute to Karavas.

After the basement was finished, construction began on the rest of the house and the store. The second, third and fourth children, Irene, Costas and Anastasia, were going to the elementary school in Karavas.

My father would come back from Nicosia to Karavas every weekend and spend time with the family from Saturday afternoon until Monday morning. I was the fifth child, and I was four years old when my father started taking me with him to the construction site, where I tried to find a way to be useful and participate in this new venture.

The workers would ask me to get them some water from the water jug and I was so excited to do that. I remember a time when three of them were on the scaffold building the wall and again asked me to get some water for them. I looked up and realized that I had to climb up the ladder to the scaffold and back down three times with the tin containers of water. I thought to myself: "There has to be a better way than going up and down." So, I took the jug and the empty tin container, and headed for the ladder. The workers saw me and had a good laugh, because the water jug was a little too heavy for me to take up the ladder. One of them came down, took the jug from me, despite my reservations, and took it to the scaffold to quench the thirst of all three of them.

I watched the workers with amazement as they prepared the mixture of lime and sand which they used as the "cement" to hold the stones together. This is what I remember very vividly: First they dug a rectangular pit in the ground, 6- by 6- by 1-foot deep. A supply of lime (CaO, calcium oxide) was placed on one side of the pit, and a mount of sand piled on the other side. Whenever they needed the "lime cement" mixture to build the structure, a worker placed a sufficient amount of limestone into the pit and poured water over it.

What I observed afterwards was something magic. The limestone started to "smoke" and opened up into a white substance that caused the surrounding water to start boiling. I remember that the workers would boil eggs in that boiling substance and I asked my father why the stone gets so hot and breaks up when you wet it. He told me that they bake the limestone in a specially constructed kiln for several days and that process makes it break down when it gets in contact with water. I remember seeing smoking kilns near my village that were baking the limestone, harvested from the mountain nearby. I would later learn in my high school chemistry class that it is an exothermic chemical reaction $CaO + H2O = Ca(OH)_2$. The white substance, which looked like very thick paste, was then allowed to cool down. They mixed that paste thoroughly in a metal basin with sand and water. The chemical reaction created a "lime cement" mixture used for building a sound stone or brick structure.

The work continued with three to four workers at a time, including my father and excluding me! I was not at the construction site all the time. Sometimes I was left behind in Karavas with the rest of the family, my mother and my grandmother.

I remember a time in the summer of 1947 when I was 4 years old. My father returned from Nicosia for the weekend and had promised he was going to take me with him when he went back to Nicosia Sunday afternoon. It was Sunday morning and I was craving an orange, so I wandered in the orchard behind the house. I looked up at the orange tree and saw an orange that was too high for me to reach. I looked around and found a palm tree branch that appeared suitable for knocking the orange down. I lifted the palm tree branch up and hit the orange very hard. Before I could even find out if the orange was knocked off the tree, I started crying and screaming. A long thorn of the palm tree branch had pierced through the palm of my left hand near my pinky.

The long thorn pierced through my flesh and still stayed attached to the branch. My father heard my cries and ran to me. He saw the thorn and used a pair of clippers to cut it from the branch and then took me, with the thorn in my hand, to the only doctor in Karavas, Dr. Psathas. This was the first time I saw a doctor and the first time a doctor saw me. Dr. Psathas cleaned and cut my skin down to the thorn and removed it. I don't remember how much I cried, and I don't know if I knocked the orange down or not. I remember that my father was trying to direct my attention outside, holding my hand firmly while the doctor worked. I also remember that he did not take me with him to Nicosia that time because of my injury, which hurt me more than the thorn.

The construction continued and all the workers, which were my relatives, were sleeping in the finished basement with my father and my eldest brother Stavros. One time when I was in Nicosia the whole group of the workers went to the old city, known as Ledra in the ancient times, to walk around and relax. While walking back to the house I tried to cross the street and was hit by a bicycle. I fell and hit my forehead on the pavement, right outside the hospital. My father walked me to the emergency room, about 100 feet from the accident. They bandaged my bump and sent me home. This was my second trip to a doctor.

The Family Moves to Nicosia

Our house and store were completed by the end of the school year, in June 1947. Our family's new custom-built castle was done, and we were ready to move in. The house had indoor plumbing with hot and cold water, a modern bathroom and kitchen, a living room, dining room and three bedrooms. One bedroom was for me and my three brothers, another for my two sisters and the third for my parents. My siblings of school age would start the new school year at the newly built elementary school in Ayios Andreas.

There was an issue, however, that had to be addressed. The family did not want my 76-year-old grandmother Eleni left behind alone. My parents asked her to come and leave with us, but she did not even want to hear it. I was chosen to stay in Karavas with my yiayia (grandmother in Greek) as her companion, and so it was. Just me and my yiayia, Yennadiena (wife of Yennadios) as she was known by all the people of Karavas.

My grandfather Yennadios had died several years earlier, before I was born. His real name was Constantinos Hadjiloukas but he was called

Yennadios because his brain was "giving birth" to a lot of ideas. (Yenno in Greek means "I give birth.") He was known as a problem solver.

The house in Karavas was now suddenly quiet. The little society that I had been accustomed to had disappeared. Stavros, the older brother I looked up to, Irene who took care of me, my playmates Costas and Anastasia. They had all gone to Nicosia. Even my little brother, two year old John, was gone. The noisy house was all of a sudden very quiet.

It turned out to be just fine. I loved my yiayia and felt very loved by her. She took me to visit relatives all over Karavas. There were so many relatives that I got the feeling that everybody in Karavas was related to us, and that was not far off the truth. Next door to us was Maritsa Orfanides and her family. Her mother Olympiada Papapetrou-Ioannides was my father's second cousin. Next to her was the Papapetrou Family. Hadjicostas Papapetrou was my grandfather's first cousin. Downhill on the road leading to the downtown area was my grandfather Yennadios's vacant house. Next door was the family of Yiannis Kozakos, whose wife Anna was my mother's first cousin. Anna's father, Athanasios Hadjiloucas, was the eldest brother of my grandfather Yennadios. Yiannis and Anna had 10 children, my second cousins.

Further down there was a coffee shop owned by my mother's cousin Kotsios, the Mouhtaris (Registrar) of the neighborhood. And a little further down was the only "Bappou" (grandpa in Greek) that I ever knew, Pieris Hadjiloukas, the shoemaker. He was the youngest of the Hadjiloucas family, and the only one I met of that generation. I have a clear memory of him sitting in a chair, as we were passing by. He always saluted my yiayia and then he was asking me if I would be treating the beautiful girls when I became a doctor, and I always answered with a resounding "yes"!

All of yiayia's children, except for Christ Loucas, and their families were also in Karavas. The eldest son Stavros owned a bakery but had spent some time in Rockland County, New York where he had a hotel in Nyack. He was the first person to buy a car in Rockland County, according to his brother Christ Loucas, who was the only brother that remained in the United States. Stavros was married to Stavrini, who was a teacher. They had no children.

Orthodoxia was the eldest of Yennadiena's daughters. She was married to Neophytos Keloglioris and they had six children. They lived on the North side of the Village close to the sea and the ruins of Lampousa, an ancient city that flourished during the Byzantine Empire. A pair of silver trays, unearthed from those ruins, found their way to the Metropolitan Museum of Art, where they are still displayed on the ground floor. More treasures found in the same ruins are displayed in the Cyprus Museum.

The second daughter Evgenia lived with her husband Antonis Kilaras at the eastern part of Karavas. We used to visit her regularly. Yiayia's stepmother, Hadjinou, was still alive and in the same neighborhood with my Aunt Evgenia, so we regularly stopped by to check how she was doing, too. Then her son Yiannis (my Uncle John) married Eleni and their house was close to the main road of Karavas.

This was an interesting part of my life that gave me the opportunity to "bond" with my yiayia, and get acquainted with my many uncles, aunts and cousins. They were all nice to me and I enjoyed their company.

All the visits to my relatives were done on foot. It was a lot of walking, but it kept my Yiayia in good shape. The most difficult part of every trip was the last couple of hundred yards leading to our house. That uphill road took my yiayia's breath away.

When we were not visiting relatives, I would play with the neighborhood kids who were my third cousins on my father's side. Stavros and Koullis Orfanides and their younger sister Elli were next door and Elenitsa and Chrysoula were two houses further. I was close to Stavros and Koullis Orfanides and we had a lot of fun together playing with a variety of toys.

All our toys were "organic" taken right out of the surrounding nature. For example, a lemon and a few pieces of bamboo made a water spinner. A long, thin piece of bamboo, much like a skewer, was placed alongside the center of the lemon from the stem to the opposite side. About six wider pieces of bamboo were then placed on the lemon at right angles to the long thin skewer. The skewer was then placed over the running water, extending from the one wall to the other of the water channel, immersing the ends of the wider pieces of the bamboo in the running water and spinning the lemon around, giving us some laughs.

Another organic toy was the spinner. A solid, unopened pinecone had a nail inserted at its tip. A length of string was then rolled around the cone and the cone thrown as the end of the string was held, spinning the cone, which touched the ground through the nail. One time a neighbor built a kite for the neighborhood kids. I saw how he did it and made many kites myself during my teenage years. A kite was also made out of long, thin sticks of bamboo frame with a newspaper attached to it. After attaching a "balancing tail" made of strips of paper tied on a string, the center of the frame was secured by another string and the kite was ready to fly.

There was an open field across the street from our houses that belonged to our neighbor, Mr. Hadjidamianos. All the kids came with me and I started running, pulling the kite with the spool as I was releasing more string. The kite climbed up and was flying, but as I was running, I tripped and fell, landing on a nest of wasps, that stormed out like a cloud and attacked me. I ran from the wasps as fast as I could but got stung once on the back of my neck and twice on my scalp. The stings burned initially but then became painful. I became my own doctor. I cut a lemon in two and started scrubbing the stung areas with the cut side of the lemon, squeezing some juice on the wounds at the same time. I thought it helped but I now believe that it was probably just in my mind.

We also played with toy cars made from sardine tins. Once the sardines were consumed, the empty tins became "beautiful convertible cars", with make believe tires and engines, that we enjoyed playing with. We had so many things to keep ourselves busy. One of them was to go on the swing that was in the back room of our house by the patio. It was a simple swing consisting of two ropes that were hanging from the rafters of the ceiling and connected to a "seat" about 18 inches from the floor. One time I climbed up to the swing and sat on the seat. My friend then pushed me a little too hard before I was ready and I fell backwards onto the concrete floor, landing on my back and hitting the back of my head, on the concrete gound. I remember I saw "stars." I ended up with a big laceration with swelling, on the right side of the back of my head, commonly called the "occipital area." My friend ran home, and I ran to my Yiayia. She washed the wound with water, placed a clean cloth over it and summoned my Aunt Evgenia, who put the herb "conizon" on the wound. Every day she cleaned the wound with water and added additional herb. It was painful but I did not make too much fuss about it. It eventually healed but left a big scar, concealed by my hair.

Another activity I enjoyed when I was living with my Yiayia was going to Mr. Klatsias's store to have the gourd container filled with wine, at least once a week. His store was at the road down the bottom of the hill. My Yiayia used to have a glass of wine every night with her dinner. At times she used to give me a little bit at the bottom of the glass too, to keep her company and knock the wine glasses to a loud "cheers!"

"Do you know why you knock the wine glasses," she would say. "Why"? I would ask. "You can see it (the wine), you can touch it, you can smell it and you can taste it, so you knock the wine glasses so you can hear it too, and have all your senses participate in the enjoyment!"

The house next door had a big room with an olive mill and every year the people of Karavas would bring their harvested olives to be crushed into olive oil. The olives were placed in a circular stone receptacle with a round millstone that had a wooden beam at its center that connected to the harness of a mule.

The mule walked around the receptacle rolling the millstone over the olives and crushing them while the olive oil poured out a spout into containers. We were always treated to a slice of homemade bread, dipped in the "freshly produced" olive oil and sprinkled on top with salt and freshly squeezed lemon juice. That was such a delicious slice of bread; a real treat! I used to watch in amazement as the millstone rolled over the olives. The mule kept going around and round.

At some point, I decided to run behind the mule, and started padding its rear thigh. That was real fun for me, but not the mule, who made that abundantly clear! He lifted one of its rear hoofs and swiftly landed it in my belly! That was the first and last time I was kicked by a mule. The kick took my breath away for a while. It hurt a lot, but I did not say anything to anybody. I had enough sense to realize that it was totally my fault, and had I complained to anyone, I would likely get scolded, adding emotional suffering on top of my physical pain. So, I kept quiet and never went close to that, or any other mule since then.

There were several olive mills in Karavas, but of more interest were the two carob mills in the neighborhood, also powered by mules. One was at Mr. Hadjidamianos's property about 50 yards uphill from our house, and the other at Mr. Rotoklis's house, on the other side, behind of our property. The uphill mill produced carob powder, which we could buy and eat as candy. It was delicious! The powder was used to make carob molasses. The other mill produced a different kind of carob candy, called pasteli, a sticky, sweet, hard carob paste, that was cut by a knife. You could buy one or two pennies worth of cut pasteli, placed on the wide leaf of a taro plant. The taro leaf served as a stick-free surface for pasteli, which had a tendency to stick to any other kind of paper or wrapper. Another delicious treat was pastellaki, a bar of processed pasteli covered with a layer of sesame seeds. These products were totally organic and very tasty.

In the meantime, the family in Nicosia was getting acquainted with their new environment. Irene, Costas and Anastasia were enrolled in the brand new Ayios Andreas Elementary School. My father and mother arranged and stocked the store shelves and opened the doors for business. In the morning, my father and eldest brother Stavros went to the farmer's central market at the Center of Nicosia to purchase the vegetables and other perishables for the store. In the beginning, they went back and forth by bus, but as business picked up, and bigger quantities of produce were needed, it became a problem.

My father's solution was to buy a commercial bicycle with a big basket and from then on Stavros carried all the perishables from the central market to the grocery store. The bike was the workhorse of the store and was also used for order deliveries to customers. Stavros was the only one that knew how to ride the bicycle. My father, however, wanted to learn, even though he had never ridden a bicycle in his life. The first try, he landed on his face and cut his lips. It was not just the pain that he had to deal with. He also had to explain to all of his customers that his swollen lips and marks on his face were not the result of a fight, but just a "bicycle accident." Some would believe it, but others would react with a tricky smile as if to say, "yes we've heard that before." Despite the terrible accident, Christos persisted and learned how to ride a bicycle.

Our family was not separated continuously. Everyone, aside from Yiayia and me, was in Nicosia, working full time at our grocery store or attending school and helping at the store afterwards. When the store was closed from Saturday afternoon to Monday morning, my father or my mother took a few of my siblings on the bus to Karavas to visit us. My father made sure he brought two baskets of groceries, one for each of my Yiayias. He would also give each of them some money to cover any other expenses. He would take me with him to go visit his mother in Lapithos, a 20 minutes walk, and take the groceries to her as well. Like all of his family, she was very welcoming, thankful and kind.

She was still living in the house where my father and all of his siblings were born. It was a one-room house, about 16 by 30 feet, with two windows. There was a hearth at one end, where all the cooking was done, and a few feet away was a table and three chairs. At the opposite end there was a bed. In the early years my Yiayia had a goat, which was tied at night to a metal ring attached to the ground near the door, inside the house.

It was a cozy home but what really made it special was my Yiayia. Her heart was much bigger than her house! Her little home was packed and filled to the ceiling with endless love. She would always give me a big hug and wish me every success and everything good in the world. During our visits, my father would spend some time with her as I went outside to play with my cousins.

There was a large parcel of land that belonged to my "Bappou" (Grandpa) and was divided among his children. My father had a piece of land with many olive trees next to his sister Polyxeni's house. The family did not own any water rights of the Spring of Lapithos, but they had their own small spring used for drinking water. The water was directed into a reservoir where it was tapped for the irrigation of their olive trees and crops. On these trips, my father would also visit his brother Panais and sisters Eleni and Polyxeni, and chat with them. You could tell that they had great love and respect for each other.

At times I would visit Nicosia on my own, taking the bus from the station in downtown Karavas. It dropped me off a couple of hundred yards from the house. I would walk home, usually to carry a message from Yiayia.

Jaundice from My Reaction to Fava Beans

One time I went with my Yiayia to visit her eldest daughter Orthodoxia and we went out to collect some fresh fava beans. I ate some as I picked them and after we were done, we took the long walk back home. The next morning, when I woke up, I felt dizzy. My Yiayia looked at me and she appeared very concerned. She had a very good reason to be. She already lost a grandson, Aunt Evgenia's son, who died after eating fava beans. She told me she was going to take me to Nicosia to see a doctor, because my color was not good.

We went downtown to the "Kallis bus service" office. There were two bus companies across the street from one another: one belonging to the Kallis Family and the other to the Tsentas Family. We normally used the Kallis bus service. Mr. Kallis was there when we got to the office and my grandmother explained to him that I was sick, and she had to take me to Nicosia to see a doctor. Mr. Kallis looked at me and said, "What are you going to be when you grow up?" "A doctor," I answered without hesitation. "No!" he replied. "It's a donkey you are going to be, not a doctor!!"

Calling somebody "a donkey" was very insulting and was reserved for stupid, hateful misfits. I was at a loss to say the least. I could not figure out what I did to this man to make him treat me so bad. I remained silent, but things got even worse. He turned to my Yiayia and said, "You have to pay me first before you get on the bus." My Yiayia told him that she did not have any money and my father would pay him when we got to Nicosia. But he would not budge. My Yiayia was at a loss over what to do, when she heard somebody calling her.

"Come aunt. I will take you to Nicosia and don't you worry about the money!" It was Yiannis Tsentas, the younger partner of the Tsentas Bus Company. "Aunt" was how older ladies were addressed as a sign of reverence. My Yiayia thanked him for his generosity and told him that he was going to be paid regardless.

When we arrived in Nicosia the bus passed by my house to drop us off before going to the hub downtown. Thinking about it now, I got a taste of the difference in people's attitude and humanity or lack thereof, which stayed with me all of my life. I experienced the behavior of a truly kind human being and in the same setting, the behavior of a "not very kind" man. From then on, we always traveled with the Tsentas Buses.

My father took me to the pediatrician Dr. Michaelides. He examined me, and then asked me to go to the bathroom in a commode. He inspected the urine and the stool and concluded I had jaundice from eating fava beans, a condition called favism, which caused a breakdown of my red blood cells. There was no medication or specific treatment other than drinking plenty of water. I followed the doctor's instructions and drank as much water as I could. It did not take me long to recover. In a few days I was back to my old self, strong and active as I was before.

Favism, which can be fatal, is an inherited condition transmitted with the X chromosome and caused by a G6PD (Glucose 6 Phosphoro Dehydrogenase) enzyme deficiency. It only affects boys because they only have one X chromosome. Girls don't get the deficiency because the second X chromosome provides enough production of the G6PD enzyme; but they are the "carriers" of the condition if they have the affected chromosome. Of course in the rare case that they inherit the G6PD deficiency X chromosome from both parents then females can have "favism" too. The deficiency causes the red blood cells to breakdown when the body comes in contact with certain substances such as naphthalene, or the ingestion of fava beans or aspirin. This condition runs in our family. When I was in medical school, I checked my G6PD and it was significantly deficient at only 8 units, far below the normal level of about 150 Somogyi units for males. I had a cousin that died from this condition, and another cousin's son almost died from it.

I stayed with my Yiayia until the beginning of the school year in September of 1949. I then joint the family in our Nicosia home and enrolled in the Ayios Andreas Elementary School in the neighborhood. My Younger brother, 4 year old John, then went back to Karavas to stay with Yiayia as her companion. Like me, he spent a lot of time in Ayia Irini Church, accompanying Yiayia to each and every service available. John managed to absorb and memorize the liturgy and all the psalms, which he recited every chance he had. He was so good at it, that, before he knew it, he became known as the "priest."

He was known as the priest, I was known as the doctor, and Costas as the airplane pilot. I was the only one that followed up on the profession I chose as a child or, to be more accurate, the profession that was picked for me by the people around me when I was a child.

The family business was doing well, but it could have been better. There were some American families living in the area, but most of them preferred shopping at the bigger supermarkets downtown. The only advantage that our business had was the fact that my father had been to the States and knew the preferences of the American shopper, more or less. On July 4, 1950, an American customer, Mr. Newman, rode his bicycle to the store to buy firecrackers for the celebration of American Independence Day. He had had a few drinks, so he was not steady on his feet, or on his bicycle for that matter. He fell down when trying to get on his bike to ride home with the firecrackers he just purchased. He got on the bicycle successfully the second time and headed wobbly for home a couple of blocks away. When he fell, a lot of money came out of his pockets. My father saw the money and realized that it belonged to Mr. Newman. He put the money in a sealed envelope in a drawer next to the cash register, telling us not to touch it because it belonged to Mr. Newman.

"Don't ever take even a single penny that does not belong to you," he used to tell us over and over again. It was a policy he learned from his parents and taught us as children. What he didn't know was that this policy would soon have a great effect on his business and his life.

Mr. Newman came back to the store a few days later. My father gave him the envelope with the money and told him that the money had fallen out of his pocket the last time he was at the store. Mr. Newman was very surprised and pleased with my father's honesty. There were a lot of American families living in Nicosia at the time, manning the consulate, as well as the "Voice of America" radio station, which was located in Karavas about 16 miles from Nicosia. Mr. Newman was so impressed with my father's honesty that he told the story to all his friends and acquaintances. He told people all about this guy from Cyprus that spent time working in New York City, came back to Cyprus and has a grocery store in Nicosia.

The business gradually became a thriving enterprise. Christos installed a telephone with the number 2106. He also bought a car at the strong urging of my eldest brother Stavros. It was a golden yellow, 8 horsepower Morris Van. He had a bench fitted behind the front seat that was removable to make more space for deliveries. Of course, like the bicycle story, my father had never driven a car before. My eldest brother Stavros already had a driver's license. In the process of learning how to drive, my father accidentally "chased" a custard cream cart vendor from his normal spot. My father was driving straight at him while trying to find and apply the brakes, so the vendor ran for dear life, and left his cart behind. He managed to stop just shy of the cart. The vendor returned to his cart, and asked my father "What made you want to kill me"?

Despite the close call, he learned how to drive and got his license. The car-related incidents or accidents continued, however. On two separate occasions, he hit a donkey that got in his way, unable to stop in time. The first donkey-related accident happened on a trip to Karavas, on the road between Nicosia and Kyrenia. There was no one on the donkey, and no visible injuries, so, as the donkey run away, we continued on our way to Karavas. The second time we were on the road from Karavas to Nicosia through the west passage of Panagra. That time, there was a man riding the donkey. My father managed to brake mostly in time and didn't hit the donkey too hard. The donkey escaped injury, but I don't know if I can say the same for the man who was riding the donkey. Right after the accident, I saw the poor man turn as pale as a white sheet and fall off the donkey. My father got out of the car and helped him up. He sat down next to the donkey for a while before he felt well enough to get on the donkey again and continue on his journey, closer to the side of the road.

There was another incident that happened on our way from Nicosia to Kyrenia. We were going downhill on a winding road with sharp 180 degrees turns. A policeman was standing right in the middle of the road at the bend area, directing traffic. My father turned, and the car appeared to be heading directly in the direction of the policeman who abandoned his position and started running for his life towards the side of the road. My father stopped and shouted to the policeman, "What's wrong with you? Why are you standing in the middle of the road? Are you trying to kill yourself?" The police officer did not respond but continued to direct traffic from the periphery of the road.

Being the entrepreneur that he was, Christos offered all of his customers the option of ordering their groceries by phone and having them delivered to their kitchen. That was a very innovative marketing strategy, much ahead of his time, sort of a precursor of today's app-based grocery delivery. He also extended the option of purchasing groceries on credit, so the regular customers could pay their bills after their payday, a move people greatly appreciated.

Things were looking great, but there was one big logistic problem that needed to be addressed. The store was too small to accommodate the size of the enterprise's new growth. As always, Christos tackled the problem decisively. He planned to extend the store, increasing its space threefold. He made the plans, got the approvals and built the additional space, connecting it to the old store.

After completion of the walls and masonry, my father hired, Savvas, a carpenter from Karavas, to build the shelves and the meat counter. So, one Sunday when returning to Nicosia, Savvas came with us to our house, where he was going to stay until his carpentry work was completed. He sat on the removable bench in the van with Costas, leaving no room on the bench for me, and Anastasia. We had to sit in the remaining cargo space in the back, next to Savvas's big toolbox. My father was driving and my mother was on the passenger's sit next to him. That was a lot of weight for that small van. Going towards Kyrenia on the way to Nicosia my father maneuvered the van around on a winding road, but due to the weight of the car, it tipped and landed on its side. It was not a violent accident; just a smooth flip of the car to its side. Some people driving by, stopped and helped everybody out.

When the car flipped, the toolbox pressed on me and Anastasia, until eventually, they opened the cargo door of the van and got us out, along with the toolbox. The passersby who stopped to help then got together and flipped the car back to its upright position. The toolbox, Anastasia and me then got back in the cargo space again, and everybody else got back in the van. We continued the journey to Nicosia and arrived safely as if nothing happened.

The carpentry work was completed expeditiously, and the structural part of the extension appeared to be complete. This was a big addition and besides the building my father needed to buy the proper equipment. He needed big refrigerators, freezers and an electric slicer for the processed meats, (ham, spam, salami) and cheese. He ran out of money. He needed another 100 pounds sterling to bring the store to the proper functional level.

He asked my Uncle Neophytos, the husband of Orthodoxia, Maritsa's eldest sister, for a loan. Neophytos was kind of rough, telling him that he would give him the 100 pounds only if he agreed to an 8 percent interest. He had no bargaining power, so Christos agreed to the terms. They signed a written loan agreement and Christos used the money to finish the new expanded Super Store.

Stavros was instrumental in the way the new store was developed and equipped. A new sign with very large letters was placed over the entrance to the store: 'STEVE'S SUPER STORE" named after my brother Stavros' Americanised name. From then on everybody started calling my father Steve, thinking that it was his name.

Before the grand opening of the new store, my father went on a weekend visit to Karavas. He watered the orchard with the water allotted to it, cut a lot of lemons for the store, and before leaving went to visit his mother. He also had a chat with his sister Xenou (Polyxeni). He mentioned that he had to borrow 100 sterling pounds from Neophytos with a steep interest rate of 8 percent. She told him that she had that money to loan him and she did not want any interest. She pulled 100 pounds from her hiding place and gave it to him. He never thought that she had saved so much money.

He was very grateful she was eager to help him. He took the money and went to Neophytos, just a week after he borrowed the money. He calculated the interest and paid the loan. Neophytos was puzzled and asked Christos why ne borrowed the money in the first place, since he did not appear to need it. My father just smiled and thanked him for his trust and help. He was so glad that his sister was in a position to help him out.

The Grand Opening of STEVE'S SUPER STORE

The expanded store had two big freezers and a new large commercial refrigerator. It was packed with frozen foods, fish, lobster tails, Birdseye brand frozen vegetables, processed meats and cuts of fresh veal and beef (veal chops, t-bone steaks, porterhouse, and filet mignon), as well as lamb cuts, chicken, pork chops and ribs. Christos knew about the different cuts of meat from the time he was working as a cook in a New York diner. The shelves were fully stocked with merchandise, with a preference for American products. Everyone in the family worked at the store, with duties delegated by my father. The new and expanded store, was received enthusiastically by the American and English clientele.

A typical day for my father always started with an early visit to the Nicosia central market. He would pick up the best and freshest produce and vegetables from Karafotias and other vendors and farmers. He then went to Emver, a Turkish butcher to get the best cuts of veal and beef. He also picked the meat for grounding into the best, fresh ground meat anybody could buy. When he was done, his preferred carrier, Hassan, would be there with his wheeled cart to carry and load the merchandise to the van. My father got everything to the store and displayed for sale, by 8:30 a.m. In the meantime, Anastasia and I were up early before we went to school to clean the inside of the store as well as the outside yard. My mother stayed in the store until my father came back from the market. After school, we helped customers at the store if it was busy. If there were no customers, we would do our homework and play with neighborhood kids. Anytime the store got busy, we were called to help out.

"You always have to wear a smile," my father used to say. "It does not cost you anything and it creates a good atmosphere and an environment of good will." So, we smiled. "Work is a blessing," he also said. "Learn to love your work and that will keep you happy."

I don't know about my other brothers and sisters, but I genuinely loved working in the grocery store. As I grew older and became a teenager, I started checking the additions of all the customer's accounts. Each regular customer had an assigned booklet where the items purchased were entered with the respective prices. The charges were added up and the original invoice given to the customer at the store or delivered with the order to their house. I checked the additions of the invoice copies, and corrected any mistakes of every transaction every Saturday afternoon, sometimes alone and other times with father or my sister Irene. I also used the commercial bicycle to deliver a lot of the nearby orders. For the orders that had to be delivered far, on the other side of Nicosia, my father used to drive me and Costas, to deliver and unload the baskets in the customers' kitchens. I remember that we always found a way to make everything we were doing funny and enjoyable.

Each member of the family had their assignments while the store was open, but we all gathered together for dinner. Mother prepared the meal for all 10 of us: Seven children, one helper, herself and our father, and she always made sure she prepared more food, just in case a friend or relative showed up, which was common. We all sat down at the table in the hall for dinner, conversation and joking around. We discussed what happened at school, if we performed well, exams we had, how the business was going and any ideas for improvements. Dinnertime was always a delightful experience, strengthening the glue that held all of the family together.

There were a lot of young American families and single American men living in Nicosia, enough to form two baseball teams. Across the street from our grocery store there was a large parcel of undeveloped land. The American customers were interested in playing baseball and asked my father if he could find out whether the owner of the parcel could rent it to them for a baseball field. My father knew the owners and in no time an agreement was signed converting the land parcel into a baseball field. A large chain link fence was built behind home plate, which was on the other side of the field than where the store was, to protect the area around it from foul balls. In no time, baseball games were being played at least once a week. One time the batter hit a very long home run and the ball landed on the the hip of a woman about to enter our store. The batter, a very athletic tall, handsome guy, ran over to see who was hit, only to find that the injured person was his wife! He saw her siting on a chair and crying, so he took her in his arms and hugged her, trying to console her. It took her a few minutes to recover, but she eventually got over it. Everybody was amazed, wondering what the chances were that the batter would end up hitting his wife with the baseball!

Every time there was a game, we had a problem supplying enough cold drinks for the players and spectators. The demand exceeded the supply by far. It did not take me long to see the opportunity. I filled big containers with beer and soft drinks and put it behind the protective fence behind home plate. Every game day, I would ride the commercial bike to the ice factory, two miles away, for a block of ice, which I broke up with an ice pick and added to the containers. That made the best ice-cold drinks any baseball player could dream of. There was never a shortage; I always replaced the drinks I sold. I reached an agreement with my father that I would buy the drinks from him at cost, get and pay for the ice and keep the profits. He was very happy with my business sense and the effective way I executed the plan. I made enough pocket money to keep me happy.

The Christoudias Family 1949

On April 2, 1949, the seventh child and third girl was born. The family reached its final shape, parents, four boys, three girls. The new girl was named Theodora after her Godmother, who was the maid of honor in my parent's wedding. In January 1950, there was a very rare snowfall in Nicosia that dropped several inches. In the 20 years I had spent in Cyprus there was never another time that snow fell in Nicosia, and none, to my knowledge since I left. There is always a snowfall of several inches or feet on the Troodos mountains in west Cyprus every year, but not in Nicosia, where the temperature hardly ever dipped close to freezing. That time when it snowed in January it was extremely cold, but we played outside until our hands and feet were almost frozen. Then we ran in the house and stayed next to the charcoal heater to warm up. Dora was 9 months old and our cousin Polyxeni, who was staying with us, was holding her, sitting close to the charcoal heater. At one point, Polyxeni got up, put Dora down on the chair and went to the kitchen. Dora moved and fell in the charcoal pit. I pulled her away from the fire but by then she sustained second degree burns to the side of her face. My father rushed her to the hospital where she was treated.

My parents had another baby girl, Eleni, in 1951. Unfortunately, she was born with a severe congenital heart disease and died seven days later. That was a sad event that dampened our spirits for a while.

My Elementary School Years

When I started elementary school in September 1949, my older brother Costas and my sister Anastasia were already attending, and I felt very comfortable having them around. The Cyprus school system was similar to the European system and consisted of six grades of elementary school and six grades of high school. I remember the teacher I had in every grade. Miss Elizabeth was my first-grade teacher. She was a young, loving, kind, caring person that had the gift of commanding the attention of the students and connecting with each and every one of them. I was lucky to have her and happy to go to school and be in her classroom. I still think of her with love, appreciation and respect.

In the second grade, Mr. Papadouris was my teacher. For some reason, he seemed to be angry at me most of the time. I remember entering the classroom as he was standing at the door. I asked him when the next time art class would be, when we got to use playdough. His answer: a smack on my face. I thought that was uncalled for, but the only thing I could do was sob. It became evident that I was getting on his nerves more often than not, so I tried not to irritate him. After a few more smacks on the face, I managed to make it through second grade. It was not a pleasant experience, though I did finish with an A.

The third grade was a pleasant year with Miss Yannoula, who was very nice and treated all the students with the same love and respect. Everybody loved her, and she loved everybody. I learned a lot from her, and she never hit me or anybody else for that matter. That was a good thing because I started thinking that getting smacked was part of the curriculum. What a difference in attitude and behavior between my previous teacher and Miss Yannoula.

In the middle of the school year Miss Yannoula got married and went to South Africa. After Miss Yannoula's departure, she was replaced by her sister, Miss Elenitsa, who was also a very good teacher. She was always nice to me except for one time when at a parent-teacher conference she was going through my spelling tests, all with a score of 10 out of 10. She told my mother that one of those perfect grades wasn't written by her, so it must have been written by me! I could not figure out what made her believe such a thing. It was simply not true. It did not affect my grade, but it affected my pride and reputation. Every single day my parents were stressing integrity and honesty, and in one sentence Miss Elenitsa questioned that. I never forgot that, but, other than that, she was a very good teacher.

During the summer recess, in 1952, we went to the movie theater and watched a Greek comedy. It was a funny movie about a bodyless creature name "Gogovios." The announcer introduced the creature: "It is not a boa constrictor, it is not a Shark, it is just the little snake, Gogovios." Gogovios grimaced and made funny faces that made everybody laugh.

The next day I pretended to be Gogovios to entertain the neighborhood kids. I took a large cardboard box from the store and made a hole at the bottom of one side for my head. I put the box over my head and sat down, so it covered my body, as I stuck my head out through the hole. And voeux la, the bodyless creature of Gogovios reappeared to the entertainment of the neighborhood kids. I made funny grimaces and my little brother John was announcing: "It's not a boa constrictor, it's not a shark, it's just the little snake Gogovios," and the kids would clap and laugh.

A day later my big brother, Stavros, heard about our "show" so he asked me to get in the box again and pretend to be Gogovios so he can take a picture for posterity. It sounded good to me, so I got in the box with my head sticking out the hole. Stavros saw me and started laughing. "Stay there, let me get the camera," he said. Instead of the camera, he came back with a bucket full of water and dumped it on my head! He laughed again, but this time he laughed much louder and harder. Joking and teasing one another and "horsing" around went on all the time in our house.

That wasn't the only time that Stavros fooled me. The truth is, I did some stupid things myself. One time I got in the box and as I tried to move, I tripped and fell. Of course, since the only part of my body outside the box was my head, I landed on my face and got a big cut on my lower lip! That ended my career as Gogovios.

The fourth grade wasn't memorable to me. Our teacher, Mr. Kosteas, was low-key, a kind man and a good educator. He taught the class well and did not smack me or anybody else for that matter.

I finally got to the fifth grade, and by then it was just me and my younger brother John in the elementary school. Irene had graduated and was enrolled in the American Academy. She excelled at school and skipped the second and fourth grades and graduated from the six-year high school in 4 years! Stavros was enrolled at the Terra Santa high school, where Costas and John also enrolled after graduating from elementary school. Anastasia also enrolled in American Academy.

As time went by and Costas and Anastasia graduated and moved on to high school, I found myself in the fifth grade with John in the third Grade. I was the strongest kid in the school from all of the "lifting" I did at the grocery store. Many kids had challenged me to a fight, and I beat them all, each and every time. My teacher, Mr. Achilleas Andreou, did not appear to have me in high regard, for reasons unknown to me. He was very rough with me and smacked me on the face several times for no good reason. Nonetheless, I was at the top of the class with very little effort. But on the midterm report card he gave me a B on spelling. I went to him and complained; he was not pleased.

"Let us check your tests," he said with a voice filled with irony. When he checked, he found that I had an A on every single test. He was forced to change my report card for spelling to an A, right then and there. His attitude changed when we were carving a large map of Cyprus on the ground in the school yard and asked me and a handful of students to help out. There were some difficulties encountered during the structure of the different components of the map, monasteries, historical sites and towns. On each and every occasion I found a solution and showed him how it could be done. He appeared puzzled but pleased. To his credit, on my next report he noted: "Very smart and inventive." I knew then I earned his respect.

Mr. Achilleas Andreou was also my sixth grade teacher, having been promoted to School Principal. Having earned his respect the sixth grade went by like a breeze, and that year I also earned the class prize in arithmetic.

My High School Years

Graduating from the elementary school was a milestone for me. In my mind it meant that I had grown up, and I was ready for high school. After scoring well on my entrance exams I enrolled in the prestigious High School Pancyprian Gymnasium. The first day at school was memorable. It started with all 800 students at a general assembly in the School Yard to be addressed by the principal. As I was standing with the rest of the students, some guy standing behind me tapped me on the shoulder. I turned around and asked him why he did that. His friend, another 'tough guy', jumped in front of him to my face and said: "Why? Do you have a complaint?" A typical schoolyard bully, he thought I was going to be intimidated. I screamed back, "You bet your ass I have a complaint!" At that point the moron attacked me. In a split second, he was on the floor, face down, immobilized, his arms twisted behind his back with me on top of him!

All the heavy lifting at the store and the calls to fight by challengers in elementary school had paid off. I had also been lifting homemade weights, which I built by putting two iron rods into a bucket of concrete. I then pulled the set concrete out of the bucket by pulling on the two parallel rods. I would then mix more concrete in the same bucket and insert the other ends of the iron rods in it. After the concrete had set, I pulled it out of the bucket and wound up with a poor man's 60-pound weights, which I lifted regularly to strengthen my upper body. So, the "schoolyard bully" had it coming! While on the floor he screamed an apology and asked me to let him go. I did. He got up and walked away, defeated. I never saw his ugly face again, and I hoped he learned his lesson. Of course, my intentions were not to have a fight the first day at high school, or any day thereafter, but I was not about to let anybody bully me. I knew that I had to defend myself any time I was attacked, so I did.

That was a lesson I learned from my mother when I was 6 years old, after coming to Nicosia from Karavas, to start school. I was playing with the neighborhood kids and one of them hit me. I went to my mother crying and told her what happened. She looked at me and said: "What are you complaining to me for? If somebody hits you, hit him back harder." This was surprising to me, because she always had taught me not to hit John, my younger brother. I realized that there was a difference and I could hit back anybody except my brother. I ran out of the house, found the kid that hit me and threw him on the ground. He never hit me again, and nobody else did either. We actually became good friends and played together.

The principal gave his welcome speech and we all went to our assigned classrooms. We were taught classical studies, math and science. We studied ancient Greek every day, covering Xenophon, Plato, Thucydides, and Homer's Iliad and Odyssey in the original texts. It was fascinating to see the evolution of the Greek language over the centuries and learn to appreciate the true meaning of each and every word. When I heard the phrase "the Greeks have a word for it" I knew exactly how and why that phrase originated. We also took Latin in the last four grades of High School, which I found relatively easy since the grammar was almost identical with the Greek grammar.

My best subjects were math and science, especially physics and solid geometry. Physics allowed me to understand my surroundings, and that stimulated my thought process in a revolutionary way. Solid geometry was even more exciting for me. For some reason when the math teacher Mr. Mavros was explaining the different theorems of solid geometry, I had the feeling that I knew it already, before I heard his explanation and analysis. After a couple of lessons, Mr. Mavros would come in the classroom, go to the blackboard, write the theorem, turn to the students and say: "Who"? Meaning who can prove it. I always raised my hand, went to the blackboard and proved the theorems, though I had never seen them before. I realized then, that I could think in three dimensions. All my classmates thought that I was attending private lessons on the subject, which was not true.

Despite that, Mr. Mavros was always displeased with my class performance. Very often he would say: "You! You don't care about school. I bet you wish your teacher dies so you get a day off school!" And, wouldn't you know it, he died towards the end of the school year, and we got a day off from school! I don't know if he meant what he was saying, but it happened to come true anyway. I was sad, because I genuinely liked the old man very much. For my part I'd rather not have a day off and have him around.

I did like math a lot, so much so, that I taught my younger brother John the Pythagorean theorem. When his math teacher told his class that she was going to teach them the Pythagorean theorem, he raised his hand and told her he already knew it. She challenged him to come to the blackboard and prove it, and if he did, she promised she would give him an A for the rest of the year. So, he went to the blackboard and proved it, no sweat. The teacher was impressed.

"Where did you learn it?" she asked. "My brother taught me," he replied. The teacher then said that it doesn't count, but John did get straight A's anyway. John was a mediocre student the first two years of high school but as soon as he started learning advanced math like algebra, geometry and trigonometry in the third year, he suddenly jumped to the top of the class. The challenging nature of the subjects woke something inside him. He was coming up with questions that I could not answer, nor could his math teacher. I guess that explains why he changed his aspirations and instead of a priest he became a structural engineer, with special interest in the nuclear power plants!

Life continued to be interesting as time went by. Every morning I would get up very early and sweep and mop the store's floor before going to school. Anastasia and the worker we had as a helper also mopped the floor, which had to be kept squeaky clean and tidy at all times. I used my bike to get to school, which was about 3 miles away. Everyone in our family helped out in the grocery store while attending school.

Stavros had found a government job when he was 18 years old, and a couple of years later, he established one of the first real estate offices in Cyprus, which became very successful. He then got involved in the import-export business and other entrepreneurial activities. After Irene graduated from the American Academy at the age of 16, she worked at the store until she was 18 and then joined Stavros at the real estate office until she got married to Socrates Socratous in 1958. Costas and Anastasia continued working at the store.

I also continued going to school and working at the store. Typically, I would sweep and clean the store, early in the morning, then get on my bicycle and go to school, which was located in the "old Nicosia," within the centuries-old medieval defensive walls. I also continued working at the store before and after school. I would either help customers at the store or make deliveries in the area. I also answered the phone and wrote down customers' orders for groceries and recorded the information in their accounts, adding up the sum of the items purchased and make the deliveries. An original invoice with the list of the items purchased and the corresponding prices and total charges accompanied each order, and a carbon copy left in the store.

The store was open from 6:30 a.m. until 7 p.m., though we routinely opened up when people needing groceries came after the closing time, since we lived next door. When the store closed, we all worked to replenish the merchandise sold, stock the shelves, and then walk home for dinner. We were always 9 or 10 people at the table every time, with Stavros sometimes eating out with clients. We talked, discussed different subjects, made suggestions on how we could improve the business or just talked about the news of the day. After dinner it was home-work time.

Every Saturday, after closing the store, we headed for Karavas. More often than not, we entertained some customers as our guests. They were treated with a tour of the village followed by a delicious barbecue lunch with large chunks of lamb, goat or chicken on a bay leaf stick skewer, rotated over a charcoal fire until cooked. A salad with fresh vegetables complemented the meal.

On Sundays Anastasia, John and myself joined some neighborhood kids and climbed the mountain to gather some wildflowers mainly Cyclamens and anemones. We also visited the mountaintop "Cave Church" of Saint George to light a candle. The cave was fashioned into a place of worship to Saint George. Other than an Icon of Saint George, donated by my parents, no other additions or changes were made to the natural structure.

My Siblings

Stavros

There were certain events and activities that revealed each sibling's character and personality.

Stavros, the eldest, was a hard worker. He started helping out when he was 6 years old, riding a donkey to the water mill, carrying a sack of wheat from our store in Karavas, where the miller ground it into flour. The flour was then loaded on the donkey and Stavros guided the donkey back to the store. He was a very active person, with a lively, pleasant and engaging personality that served him well in his business in later years. He liked to joke around and commanded everybody's attention with his upbeat disposition and optimistic attitude. He also liked to go out at night regularly and nap during siesta time in the summers. He was a successful entrepreneur and developed several businesses from scratch. Aside from the real estate office, he founded a business exporting lemons and oranges to Europe. He developed another import business for alcohol and tobacco products. He was always very restless and kept busy all the time.

Costas

One evening Costas decided to go to the movies with our cousin John Koudounas who was helping at the store and staying with us. As they got dressed and ready to leave for the cinema, John demanded to go too. Costas did not want to hear about it, and left him behind since he was too young to fit in.

John was upset with Costas but figured out a way to get even with him. He filled a bucket with water and placed it on top of the half-opened door of Costas's and the boys' bedroom. When Costas returned, he would open the door and the bucket would flip and pour the water on his head. The plan worked perfectly except that the next person to walk into the boys' bedroom was Stavros, who had a date that night. He took a shower, put on his best clothes and went to the bedroom to use his cologne. But when he opened the door, he was treated to a second shower courtesy of John, only this time it was with cold water, while he was fully clothed!

Stavros figured out that John was the culprit, even though he was asleep in his bed. John was known for his practical jokes; my mother used to call him "Captain Trouble" for good reason. So, Stavros filled the bucket up with water, went back to the bedroom and emptied it on John! John was stunned but he did not cry. He got up, put on dry clothes and went to sleep on the dry floor. I guess he realized that he had to deal with the complications that resulted from his machinations. He was a little boy, nine or ten years old, but took it like a man!

Costas was kind, hard-working kid and fun to be with. We worked together, played together and had fun together. He was the handsome one and I remember when we were kids, many people that knew our grandfather Yennadios commented that Costas looked very much like him. Costas liked the grocery store and eventually inherited the business, which at one point struggled. Stavros helped him liquidate the stock and pay the debtors. He worked for Stavros for a bit, before Stavros helped him develop his own logistics business. His hard work, outstanding service, honesty and integrity, turned the business into the biggest logistics enterprise in Cyprus.

Irene

My sister Irene was the smart one, but she was always very demanding. An outstanding student, she went through the six grades of American Academy high school in four years, skipping the second and fourth grades. She excelled at everything she did.

At one point, Anastasia, me and John were sleeping on a double bed in the east bedroom. I was sleeping on the side close to the wall, John in the middle and Anastasia on the open side of the bed. Irene had her own bed in the same room.

One night it so happened that, for some reason, I slept in the middle and John slept on the side close to the wall. Everybody was in bed, and the lights were out. I fell asleep in no time. Anastasia and John were talking, joking and laughing as usual, irritating Irene and keeping her up. She repeatedly ordered them to "shut up and go to sleep," but they were having too much fun to listen to her.

As they carried on, Irene got mad. She got out of bed, came over and started beating me up, thinking she was hitting John! She did not realize that I had changed places with John that night. I woke up crying, asking her why she was beating me up. It was very funny, unless you were on the receiving end of the beating, like I was. That's why I was the only one crying and everybody else was laughing, including Irene!

Anastasia

Anastasia, the fourth child and second girl, with blond hair and blue eyes, had a stunning resemblance to our grandfather's twin sister, Yallourou, on our father's side. Kind-hearted and eager to help everybody, Anastasia was very pleasant, always fun to be around.

Anastasia, me, and John or, as mother called him, "Captain Trouble" did a lot of things together. When she was 10, I was 8 and John was 6, we decided to make almond dessert. We saw our mother do it, so we figured we could do it too. We ground about a pound of almonds and put them in a pot with a lot of sugar and water. We stirred it over the fire until we got tired and then I carried the boiling dessert to the side. John was right next to me, observing carefully so he also could learn how to make the almond dessert. As I lifted the pot, I lost control of it and spilled the boiling dessert on John's back! I was scared but quickly removed John's shirt and placed him under the water faucet. We let the water run on his back as we picked up the scolded skin. We begged him to stop crying because we didn't want our parents to hear him and beat us. But my mother heard and ran to us, and once she saw the burns on John's back, she called our father and he took John to the hospital.

I went to hide first in the basement and then in the bedroom under the bed, because I knew I did something very, very bad, that deserved punishment. I wondered how John was, and what was going to happen to me, when all of a sudden, he looked under the bed where I was and said, "George, come out! I am okay! Because of this, they took me on a nice ride to the hospital and fixed me up!"

I got out from my hiding place and saw poor John covered in bandages from the neck down to his waist. For some strange reason I did not receive any punishment, though I was convinced that I deserved one. The incident reminded me of a story my mother used to tell us every so often.

A woman gave her son a clay jug with a spout and asked him to go to the spring and fill it up. At the same time, she smacked him across the face and told him to be careful not to drop and break it. "Why are you hitting me? I did not drop it, and I did not break it," the son complained. She explained, "It will be no use hitting you after you break the jug, because it will not put the clay jug, back together! Slapping you before, will make you more careful, and thus, you will bring the jug back intact, and filled with water!" That is the reason I did not receive a punishment I guess, because it would not have served any purpose.

I realize now that taking John's shirt off and placing him under the cold water to wash off the hot almond dessert was the appropriate thing to do, medically speaking.

There was another time, about a year later, that I had to take care of my little brother but this time I did not cause his injury. One of our chicks ran out of the chicken coop. John ran after it but he could not catch it, so he dove to grab it, and in the process landed on a tin cover. He got a laceration about an inch long on his knee. There was a lot of blood but that did not scare me. I ran to the store, got a bottle of Dettol (medical antiseptic) and some cotton and went back to John. I cleaned the wound with the antiseptic and covered the wound with the cotton. In the meantime, my father heard the commotion, saw the big laceration and took "Captain Trouble" to the hospital for another pleasant ride and wound care.

John

John was the most creative master of practical jokes. He had a teacher who used to pace back and forth in the classroom between the desks. John went to school earlier than usual, before the teacher was scheduled to be in the classroom. He brought a pound of sugar from the store and sprinkled a thick layer in the corridor between the desks. When the bell rang and the students filed into the classroom, the teacher started talking and walking as usual. With every step, you can hear "crunch, crunch, crunch" and everyone started laughing. The teacher got furious, but no one actually knew who sprinkled the sugar. And no one ever found out! The whole class ended up getting detention, but no one suspected that John, the quiet, skinny boy, was the guilty party.

Another time some field mice were caught in a mousetrap in our garage. John once again went early to school, bringing a mouse along to tuck into the drawer of his teacher's desk. When the class convened, the teacher sat at her desk and as she opened the drawer, the mouse jumped out and landed on her lap! She leapt from her seat screaming! No one except John knew how the mice got there, and no one ever found out.

In another incident, John pulled a prank on the store's bread delivery-man. One day while the deliveryman was having his usual chat with my father, John tied a few empty cans onto a string and tied the other end of the string to the back fender of his van. When the delivery-man took off, he stopped the van after hearing a terrible noise. He had assumed it was his vehicle because when he stopped the van, the noise also stopped. He checked under the van and when he didn't see anything, he tried to continue on his way again, but the noise continued. He once again stopped but this time he saw John laughing and noticed the cans tied behind his van. He started laughing too, cut off the string with the cans and went on his way.

When John became a teenager, he always got up early to go to the central market with our father before he went to school. By the time he was back from the market, I was just getting up. One day I woke up, washed, got dressed and went to put my shoes on. The day before it had rained, so my shoes were kind of muddy. I looked at my shoes and one was shining perfectly allover, including the sole of the shoe, while the other was muddy. I heard John laughing aloud but I did not need to hear his laugh to know that he was the perpetrator. I grabbed him by the ear, and took him to my shoes, gave him the shoe-shining equipment and told him to finish the job. He did while he continued to laugh. I guess he was highly entertained by the expression on my face when I saw what he did.

During Christmas we always decorated a Christmas tree using stretched cotton as the snow.

One time, John decided to create a raffle to raise some money. The prize was a large box of chocolates. The raffle numbers were sold out and John cleared a profit of one- and one-half pounds, which was the equivalent to a couple of days' salary of a worker. He went to our father and showed him the money and asked what he could buy with that amount. My father thought for a minute and then told him that he could buy happiness for a poor, paralyzed lady for the Christmas season.

"Give me that money," my father said, "and I will give you food and other things at cost price, which you can take to Anastasia, daughter of the "barefoot," a term that was the nick name of her father. This poor old lady was bedridden and paralyzed from the waist down, for unknown reasons. She lived alone at the outskirts of the village in her tiny, one room home. She had to rely on the generosity and kindness of her neighbors to survive. Neighbors provided food and care to the best of their ability, but they too had limited financial resources.

John gave the money to our father in exchange for a large basket filled to the brim with groceries: bread, processed meats, cheese, and other processed food supplies, items that would come in handy in the celebration of Christmas. On the following Saturday when we went to Karavas, a couple of days before Christmas, John delivered the food basket to bedridden Anastasia.

"Mrs. Anastasia, I brought some things for you for Christmas," John said. She was touched by the generosity of this little boy but even more, she was moved by his thoughtfulness. She appreciated the fact that he thought of her and cared about her. She knew him and all of us, because every time we passed by her house, we stopped to say hello and wish her well.

She could not thank him, praise him enough or wish him well enough. She said she will pray enough for him for being so good to her. This is how we were brought up. Always be kind, be honest and caring. Always help people as much as possible, when our help is needed most. When any of us did a good deed, my mother would pray aloud for us and ask God to guide us to become useful to ourselves, our family, our society and our country. I am delighted to say that God answered her prayers.

Dora

Dora was the youngest of the bunch, and we always took care of her and treated her well. She had a talent for the arts and she eventually studied to become an interior decorator.

Life with My Siblings

Anastasia, me and John were close in age, so we got into mischief together. As we grew older, Stavros moved out of the house and John and I moved into the "boys" bedroom. Each room had a light at the center of the ceiling and one switch on the wall by the door. We had no bedside lamps or other lights. At night, before going to sleep, somebody had to get out of bed and turn the light off. The light switch was close to the door and turning the light off, became an issue every night. We used to call Anastasia to come over because on the premise that we had something very important to tell her. She would run from her room, come over and ask: "What is it?" We would then laugh and say, "Turn the light off."

She fell for it a couple of times, but soon started to respond to us with "if you have something to tell me, come to me." So now all the pressure was on the younger brother. He had to get up and go turn the light off every night, so he devised a way to do it without getting out of bed. He put a nail in the wall above the side where he was sleeping. He then tied one end of a string to the nail and passed it over another nail above the light switch, and then down to the light switch itself, onto which he tight the end of the string. By pulling on the string he could turn the light off from where he was sleeping, and that solved his problem.

There were some special occasions, like Thanksgiving, that remain vividly in my memory. Although we did not really celebrate it per se, we were involved with the preparations for our American clientele. Starting two weeks before Thanksgiving, we started receiving orders for turkeys to be delivered the day before the holiday. In Cyprus at the time, there was no place where you could buy a ready to cook turkey other than at Steve's Super Store. Yes, we were the only store that carried ready to cook turkey.

Based on the number of orders we received, my father had a Turkish man named Leyla deliver the live turkeys to our store. We then weighed them, one at a time, with a hand scale. The turkey was suspended from a hook on one side of the scale and a metal weight ran along the marked lever on the other side to reveal the weight of the turkey. While I was holding the hand scale, Leyla would then suspend the tied-up turkey on the hook and our store helper Sotiris, would run the metal weight on the lever and record the weight of each turkey. It all worked well as long as everybody did their part of the assignment. Otherwise, the process could result in "a tragic comedy," as it did one time.

I was holding the scale, Leyla was suspending the turkey from it and Sotiris was trying to place the weight on the lever, when he accidentally dropped the weight on Leyla's foot! Leyla screamed with pain, dropped the turkey, and jumped about two feet off the ground as he grabbed his ailing foot, and Sotiris broke into a loud nervous laughter, while I was looking at the scene with disbelief! Accidents happen but squashing the man's foot and laughing aloud was too much to take for me. So, I slapped him, but surprisingly that didn't stop his laughter, which went on for a few more moments.

We took a break until the sting of Leyla's injury got better, and then continued until all of the turkeys were weighed and recorded, one at a time. Leyla, wisely stayed further away from the scale, just to be on the safe side. The total weight was then added up and the amount payable determined. Leyla got paid and went on his way limping, with a sore foot.

The turkeys were then placed in the chicken coop at the back of our house, fed and given water. The next day, the Wednesday before Thanksgiving, Costas and I slaughtered the birds in the backyard, and the whole family helped pluck off the feathers and clean them before putting them in the store refrigerators. The intestines and other viscera were removed as part of the cleaning process and placed on the side. Our three dogs got to have a feast. We prepared 30-40 turkeys every year for Thanksgiving and there were plenty of viscera for the dogs. They ate so much that they could not stand on their rear feet! It took them a full day to recover and be able to stand and walk again.

I got so much enjoyment working in the store and I learned so many things. I learned how to interact with all kinds of people—young, old, rich, poor, good and bad—while also learning how to buy and sell merchandise. I learned to take precautions with people I didn't know, and learned how to treat our customers with honesty, integrity and respect. I also learned the English language by practicing it every day with our American and English customers.

I really loved school, but I also loved working at the store. At some point I started entertaining the idea of forgetting about medical school and medicine and going into business. As far as being a doctor, I was concerned about having to get out of bed in the middle of the night to attend to patients. Being awaken in the middle of the night was a terrifying idea for me at the time.

The Resistance & The Cyprus Conflict, 1955–1959

In 1955 an armed struggle erupted against the British occupation of Cyprus, demanding the unification of the island with Greece. The struggle lasted until 1959. The British underestimated the resolve of the population to achieve self-determination. The entire population was in favor of the resistance with a very wide participation in the organization that was fighting the British. In our school more than 50 percent of the students were members of the organization, and the non-members were definitely sympathizers.

I was a leading member of the Resistance. Our duties were to display Greek flags in the main streets of Nicosia during the Greek Holidays, such as the GreekIndependence day, and the OXI (Ohi= no) Day commemorating the response of the Greek Government to Italian fascist Mussolini's demands that Greece surrender the country to the axis. We also helped enforce the passive resistance which included boycotting British products, supporting the sale of local products, and making sure that the local companies did not use the English language in their stationary or signage. The higher ups of the organization would give me a listing of local businesses that were using stationary or invoices in English. They likely received the information by workers of the printing company, with an explicit order to visit the perpetrators and demand that they stop using documents in the English language.

All the orders coming from the top of the resistance wrote the instructions of what action to take. All of our grocery store's invoices and stationery were in English, since our clientele consisted mainly of American and British customers. It was not surprising then, that one of the orders I received of businesses to be contacted for English print, included the business of "Steve's Super Store, 12 Kassandra St., Nicosia," which was our store.

I pocketed the order and tried to figure out what to do. All this activity was "passive resistance," modeled after the great Indian leader Mahatma Gandhi. But our duties in the resistance expanded beyond this. We coordinated and organized demonstrations in the streets with students from other high schools.

In January of 1956 several students were arrested in one of the demonstrations. In response students at my high school and other high schools, prepared for a giant response, that would express the defiance to the occupying British forces. The preparations started on Jan. 26 by piling rocks, bricks and pieces of wood on the roof of the school library, at the corner of the main school building, overlooking the underlying crossroads junction.

On Jan. 27, 1956 the students again poured into the streets and started demonstrating in solidarity to the arrested students and against the occupying British forces. Several vehicles with British troops responded to the events and tried to disperse the students, attacking them with clubs. The students retreated back into the school and the others stationed on the roof surprised the British troops with a barrage of stone and bricks. The British captain in charge of the troops then called for reinforcements to "the bloody school" as he was heard characterizing our school. The "battle" continued until the reinforcements arrived in the form of a newly formed, and newly trained "assistant police force" exclusively made up of poorly qualified and trained Turkish Cypriots.

The students retreated back to the school grounds as the British commander ordered the "assistant police forces" to attack the students inside the school. I had just celebrated my 13th birthday and was not even aware of what was going on outside the school until the "assistant police forces" entered the building. As the assistant police forces attacked us with shields and clubs, we retreated to the schoolyard, which was enclosed by an eight-foot wall. The assistant police leadership made a big mistake when their officers directed them to attack us in our own schoolyard.

As they entered our territory and started storming towards us, clubs and shields in hand, they faced several hundred of us, sticks in hand, disgusted and angry for their audacity to invade our "home." We attacked fiercely like a huge angry wave. When they saw several hundred teenagers running towards them, they dropped their shields and clubs and started running, but not all of them got away. A few of them were caught and beaten mercilessly as pay back for all the beating we received by them in the streets.

The next phase of the conflict involved the British occupying forces. They entered the schoolyard, not with clubs and shields, but with machine guns. They started shooting in the air, and I remember seeing tree branches falling down after being severed by the speeding bullets. Now it was our turn to run, though there was no place to go except the acre-sized schoolyard. Instead, I climbed the wall and jumped to the side of the road behind the school, about 10 feet below. From there I walked away and back home, about three miles away. The injured assistant police officers were picked up by the ambulance and taken to the hospital as a new unit of police came back to the school yard to finish what they were up to earlier: beating the students mercilessly. And they did. One of my best friends, Nicos Polemidiotis, was on the receiving end, and remained black and blue for weeks.

In response to the student demonstrations and the ensuing troubles, the occupying British forces shut down our high school. But they accomplished what they were after: Position the Turkish Cypriots against the Greek Cypriots. Divide and rule imperialism, a strategy the Romans used 2,000 years ago: "Divide et impera!"

Closing our high school was a big blow to the population. But we were not about to lose a year of our studies because of the imperialists. A new system was developed, by which students were divided in small groups of six to eight. The students reported to teachers' homes and were taught different subjects to cover the curriculum. It reminded everybody of the "Krypho Scholeio"—the "secret school"—that was administered at night by the priests during the Turkish occupation of Greece, to teach the children writing, reading, history and Religion, things, which were strictly forbidden by the Turks. The school remained closed until the new academic year started in mid-September of 1956.

The activities of the resistance continued throughout the school closing and beyond. In addition to the "passive resistance" it included destruction of government property, such as setting government vehicles on fire. My team, which included my classmates Nicos Polemidiotis, Stelios Papantoniou, George Dracos and Koulis Papachristoforou, had carried out an arson of a car belonging to a British officer. I did not actively participate in that one.

On another occasion, I with Koullis planned our second attack. We bought a gallon can of gasoline and went around looking for the new target and thought about the government public works van that was often parked by the soccer stadium. The day we went looking, gasoline in tow, the van wasn't there. We decided that it was too risky to be going around with the gasoline container in my school bag, because there were a lot of British patrols in the area that could stop and search us any time. Instead, we looked around for a hiding spot for the gasoline and found an empty construction site. It was late afternoon and the workers had left for the day. We looked around and saw a piece of plywood in the yard under which we could hide the gasoline and still have easy access when we needed it.

As we walked away from construction site, we heard the screeching sound of car brakes. We turned around and saw four British officers jumping out of their station wagon and running towards us.

"Hands up!" they yelled. We dropped our school bags and raised our hands. They searched us for weapons and found nothing. Then searched our school bags and still found nothing.

"There is nothing in the bag," one officer said, "but I smell petrol. They must have hidden it in the construction site."

One of them stayed behind to stand guard, pistol in hand, as the other three went inside the construction site and did an extensive search of the unfinished building that took more than an hour, finding nothing. Koullis and I were feeling good because we knew they would find nothing since they were looking in the wrong place. Then, just as they were leaving, one of them, frustrated, kicked the plywood in the yard uncovering the can of gasoline. They took it and arrested us.

In the meantime, I pretended I did not understand English. They cramped us into the cargo space in the back of the station wagon, as the four of them got into their seats and headed for the C.I.D.—the Criminal Investigation Department. I heard the officers talking about me and Koullis. They were saying that since they did not find the gasoline in our possession they could not prove that we were the ones who placed it there. They had no case, which made me very happy to hear. I remembered that I had several "orders" in my pockets, coming from my superiors in the organization. I knew that the British in the CID would do a much more extensive body search, and in all likelihood, would find the documents. I remembered reading some spy stories where people would swallow paper documents so that they wouldn't fall into the enemy's hands. I decided to remove the three documents handwritten in Greek. I crunched one into a ball, thought to myself "kali orexi" meaning "bon appetite" in Greek, and put it in my mouth. I tried to chew but the darn thing was not chewable. I tried to swallow it whole, but it just would not go down. It became evident to me, that the writer of the spy story had a lot of imagination, and if I wanted to prevent the documents from falling into the enemy's hands, I needed a better plan.

I looked around the cargo space and noticed the spare tire right next to me. This would make an excellent hiding/disposal place, I thought to myself. They are not going to find these documents any time soon, unless they have a flat tire, which could be a long time from now. So, I squeezed each document into a ball and squeezed each one of them next to the rubber of the tire. In the meantime, I talked to Koullis in Greek, telling him our story. It was very simple. "We finished school, and we were just walking around to look at girls. We had nothing to do with the gasoline. We were coming out of the construction site because we went there to pee, since there were no public toilets around." One of the officers kept telling me to "shut up" but of course I did not understand English and, after all, this was my country, not his!

We arrived at the CID building and they escorted us into the interrogation area. They emptied our pockets and did a body search. In my pockets they found one order that I overlooked and failed to dispose of. Luckily, it turned out that it was the order regarding the use of English language stationery and invoices. We had to visit the 10 businesses and ask them not to use the English language on any of their documents. Guess which company was at the top of the list? "Steve's Super Store, 12 Kassandra St., Nicosia. I breathed a sigh of relief, because I thought that this gave me a way out. There was this huge British guy with a lot of muscle that started asking me questions, and every question was followed by a punch in the stomach. It was end of November 1958. I was two months shy of my 16th birthday and in tip-top physical shape. I was doing heavy lifting working in the grocery store and did more lifting with my cement weights on top of that. Every time I saw the punch coming my way, I tightened my six-pack abdominals and protected the insides of my abdomen, avoiding internal injuries.

"Why is this note in your pocket?" he asked.

"Because the first business on the list is my family's business, so somebody put this note on my desk to relay the message. I found that note on my desk, so I put it in my pocket," I answered.

73

I don't think they believed me, but I was sure it made a very good argument. The beating and questioning went on for some time but, as everything in life, it finally came to an end. My belly wall was sore from the beating, but thankfully, I did not have any pain inside.

By the time they finished the interrogation, it was very dark, well past the nightly curfew of 6 p.m. to 7 a.m. that applied to anyone between the ages of 14 and 40 years old. They called my father to come and take us home. When my father arrived, they gave him an earful that the resistance was turning the son against the father. Eventually they let us go with a pass of exemption for the curfew. We dropped Koullis off at his house first before we went home.

A few months later in 1959, an agreement was reached to establish the Democracy of Cyprus as an independent state. The seeds of division between the Greek (82 percent) and Turkish (18 percent) communities planted during the British occupation were also incorporated into the constitution of the new republic. The 18 percent Turkish minority received a 30 percent share of the government and veto power while Turkey, Greece and Great Britain became guarantor powers. These terms, should have never been accepted by our leader Archbishop Makarios, who accepted and signed the Zurich Agreement. He was under duress by the Greek Prime Minister Karamanlis to accept the terms. It was incompetence at best. When more rights are given to a minority beyond what they were entitled to, you are inviting discourse and trouble.

With the end of the hostilities and the establishment of the new republic of Cyprus, we entered a new era of Cyprus History, with high hopes for lasting peace. Steve's Super Store was doing fine, and the family continued to work in the store and attend school. Stavros was running a real estate office and was doing very well. Irene graduated and was working for Stavros. Costas and Anastasia were working at the store full time and Anastasia was also helping our mother with the house chores.

My Father's Illness

I was in the fifth grade of high school, and once again seriously entertained the idea of going into business instead of medicine but then something happened. It was the end of Spring in 1960 and my father started having some abdominal discomfort and cramps with severe pain every now and then. He went to a doctor who diagnosed a probable malabsorption syndrome and instructed him to eat a lot of fried and fatty foods. My father followed the doctor's instructions but saw no improvement at all. He started losing weight. He went to another doctor who also happened to be the Mayor of Nicosia, Dr. Dervis. His diagnosis was that my father had a peptic ulcer, so the doctor instructed him to avoid fried and fatty foods.

"Doctor, the other doctor told me that I should eat fried and fatty foods, and you are telling me not to. What should I do?" said my father.

"Go ahead and eat and to hell with it," Dr. Dervis told him.

It would have been funny if it were not so tragic. My father continued to deteriorate, so he took a week off, and went for a vacation for the first time in his life. He returned to our house in Karavas. He had severe constipation alternating with diarrhea. But the vacation did not do him any good either. The advice of the doctors in Cyprus proved useless, so he decided to go to England to seek proper care.

He arrived in London in October of 1960 and saw Dr. Himonides, a Greek doctor and general practitioner, who referred him to a surgeon, Dr. Handley, at Middlesex Hospital. Based on my father's history, the physical examination and the work up, he was diagnosed with an obstructing tumor of the colon and advised to undergo surgery. He knew that he had no other choice, so, with the advice of Dr. Himonides, he consented. In November 1960, he underwent an exploratory laparotomy and a resection of the sigmoid colon with the obstructing tumor.

The only thing he took to the hospital was a picture of his wife and every one of his children. As he told us later, he cried as he was going through the pictures except when he got to the photos of Anastasia and of John (Captain Trouble); those got him laughing. Anastasia and John always brought a smile to everybody's face. His days in the hospital were very tough. He was used to a house filled with his loved ones, never a dull moment. Now he was in serious pain, all alone, in a strange place, not really understanding what was going on. Dr. Himonides and the surgeon, Dr. Handley, were nice to him, but it was still a difficult and traumatic experience.

He slowly recovered and as soon as he had his strength back, he returned home to Cyprus. What a relief! He was healthy again, eating well and getting stronger by the day. Life returned to normal.

Now a senior and having turned 18 on Jan. 16, 1961, I got my learner's permit to drive. By this time, Stavros had moved to his own place but came home to take me for a driving lesson. One time after the driving lesson, he told me to drive to his office. "Park the car and get out," he said, when we arrived. "I have something to show you."

We went inside his office and sat down when he handed me a piece of paper from his drawer. It was a letter from our father's surgeon, Dr. Richard Handley, addressed to Dr. Papanikopoulos, who was the Cyprus contact. It read:

Dear Dr. Papanikopoulos,

I think you know that I operated on Mr. C. Christoudias for a carcinoma of the colon. I enclose a copy of my letter to his doctor in England Dr. Himonides, which will tell you about the operation. I am afraid the letter is a gloomy one from the long-term point of view but from the short-term point of view I think we have had a very satisfactory result.

Mr. Christoudias has recovered well from the operation and both his bladder and bowel are working normally. I think we have given him at any rate some months of fairly normal life, but it is certain that sooner or later the tumor in the liver will give rise to symptoms. Mr. Christoudias is taking his X-rays with him for you to see. I have not told him the full situation but have explained that he had an obstruction at the colon, which I have removed, and he has not asked me what the nature of the process was that had caused the obstruction,

Yours Sincerely,

Richard Handley

Stavros also gave me the letter sent to Dr. Himonides.

The letter read as followes:

copy Mr. R. S. Handley

16ᵗʰ November, 1960

Dr. G.J. Himonides.

75 Porchester Terrace,

W.2.

Dear Dr. Himonides,

As you already know, I operated on Mr. Christoudias last Saturday. I am sorry to say that I found hi (the) liver to contain a number of secondary deposits. I should think about ten separate nodules being palpable. However I felt that in view of the likelihood that the bowel would very soon obstruct that we ought to resect the primary tumour and I therefore did this. It was infiltrating the bladder and I had to excise a piece of the bladder wall about the size of a penny. However the removal all went quite smoothly and I think that it was the proper thing to do because it will give Mr. Christoudias extra months of life and his death will be very much easier from the liver condition than it would have been from bowel obstruction. I am sorry that the outlook here cannot be very good, but he is recovering well from the operation.

With kind Regards,

Yours sincerely,

"There are multiple liver nodules" and "secondary deposits".

I had not seen the words before, but I knew exactly what they meant. As I read and started digesting the content of the letters, my world collapsed around me. The message was clear. The man who was my hero, my role model, and whom I loved with all my heart, had a death sentence.

My father only had a few months to live and he did not even know it. Though he was feeling well at the time, there were difficult and painful days ahead of us. Stavros told me that no one else knew the truth about our father's condition and suggested that we keep it a secret for as long as we could. I agreed. The more people that knew about it, the more likely it would be that our father would hear about it. And how do you tell him that he only has a few months to live? How is he going to react to such terrible news? How is our mother going to take it? How is his condition going to deteriorate and when? What do we do when that happens? There were a ton of questions but no answer in sight.

I dreaded the time that my father was going to get worse. I prayed that time would stop, and life would remain stable with him alive and with the family. But time was like water running down a slope, with its own rules and natural laws to obey, oblivious to our prayers and wishes.

In March of 1961, four months after the operation, my father had an acute shortness of breath episode. He gasped for air and had to sit up for relief. We called a doctor who gave him an injection of morphine, which improved his symptoms. I panicked when I saw him suffering. I wanted to help him, but I was completely helpless. It was a feeling I couldn't describe in words, a feeling of being completely unable and powerless to intervene and sooth the pain of the person I adored and loved with all my heart.

From then on, everything went downhill. His appetite was gone, his strength evaporated, and he became jaundiced. He showed me some hard lumps that he had noticed in his belly. I palpated them. They were rock hard tumors in his right upper abdomen, which I now know were cancerous tumors and growing in his liver. The cancerous tumors blocked the bile tubes and caused bile to back-up into the blood stream, giving him that dark yellow color of jaundice.

In the middle of the night, he had pain again and called to me, "Come George my son, come." I jolted awake, my eyes wide open, hearing his cries of desperation. I felt completely useless and powerless, totally unable to help the person that meant everything to me. I stayed in bed, wide awake, with a heavy heart, and a feeling of desperation that I could not help my father. Or so I thought.

The knowledge and experience I have now has made me better able to understand my father's cry for help. He was not calling me to go cure him; he just wanted me to be next to him at his time of suffering and maybe hold his hand or utter a kind word to help sooth his pain. But what I know now I did not know then and I did not answer his call. I feel like I let him down and it's something I will carry with me and regret for the rest of my life.

My father's condition deteriorated fast, to a point where he could not stand or walk without help. He died at home, on April 28, 1961. We kept vigil overnight.

The funeral was the next day and everything seemed like a bad dream. I had mixed feelings about his death. On the one hand I was devastated that I lost my father, yet on the other hand I was relieved that he was not suffering any more. Three of my high school classmates, Nicos Polemidiotis, George Drakos and Stelios Papantoniou, came to the funeral for moral support. I could tell they understood my pain and desperation. Their presence was greatly appreciated.

Not everybody was sympathetic for my loss. A friend told me that a wise guy named Antonis, when he heard of my father's death, had said, "Let him go to hell." I was surprised and disgusted. How could anybody be so callus as to not respect the dead? I decided I had to teach him a lesson and told my friend, "Give Antonis a message. He is the one going to hell. He should expect a beating from me."

I had some political differences with Antonis but we used to be friends and I never thought he would stoop that low. The next day when we were leaving school, I saw him.

"You said you were going to beat me up! When is that going to happen?" he said sarcastically.

I could not believe it. This guy was really stupid! He was asking for a beating or he thought I was not going to keep my promise. He was so wrong!

"Right now," I responded. "Let's go to the square."

We rode our bikes to the square by the church, which was a few hundred yards from the school. We parked our bikes and faced each other. Then we attacked each other at the same time. He was no match for me! My first punch landed on his face, at the left eye socket. He was stunned but came back at me with some "air punches" while my fists kept landing on his chest and face. Suddenly his friend arrived and joined the fight, but I was able to manage both of them. In the meantime, other students passed by and separated us. Antonis and his friend got on their bikes and rode away. Antonis had to wear dark glasses for 6 weeks to hide the black eye that I gave him.

I did not mind that other students separated us and stopped the fight. I kept my "promise" to beat Antonis up, though it was more like a promise to my father's memory rather than to this jerk. My only injury was a swollen right hand at the base of my index finger that had landed on Antonis's face. That's what happens when a fist lands on somebody's face with a great force. That's Newton's Law: "To every action there is an equal and opposite reaction." From then on, every time I saw Antonis he never made eye contact with me. He just turned the other way and got out of my sight! That was fine with me.

With my father's passing, the family had to honor his memory by finding a way to successfully carry on. Stavros took on the role as leader of the family, managing the finances, and other matters of our father's property, such as the care of the orchards and the annual sale of the lemon crop. Irene had already gotten married in 1958 and was busy with her two girls, Mary born in 1959 and Cleo born in 1960. Costas ran the grocery store, as he had during our father's sickness, and later hired another employee. Anastasia helped out in the store, and also assisted our mother with the house. John and I continued to work in the store after school, helping customers, stocking shelves, filling orders and making deliveries.

Before he died, my father sold the olive grove in Lapithos he had inherited from his father for 600 Cyprus Pounds ($1,800). He deposited that money into a bank account he had opened in my name for my studies. He wanted me to study medicine and wanted to give me the seed money to start my education. My father made Stavros promise that he would help me study. At this point, I was very close to high school graduation and had to make a decision about my pathway to becoming a doctor.

Part 2: My Journey into Medicine

My College Years and Medical School

Pre-Medical Classes

I realized that the decision about my future was sealed with my father's death. Between the mismanagement of his condition by the doctors in Cyprus, and my own uselessness to answer his call for help, I knew I had to become a doctor and be of service to humanity. I knew I could not save the world, but I also knew I could definitely save some people and all of the thoughts I had about going into business evaporated into thin air. I knew what I wanted to do in life, and I knew that, no matter what, I was going to fulfill my dream of becoming a doctor. I had two choices for medical school—England or the Athens University Medical School. I wrote letters to several English medical schools about entrance requirements and learned that I needed to pass the GCE (General Certificate of Education) and all of the required subjects.

The GCE I could take in Cyprus by joining a special program at the English School in Nicosia. The two-year program was tailored to high school graduates that wanted to study in the UK. The less expensive way was to first meet the GCE requirements in Cyprus and then head to medical school in the UK.

I applied and enrolled in the English program and took the necessary subjects needed for medical school. It was an interesting experience studying advanced level biology, chemistry and physics. I had always loved physics when studying at the Pancyprian Gymnasium but did not care much about biology and chemistry. But when I studied those subjects at the English school, I came to love chemistry and biology in addition to physics. I had realized later that the earlier chemistry and biology teacher was not qualified, and we never got deep into the science. At the English school, I discovered that both chemistry and biology were interesting and intriguing.

In biology, one of the first things we did was dissect a Squamus Acanthias—a dogfish—and identify the different parts of its anatomy. The fish was preserved in formaldehyde, which was irritating to the nose and the eyes. Squamus Acanthias was different from other fish, because it has a skeleton of just cartilage and no bones. Further, it did not lay eggs, but gave birth to live offspring. It is a small fish, about 12 inches long, and readily available in the central Nicosia fish market.

Like our father earlier, Costas was going to the central market every day to buy fresh vegetables and meats for the family super store. I asked him to buy a few dogfish so I could dissect them at home; he got me plenty. One of the fish seemed kind of fat, so I opened it up. I found two pouches filled with baby dogfish. I stopped dissecting and brought it to school the next day. It was then preserved in formalin so it could be displayed in the lab for future classes. One day after finishing classes, I decided to dissect another dogfish at home. I gathered a fresh dogfish along with a board, some pins and my biology book with the squamous acanthias anatomy and brought everything to my bedroom. I placed the dogfish on the board and secured it with the pins like we did in the lab. I then turned to the book's dissection information and opened the fish with a scalpel. It was like being in love!

Before I could go further with the dissection, I heard Costas calling me. "George, I need some help!" The store had gotten busy and he needed an extra hand. I left everything in place and closed the bedroom door behind me. I stayed in the store for a couple of hours until it slowed down again and then headed back to my project of dissecting. As I reached the bedroom, I was surprised to see the door open; I knew I had closed it. I went inside and saw the board and the biology book but instead of the fish, there were three cats licking their lips! John had been curious about what I was doing in the bedroom and went in my room to check it out. He saw the opened fish and left but did not bother to close the door behind him. He inadvertently treated with a feast, three of our seven cats (we also had four dogs).

John showed up shortly after and told me he found what I was doing very interesting. I was a little upset that I had to start all over again with a new fish, but I seriously could not get really angry with John. I yelled at him for what he did, but he just laughed. I decided laughing was better than yelling so I laughed along with him!

This incident was like the times he would call all the dogs and cats and then throw a piece of meat in the middle to see them battle it out. Or when he poured black pepper on the cat's nose, causing it to sneeze repeatedly while trying to push the pepper off his nose with his paws.

Another time he gave one of our cats a hot piece of meat he pulled from a skewer, right off the fire. The poor cat was grabbing the meat, and then dropping it, over and over again, realizing it was too hot. Meanwhile, "Captain Trouble" was entertained, laughing his head off. Despite this, captain trouble actually loved our cats and dogs and treated them like family.

There was a big void in our lives with our father gone, but strangely enough I always felt he was next to me, teaching me his lessons: "always do what is right"; "treat people with respect"; "always wear a smile"; "fight for your rights"; "you can do and be anything you want in life if you are willing to work hard for it"; and "be kind to the needy." My father and I shared a special bond, which at times was resented by my siblings. I loved him so much! That bond lasted through my life and it will go on until my death.

Life went on, and the family continued its course. In 1962 Stavros took on the Mattar's Camp Hotel in the Troodos Mountains to run as another business. The 100-bed camp hotel was only open from June through September and always had 100 percent occupancy in August. It was the highest hotel in Cyprus at about 6,000 feet, where people from the low valleys could find a cool refuge and escape from the scourging heat of the Cyprus summer. The top of the mountain is 6,404 feet, and gets covered with snow every winter, making it accessible to skiers and snowboarders.

I went to the hotel every weekend and delivered food and supplies from the store and helped out with whatever was needed. The next year at Stavros's request, I ran the hotel. He added a nightclub with a live band, but the expenses ended up being too high and the operation period too short for profitability. Overall, the entire hotel enterprise was not profitable for Stavros and he just about broke even. At the end of the season he asked me to join him in his business endeavors, which included real estate, a travel agency and an import export enterprise. I declined. I knew my path to the future was already decided, having been influenced by our father's terrible experience and suffering. I was going to be a doctor.

When our father was alive, he bought a building lot in the same area of Nicosia where we lived, to build a house for Anastasia. Providing a house by the parents to every daughter as a dowry, was traditional in Cyprus. My father had already built a house for Irene before she got married. He intended to build a house for Anastasia, and give the youngest, Dora, the original Nicosia home. In 1962 our mother sold an olive grove she had in Karavas for 2,000 Cyprus pounds, which was used to build a house for Anastasia. Stavros asked me to give him $300 Cyprus pounds from the bank account my father had opened for me. He said he needed it to finish Anastasia's house so I did not question his intentions. After giving him the amount he asked me for, I was left with an account balance of 300 pounds.

Medical School

The time came in September of 1963 to make a decision about where I was going to study. I passed my GCE exams, but the expenses were too high to study in the UK. I decided to go to Athens University Medical School, which was significantly less expensive. Additionally, the University of Athens gave preferential treatment to non-Greek citizens from abroad, allowing them to enroll in the school of their choice without taking the entrance exams. The only requirements were to be a graduate of a high school that was approved by the Greek Ministry of Education. I was a graduate of the Pancyprian Gymnasium High School, which had the Greek Ministry of Education approval, so I qualified.

I made an arrangement with the Bank of Cyprus to remit 30 pounds a month while I studied. I got all my documents in order, packed my suitcase, and bought a boat ticket to Piraeus for 7 Cyprus pounds (about $20), for the 36-hour "on deck" trip. Stavros and our mother drove me to the ferry Pegasus in Limassol, and we said our goodbyes. As I embarked for Greece on the boat's deck, I at first felt a little dizzy and nauseous, even before the boat took off. It was my first trip out of Cyprus and the first time I was on a big boat. My high school had organized a trip to Greece in the summer of 1960 when my father was sick, but traveling wasn't a consideration for me at the time.

I eventually got over the dizziness and nausea and started feeling like a happy sailor, enjoying every moment of the cool September breeze of the Mediterranean and the Aegean Sea. When the ferry arrived in Piraeus, I took the train to Athens to see my high school friends Stelios, Nicos and George. They welcomed me and showed me the medical school, restaurants and some Archaeological sites. While eating at a restaurant later, we went down the memory lane of our high school days.

The next day I looked for an apartment and rented an affordable small studio in the basement of a private hospital. It was the perfect location, in walking distance to the medical school's basic science building

I needed to attend every day. After that I went to enroll in the medical school and presented my high school diploma as required. I was officially enrolled as a medical student at the end of September 1963.

The basic science subjects were easy for me because I had studied them at the English School on an advanced level. My first year quickly breezed by painlessly. Other than my friends in Athens, I also had relatives. My Yiayia Eleni's brother Christodoulos went to Athens, got married and had three sons, Stavros, and his twin brother Achilleas, and the youngest Andreas. Stavros's wife, Rita, was sweet, kind-hearted, welcoming and polite. I had an open invitation to lunch every Sunday and I kept it. It was such a pleasure to spend practically every Sunday with my family in Athens. It was Stavros, Rita, their son Costas, and Stavros's aunt, who had never married, because her fiancé was killed by the Nazis during the occupation of Greece (1941-1945), in the second world war. Sometimes Stavros's first son Christos from his first wife was also there.

I enjoyed listening to the stories uncle Stavros told us. They were stories he had heard from his father Christodoulos and one in particular stuck in my mind. The story was from probably around late 1870's, early 1880's, when uncle Stavros's father was a small child. He was growing up in the same house I was born and Christodoulos went to play in the ravine next to the house. His father, Stavros, my great grandfather, went looking for him to no avail. He finally showed up wet and happy, but his happiness did not last long. Stavros grabbed him, tied him up and suspended him from a hook hanging from the center of the ceiling. Stavros then took a stick and started beating him up. With every strike, a crab fell from his pants! When he was at the ravine, he had been catching crabs from the water and placing them in the crease of his pants, which he formed by rolling the waist. He planned to cook them in the charcoal and eat them but unfortunately, things did not work out for him. No wonder he left home for Athens when he reached the age of 17.

The Sundays I spent with these lovely people, made my life so much easier and more enjoyable. Support also came from my mother Maritsa and my sister Anastasia who wrote detailed letters regularly about family life and whatever was happening in Cyprus.

The year went by fast and I passed all of my tests in all the subjects. I returned to Cyprus at the end of June 1964. I worked at the store or at Stavros's office, wherever I was needed, and I enjoyed the work whatever and wherever it was.

Stavros took a mortgage on Anastasia's house to buy a parcel of land with another partner. He told Anastasia the land could be subdivided into 24 building lots by the sea, netting 12 lots, which could then be shared equally with six lots each. Anastasia was now working at Stavros's office with no salary.

In September of 1964 I returned to Athens to start my second year of medical school. This time I found a place to live on the second floor of a rooming house for 400 drachmas, or about $13 per month. The second year's subjects were anatomy, histology-embryology, biochemistry and pathology. I liked all the subjects and I asked my brother Stavros to buy my medical textbooks in English, the next time he went to London for his business. He obliged and I was very happy to have English textbooks in all the relevant subjects. I liked having more references to review while also keeping up with my English.

The Cyprus intercommunal Trouble

Everything had been going smoothly until final exams. There were rumors that the Turks in Cyprus, with the support of Turkey, were going to revolt so Turkey would intervene and partition the island. General Grivas, the military leader of the Cyprus uprising against the British, decided to provide combat training to all Cypriot students in Athens. He wanted to form his own army and take us back to Cyprus to defend our country. We were taken to the Chalkis Military base and trained intensively for 40 days.

I was assigned a heavy Bren machine gun and had to carry it long distances every day and sometimes during the night. The food was inadequate, and the training intense and demanding. All my friends, Nicos, Stelios, and George D., were in the same squad with me. We had fought the British before as high school kids during the resistance, with a much different role. Now we were men, and this was the real thing. I was exhausted. I lost a lot of weight, felt weak, and had difficulty carrying that heavy machine gun day after day. The sedentary lifestyle of prolonged studying, threw me out of shape. Everybody else was carrying a rifle or a Sten gun, both much lighter than what I had to carry. The only thing heavier than the Bren was the Bazooka.

My friend Nicos realized my difficulty so one time he was considerate enough to exchange his rifle with my machine gun, to make things easier for me. I thanked him very much for his care and consideration and accepted his gesture with gratitude. This did not last long. The staff sergeant, who had fought valiantly in Korea, pointed his finger at me, and two others: "You, you and you," he said. "Carry the bazooka back to the camp." I did not know why these things happened to me! Maybe it was because I could deal with them. I did not know whether I should laugh or cry, but both would be a bad idea. If I laughed, that would insult my superior, and if I cried, that would insult my manhood. Men don't cry, so neither did I, not that time anyway.

I just spoke to the staff sergeant in a nice way. "Sir, I have been carrying the Bren gun every single day, and that got me exhausted. My friend just a couple of minutes ago gave me his rifle and took the machine gun to help me out. I would love to carry the Bazooka, but I am afraid I am too weak to do that. Please assign somebody else to do it." He looked at me for a second and pointed to another guy. "You," he said and picked somebody else for the job.

The intensive training lasted 40 days. About 600 of us, then boarded a ship and headed for Cyprus. Though we did not know it at the time, General Grivas was on the same ship with us. We arrived at the port of Limassol the next day and transferred to buses headed for Nicosia. After giving them our contact information, we were told to go home, stay put and wait for new orders.

A fundamental disagreement about the best course of action bubbled to the surface during a meeting between General Grivas and the President of Cyprus, Archbishop Makarios. From what I heard, Grivas wanted to use us as the army of Cyprus, but Makarios had serious doubts about a plan that utilized students as the army—"these young adults represented the future of the country". Instead, Makarios proposed forming a new army with mandatory service for all young men and send the students back to their studies.

And so, it went. We were told that a National Guard would be formed with obligatory service and if we wanted to enlist, we could, but if we wanted a deferment, we could do that too. I applied and received a deferment and returned to Athens to continue my studies. I believed I had a destiny to fulfill. I missed the exam period, but special arrangements were made for the Cypriot students that had gone for military training.

Life as a Medical Student

I studied very hard and I believed I had solid grasp and knowledge of the subjects. Some of the exams were oral and given by the professor. I was very confident that I was going to have no problem passing my exams in all subjects except for histology-embryology, not because I was not well prepared, but because I heard some crazy, strange things about the professor, Mr. Sklavounos. The word was that he was kind of a racist and unpredictable. If you were of a fair color and blond, he was inclined to give you a passing mark. If you had dark skin and features, you would have some difficulties passing. I did not really believe that, thinking that all the talk about it was nothing but exaggeration, but at the same time, I could not completely ignore the warnings, so I was nervous.

The day of the histology-embryology exams came, and students gathered in the hall by the professor's office, waiting to be called in for the test. The messenger showed up and called five names including mine. After handing in our ID-registration booklets, we were escorted into the histology-embryology lab where the professor was sitting at his desk. There were five chairs lined up in front of the desk and we were seated in the order we were called in. The booklets were used for student identification but also had subject tabs for exam grades. The passing mark was any number between 5 and 10. A number of zero to four was a failing mark.

The professor separated us into two groups; I was the third student of the first group. He then opened a German Journal of embryology and placed it in front of the first group with the instructions/command: "Study the specimen." He turned to the other group and spent several minutes asking the two students different questions. The three of us that had to "study the specimen" weren't paying much attention to his questioning. We were too busy checking out the picture in the embryology journal opened in front of us. There was a line drawn from each of the embryo's parts to wording that described and identified the parts but written in German. I studied German for six months at the Goethe Institute in Athens, not enough to speak fluently but enough to understand that the picture was a cross section of an embryo in its fourth month. I also understood enough to identify the other parts. Scientific language is similar to English, Latin and Greek terminology. I whispered all the information to the other two students while the professor was busy shooting questions to the second group of students.

He then turned to the first student of my group. "Identify the specimen," he said sternly. The first student told him whatever he remembered from my whispering. "You don't know anything," the professor said.

He turned to the second student. "Identify the specimen," he told her. She recited the different parts one by one but did not mention that it was a cross section of a four-month-old embryo, nor did she identify the placenta.

The professor said nothing as he turned to me, handed me a pointer and said, "You!" I pointed to each structure and said, "We have a cross section of a fourth month embryo, and this is the placenta."

"Is that all you see?" he said irritated. I had only mentioned whatever was missing, from the answer by the previous student, but I recovered very fast.

"There are more! This is the heart, these are the villi of the placenta, this is the amniotic sac."

He took the pointer from my hand, pointed to the placenta and said, "This is the placenta." He gave the pointer back to me saying, "Show me the placenta."

I pointed at the placenta repeating what he said. "This is the placenta." This scenario continued for a few times—him pointing to a part, identifying it and then asking me to do the same.

I had already identified the parts, so it did not make any sense. It was like a comedy.

He then addressed all of us. "The examination is finished, go."

We left the lab and waited outside the building for the messenger to come out with our ID-registration booklets and receive his tips. We did not know what to expect, so we all were very nervous and anxious. He finally showed up with some information. Coming down the stairs, he exclaimed:

"Mother, oh mother cry for me!" That was bad news. He gave each one of us his booklet. Four students failed and just one passed-I was the one! I passed with a grade of 8 out of 10. Everybody else got a failing grade of 4! Now I had a personal experience of this professor's eccentricity and realized that everything I heard about him was true.

I passed every subject and that opened the door to third year classes. The third-year curriculum had one of the most difficult subjects in medical school: Pharmacology. The medical school system allowed students to carry over a total of two subjects from any year until senior year. They could fail or not take the exam until senior year, but they could not graduate until they passed the exams of every single subject in the six-year curriculum. All exams were given in the end of spring-early Summer and in the fall, and there was no limit of how many times students could take an exam. You could advance to the next year as long as you did not have pending exams in more than two subjects.

There were about 600 students who had passed all of the six-year curriculum subjects except for pharmacology, which was the only thing holding them back from their diploma. The difficulty of pharmacology was that there were hundreds of chemical formulae that needed to be memorized, as well as the actions and side effects of every drug in the formulary. I knew that I had to develop a new study strategy if I was going to successfully take the pharmacology exam.

Up until that point, I used to get up at 9 or 10 a.m., go to a lecture or two, have lunch, rest for 30 minutes and then study for about 3 hours until 6 p.m. . I then paused for supper. By the time I went to the restaurant, had my supper and got back to my apartment, it was about 8 p.m. I would rest for 30 minutes and then study until 2 or 3 a.m. This schedule provided 5-8 hours of useful study time daily, about 30-48 hours per week, or an average of 39 hours per week. The problem is that the day and evening hours were associated with a lot of disruptions, so they were not enough to provide adequate familiarity of the subjects, especially pharmacology.

I calculated that I needed to study a minimum of 60 hours per week in order to study, assimilate and pass all my third-year subjects including pharmacology. I heard one of my classmates mention that he was getting up at 6 a.m. to study and found that very productive because there were less disruptions that early, and he was also fresh and able to assimilate things better. I found that very intriguing, so I started thinking about it. I figured out that if I got up at five a.m. daily, had my coffee and toast and started studying by 5:30 a.m., I could concentrate and work for seven straight hours until lunch at 12:30 p.m. That would give me seven hours of study daily, so I would just have to do three more hours of work in the afternoon or evening to meet my target of 10 hours a day, or 60 hours per week of studying.

The 10-12 hours per week spent at lectures or in the lab, were over and above the study time. This schedule appeared to be a winner for me, so I implemented it. I moved to a studio apartment in the basement with a large window facing a flower garden and a door leading to it. I bought a folding desk for 150 drachmas ($5), plus 20 drachmas (67 cents) for delivery. I placed the desk by the window facing the garden and put my study plan into effect.

I kept a record of the time I spent studying. In the evenings, I got together with another student and we threw questions at each other as a way of training for the exams. The pharmacology exam, however, was written and the results would depend on students' knowledge of the subject, rather than on the idiosyncrasies or the mood of the professor.

I managed to keep my schedule on tract. I studied for six days, 60 hours per week. On Sundays I went to see Uncle Stavros and Rita and for lunch and family interaction. If, for whatever reason, I failed to reach the 60-hour mark for studying in any given week, I made up for it by studying on Sunday. Most of the time, however, I surpassed my 60-hour target.

The days were hard. I remember that every time I got out of the house to go for lunch or dinner, I felt like I was getting out of jail or detention. The weather was so beautiful in the spring and there I was, stuck in a chair studying, fighting the urge to go out and wander around the beautiful sites of Athens! It was really hard work, but I expected it to deliver the rewards when the time came, and it did. About 600 students took the written exam in pharmacology in June 1966 but only 36 of us passed! I was ecstatic! I was successful on my first try! The rest of the subjects were relatively easy, and I had no problem passing each one on my first try too.

From then on, I did not have any missteps except for the time that I took the oral exam in radiology, a subject that I liked a lot, studied well and I was familiar with. I gathered with the other students outside the radiology professor's office waiting to take the exam. The messenger came out and took seven of us into the professor's office. We gave him our ID-registration booklets and were seated in the seven chairs lined up in front of the professor's desk. The examination consisted of questions addressed to the first five students back and forth for about 30 minutes. He did not ask me a single question. He then started marking our "performance," starting with the first student. I was the seventh, the last student, and I was wondering what he was going to do with me, since he did not ask me about anything.

My curiosity was quickly satisfied, though not to my liking. He turned to me and said, "You did not tell us anything!" He was right about that, but he also did not ask me anything and did not give me the opportunity to point that out. "Three!" he said. Out of 10, it was a failing mark.

I was disappointed, but it was not the end of the world. I knew I could pass the exam if he only asked me some questions—and I knew how to accomplish that. The next time I took the exam, I decided I wouldn't go into the professor's office unless I was first in line. That is what I did on my second try in the fall, and it worked. He asked me a lot of questions, I answered them and passed the subject with no problem.

To gain practical exposure to clinical medicine, I used to go to the hospital that handled all of the daily emergencies for the day, and help the resident doctors on call with the scat work. The health care system in Athens consisted of hospitals rotating 24-hour periods to handle all the emergencies. In this way the hospital "on duty" was prepared to handle emergency visits and admissions by having all its personnel available to take care of the expected heavy patient load.

The "on duty" days were indeed very hectic, because of the large number of emergency visits, so the doctors were frequently over-whelmed. Having taken classes at the Laiko University Hospital, I got acquainted with the doctors working there. They were the ones who had to do all the work when the Laiko University Hospital was on duty. I approached the doctors and asked if they would allow me to come and help out by taking a new patient's history and handling the initial exam. This way I was helping out by doing some of their work, under their supervision, and at the same time I had the opportunity to be exposed to real life clinical situations that would help me appreciate the patients' problems and the proper course of care. Dr. Andreas, one of the internal medicine residents, was very receptive to my request and I got my chance to spend time at Laiko Hospital every time it was on duty. The plan worked out very well. When patients were brought to the unit, I was the first to see them, take a detail history, examine them and then give a report to Dr. Andreas. If a patient was in distress, Dr. Andreas stepped in at the beginning. This worked out great for me because I was able to develop the clinical skills necessary for patient evaluation and management. It was during those voluntary days that I felt like a real doctor for the first time.

One such day, a tourist from Scandinavia was brought in in a coma-tose state, after what was an obvious suicide attempt. An empty bottle of barbiturates was found next to his bed. As soon as he was brought to the unit, I called Dr. Andreas who rushed to his bedside. The diagnosis was made, and Dr. Andreas asked me what the antidote for barbiturates was, and how it should be given. He was checking my knowledge.

Pharmacology was a subject I had spent countless hours learning and memorizing, so my answer was fast and to the point: "Picrotoxine, injected very slowly, intravenously." Once the picrotoxine was brought over by the nurse, Dr. Andreas gave me the syringe to draw the medication, and then asked me to inject it intravenously "very slowly." Under his direct supervision I injected the medication a little at a time, taking a long time to administer the recommended dose. The patient was comatose and completely unresponsive when I started the injection. By the time I finished he opened his eyes, looked around and started talking to us. I was amazed! A lifeless body was transformed, talking to me in a matter of seconds from finishing the injection! It gave me so much joy to have the opportunity to actively participate in saving somebody's life. It satisfied my desire for purpose, accomplishment, and service to humanity, feelings that I enjoyed throughout my medical career.

A great aspect of the University of Athens Medical School was that it gave me a broad spectrum of knowledge. Every student that got to enroll and graduate from this prestigious institution was indeed fortunate. There were no electives; the curriculum covered every branch of medical science, both clinical and basic sciences. Every single branch had to be taken and the respective exam passed before a medical degree was earned. The four main clinical departments were internal medicine, surgery, pediatrics, and obstetrics and gynecology. Additional mandatory subjects taught were cardiology, ophthalmology, otorhinolaryngology (ear, nose and throat), urology, orthopedics, neurology, psychiatry, dermatology, public health, toxicology and forensic pathology, pathology, radiology, anatomy, histology and embryology, physiology, and pharmacology.

Professors and other faculty had unlimited access to large amphitheaters at every teaching facility that could accommodate several hundred students. The attendance at the lectures varied significantly, depending on the subject, the lecturer and the time of the presentation. The lectures usually started at 9 a.m. and continued through the afternoon. The professor of ophthalmology was the only one that gave his lectures at 7 a.m., so, out of several hundred students, only about 30 of us attended his lectures. I remember the first statement he made at the first lecture of the year. "Ladies and gentlemen what's happening here today is the same thing that happens in society, which is, only a small segment of the student body is working, while the rest are goofing off." That was an interesting statement, which sounded just about right.

The senior year of medical school involved a rotating internship in the four basic departments of the medical arts: internal medicine, surgery, pediatrics and obstetrics and gynecology. Three months were spent in each subject, before the students became eligible to take the final exams for their diploma.

In the meantime, there were new family developments in Cyprus. John had enlisted in the army in 1964 and fulfilled the mandatory 13 months of service. He wanted to study civil engineering but had not finalized his plans yet. He graduated from the Italian Terra Santa High School, which met the standards of the Greek Ministry of Education. John had already secured enrollment at the prestigious Milan Polytechnic but entertained the possibility of attending the Metsovio Polytechnic of Athens when he visited Greece in September of 1965.

When he inquired about it, he discovered he would have to take an entrance examination in the spring. That precluded enrollment for the academic year of 1965-66. I suggested that he consider studying medicine instead at Athens University Medical School, but he did not like the idea. He stuck to his choice of studying civil engineering. He continued his journey to Milan, and enrolled in the Milan Polytechnic, where he earned a doctorate in civil engineering. He graduated in 1970 and returned to Cyprus.

Costas got engaged to Stavroula, who was Anastasia's classmate at the American Academy. They got married in July of 1965, and had their first child, a son, on Feb. 20, 1966. They named him Christos, after our father, and I had the honor of being his Godfather. A second child, Evgenia, was born on April 27, 1970.

Stavros was working hard and playing harder, but he finally met his match. He got married to Constantina Panayiotou in the summer of 1966. They had their first child, Maria on Dec. 7, 1966 and their second child Charis, on Dec. 16, 1968. His business included import export, alcoholic beverages and tobacco products, a real estate office and real estate development.

Anastasia got married on Aug. 27, 1967, to Angelos Agathangelou who had roots from Karavas; his family was well acquainted with ours. His mother, a seamstress, had actually sewn my mother's wedding gown! Angelos was employed by Stavros but was let go after he got married to Anastasia, so he went back to his previous employment as a high school teacher. They moved into our house, which was assigned and titled to Theodora as her dowry. Anastasia's house rent, which was previously collected and used by Stavros "to help us study," was now directed to Anastasia.

Theodora graduated from high school in 1967 and joined me in Athens where she enrolled at the Vacaleau School of Fine Arts, to study interior decorating.

Military Rule, Paying for Medical School

A lot of things happened in 1967. In the early morning of April 21, I got up, had my coffee and sat down at my desk to study. Soon after, I heard some cracking noises, which sounded like pieces of wood thrown down at a nearby building construction site. I turned my radio on, and I was stunned to hear an announcement that the government was dissolved, and the country was now under military rule, and that people should stay home because Athens was under curfew. I had experienced "curfew" before, during the British occupation of Cyprus, but did not expect to live through it again in Greece, the birthplace of Democracy! I did not know what to make of it. I was foolish enough to run to my high school classmates who lived about a block away, wake them up and tell them that Greece was now ruled by a military junta.

"You are kidding," they said. "We don't believe you." When they turned on the radio, they were still in disbelief. The members of the overthrown government were arrested and jailed. The reporters of the opposing media were named as enemies of the people, like in every dictatorship, and arrested, as was anybody who dared open his mouth against the dictators. It did not take long for multiple jokes to pop up. Here is a typical one:

"If you need to have your tonsils removed you have to go to a proctologist, to have them removed through your rear end."

"Why?"

"Because if you open your mouth you go to jail!"

It was sad to see the land where Democracy was born fall into the chaos of dictatorship, which can never result in anything good.

The time period of 1967-68 was trying not just for Greece, but also for our family. It started with Stavros's demand that our lemon grove property in the valley, which was producing an income of 600 to 1,000 Cyprus pounds per year, be registered to him, for helping me and John with our studies. The rational was that Irene was given a mortgage-free, custom-built house as a dowry, while our father was still alive. Costas inherited the grocery business. Anastasia had a custom-built house, which was built on a lot purchased before our father died. Our mother sold an olive orchard in Karavas and the proceeds were used to build the house in 1962. That house was used as collateral for a loan to purchase a piece of sea-front property, which was subdivided into 12 building lots. Anastasia and Stavros were partners in this venture in 1963, which yielded six building lots for each of them.

John and I were happy to be funded for our studies with the property income and had no other claim or demand. Theodora received the family house and store property in Nicosia. We all thought it was reasonable that the lemon orchard in the valley be given to Stavros. His rational was very simple. He was paying for my, and John's studies and expected that the final total cost for both of us would reach 6,000 Cyprus pounds. He appraised the value of the lemon orchard at 6,000 pounds, so if the family gave him the property it would cover our expenses. Of course, he did not calculate the income he already got every year from the crop sale plus the rental income from Anastasia's house. Regardless, everybody agreed and signed over the property to Stavros, except Irene, who harbored severe reservations and refused to sign her share over. Stavros threatened that he would stop supporting me and John if she did not agree to sign the transfer, though in a letter to me, he stated clearly that no matter what, he intended to support me and John financially until we finished our studies. Irene eventually agreed with the distribution of the inheritance and the lemon orchard was transferred to Stavros at the end of 1967.

At about the same time, Stavros started selling some of the building lots of the sea front property and demanded that Anastasia transfer all her lots to him, because "it was his idea to buy that property." When that came to my attention, I got upset, and wrote a letter to Stavros, in which I raised my strong opposition to his demands and his tactics. I pointed out that if Anastasia's house was not used as collateral, he would have not been able to secure a loan for the purchase of the property, and he would have had no building lots, period. It was only fair that if her property was at risk because of the loan she should get the appropriate rewards when the venture proved successful. This was in the spring of 1968. I expected that my letter was going to encourage him to rethink his position, but I was so wrong! In May of 1968 I received his response in a letter.

> *"Dear George, I want to let you know that I will not be able to provide financial help for your studies anymore. If you want to continue your studies, you have to look for funds elsewhere."*

What a surprise! All the big promises that he "would be there for me no matter what" had evaporated. All the love and respect had disappeared, and all the caring was blown away by my objection to his greed! This was a very unsettling development, to say the least.

Stavros's behavior threatened to blow away the cohesiveness of the family and dissolve the mutual feelings of love, respect and care, which were a part of our family for as long as I could remember. I could neither believe what he did to me, nor understand why he did it. He proceeded to manipulate the situation so that Anastasia was compelled to sign all but one of her building lots to Stavros.

That behavior was inappropriate, but there was no time to be wasted on my part. In a few weeks I had to start my senior year, with the four 3-month rotations before graduation, and, all of a sudden, I did not know if I was going to have any money for rent and/or food. At least I did not have to worry about tuition fees since the government under George Papandreou made all state universities tuition free. What it boiled down to, was that I had two options. The first option was to demand that he live up to his commitment and continue to support me until I finished medical school, as he had promised just a few months ago. After all, that was the reason that he demanded and received possession of the precious lemon orchard.

That was the just and appropriate option, but at the same time it was the worst option, because it was going to tear our family apart, with a possible ongoing family feud. Besides, I needed to focus on my studies, as I was ready to enter the most critical part of my education, which would determine my success and future career.

The second option had two parts: a) I had to secure some money for my immediate needs for food and rent, and, b) I needed to secure a source of funds to carry me to my graduation, which in plain English meant "I needed to find a job."

For me this was a no brainer. The first option was rejected for obvious reasons. The second option was the most appealing for several reasons. First, I was trained by my father since the time I was a small child, to work, and work hard, so I had no problem with working, if I could only find a job. Then, I was also trained by my father, to persist in achieving my goals, irrespective of any and all difficulties, obstacles, or adversities. There was a big advantage in finishing my studies without any help from Stavros or anyone else for that matter. My medical school graduation would be solely my accomplishment, and nobody else's. I was thinking of my dead father as I was saying: "Where are you my father? Where are you to see me in all my glory, how I will get through this storm and come out triumphant, in bright sunshine, to the finish line, like you have, so many times!" I know my father had very high hopes for me. He thought I was going to be a very successful member of society. I imagined him saying: "Go on my son, show the world who you are. I taught you well. Don't bow to anybody! Prove to everybody what you can accomplish, irrespective of the circumstances. I will always be by your side!" Never for a minute did I doubt that I was going to stay the course and graduate from medical school despite any difficulties or problems.

I wrote a letter to my brother John, who was studying in Milan, and asked if he had any money that he could send me. His answer was swift. He had saved some money, as he always did, so he gave it to another student from Athens. The brother of that student came to my apartment and gave the equivalent amount in drachmas to me. Not only did John solve my immediate financial needs, but in a letter that came a few days later, he had also figured out a long-term solution too. He suggested that he would interrupt his studies and go to work for a year. He would send me the money he made so that I could finish medical school. Then, after I graduated, I could support him to finish his studies.

His offer was very moving but had no practical value at all, because there was no way that I would let him sacrifice the continuity of his studies to subsidize mine. Besides, Stavros had no more money for my studies because I stood up to him, but he was still willing and able to support John in accordance with the original agreement when he received the lemon grove. John's offer, however, had a huge moral value. It proved to me that our family values, the care, love and respect among us were still alive and well. I was deeply touched and appreciative of his gesture but there was no way I could even consider it. I thought that his valuable and immediate help with the funds he provided to me in my dire need was all I needed to recover from the shock of Stavros's rejection.

Despite the fact that this development happened at the worst possible time, during final exams, I was determined to secure employment to help me graduate. I first went to the Cyprus Student Federation in Athens and asked whether they had any information about job availability. My determination must have been very obvious because the guy appeared to look at me strangely.

"There are jobs," he said, "but you need to get a work permit from the Department of Labor." Translation: "You are going to starve to death before you secure a work permit, if you take into consideration the Greek bureaucracy." Strike one! I wasn't sure what to do next.

I knew there were many students that were working so I asked around and approached every classmate I saw to inquire whether they knew of anybody that had a job for a medical student. I was convinced that there was a job for me out there, somewhere, and I was determined to find it and take it! One of these classmates was Vasilis Politis. "Yes," he said, in response to my question.

"I work at a psychiatric clinic near the airport. The other medical student who works there is leaving because he is graduating now. Are you interested?"

"I certainly am!" I replied. "What do you do there?"

"You have to work in-house from 6 p.m. to 7 a.m. three nights a week and every other weekend. You have to address any medical emergencies and sometimes administer intravenous injections of medications. The clinic provides meals when you are there, and a room for the on-call doctor on duty," he explained. "Why don't you come with me this afternoon? I am on duty tonight, so I can show you the place and explain what your duties will be. You can also meet the director for an interview."

Working at The Psychiatric Hospital

And so it was. That afternoon we took the bus to the area of the acropolis by the Olympic Stadium, where the first modern Olympic Games were held in 1896. From there we took a second bus that passed by the psychiatric clinic, about 15 miles away. The clinic was a short distance from the bus stop. We went inside and Vasilis introduced me to the head nurse and the Medical director. The institution was a small private hospital housing about 20 non-violent psychiatric patients. The director and co-owner of the clinic was a nice polite man, very pleasant, who did not ask many questions. He wanted to know what year of medical school I was in and where I came from.

"You don't have the Cyprus accent," he said when I told him where I was from. The Cyprus dialect has a very distinct accent with idioms closer to ancient Greek. I guess after five years in Athens I adopted the Athenian accent. "You can start tomorrow," he said. "Your salary will be 3,000 drachmas a month, and a thirteenth salary (bonus of one month's salary) on Christmas."

That was enough to take care of my basic expenses, as well as Theodora's, such as rent and food. Vasilis then took me around the small hospital and introduced me to the rest of the staff. He showed me the on-call room and introduced me to the kitchen and dining room personnel. The on-call room had a comfortable bed and a desk, which was perfect for studying when there were no emergencies to attend.

I stayed at the clinic for a few hours to see what kind of emergencies Vasilis faced and how he managed them. It did not take long for the first emergency to occur. A patient was getting restless and combative. Vasilis administered a glucose hypertonic solution intravenously to the patient. That resulted in a complete change in the demeanor of the patient, who became very calm and cooperative. The patient then stared at me for several seconds and pointed at my hand. I was holding a cigarette, which I lit because I got nervous by the situation. I did not know why he was staring and pointing at me, saying nothing.

"He wants a cigarette," Vasilis explained. "Under normal circumstances, he is a good, nonviolent man."

I gave him a cigarette and used the next couple of hours to find out about the inner workings of the clinic and the problems Vasilis encountered with each of the patients. I thanked him for finding me a job and left the clinic. It took me about an hour to get back on the two busses, which meant that two hours were needed for commuting every time I had to work.

I was so relieved that my immediate future was now clear. The short-term needs were satisfied by John's generosity, giving me everything he had saved for a rainy day. Plus, my financial needs until the day of my graduation were now secured with the new job that my friend and classmate Vasilis had helped me find. Everything now was totally dependent on my abilities to work and also study and attend the rotating hospital assignments of my senior year. That made me very happy.

Having taken psychiatry with substantial practical applications under the psychiatry professor Dr. Scarpalezos, I felt comfortable, qualified and confident that I could successfully and accurately understand and address any problems that might arise at the psychiatric clinic. The endless hours I had spent volunteering at the hospitals were also helpful in giving me practical medical application experience. The voluminous theoretical teachings in all different specialties at Athens University Medical School also helped me significantly.

When I was commuting, I studied. I also found time to study on the nights I was on duty, as the number of emergencies, were few and far in between. I made rounds with the nursing supervisor, who gave me a report on all the patients when I arrived at the clinic in the late afternoon. I then had dinner, courtesy of the clinic, and sat down at my desk, hard at work to stay ahead in learning the material necessary for the hospital's clinical assignments.

It was hard work but that did not bother me. I always thrive under pressure. I had been training for a situation like this all my life, by the best mentor anybody could have dreamed of, my father! Despite the fact that he was dead for more than seven years, I always felt that he was right next to me, advising me, calming me down and cheering me on! Besides, being stuck at work for overnight duty kept me focused on my studies and away from everyday distractions, such as rest and entertainment.

I started working at the small psychiatric hospital, Ayia Glykeria. Theodora had finished her first year at the School for Fine Arts and returned to Cyprus in June of 1968. My work at the hospital didn't involve many serious events but at times there were incidents that needed my urgent attention, like the time an old man was beaten up in the wee hours of the morning by his younger roommate. The nurse woke me up to address the problem. I went to the room and asked the young patient why he attacked the poor old man.

"He was stepping on the Cross," the younger man said.

The old man was sleeping outside the covers with his legs crossed. The young roommate was offended because he misinterpreted what he saw. I examined the old man and thankfully he did not have any serious injuries, only some bruises on his face. I asked the nurse to transfer the old man to a different room, which solved the problem, though the old man had to deal with the black and blue discolorations, all over his face.

Senior Year Clinicals

My first senior year clinical assignment was in Obstetrics and Gynecology at the Areteion Hospital. It was an interesting rotation, but I was not particularly interested in that specialty. We had to be at the Hospital at 8 a.m. to take care of patients in the wards, or scrub in the operating room until 5 p.m. Just to make it on time I had to get up at 5 a.m., have breakfast, see the patients, and get to the bus stop by 6:45 am, to catch the bus to the Olympic Stadium, and then the second bus to the hospital, causing me a lot of anxiety of missing the bus. Even now, over 50 years later, though infrequently, I still have nightmares that I miss the bus, get on the wrong bus, or missing the bus connection to the Hospital! Even though I had no special interest in the specialty, I received substantial exposure to the workings of obstetrics and gynecology, which helped me a lot later, during my internship in Jersey City, N.J.

The second, three-month, clinical assignment was in General Surgery. This was a specialty I had a keen interest in, since it stimulated my imagination immensely. It made me very happy and I was certain that I wanted to become a surgeon, and a top one at that. I was assigned to the first surgical service, but I was eyeing the second surgical service, headed by a world-renowned surgeon and researcher, Dr. Constantinos Tountas. He had a reputation of being very tough and demanding, with high expectations from his students and his associates. It so happened that another classmate of mine, Solomos Spyrides, also from Cyprus was assigned to Dr. Tountas at Areteion Hospital but he was not particularly interested in a tough professor. He actually asked me if I was interested in exchanging assignments. Dr. Tountas and his service was my kind of stuff. Give me difficult, give me tough, give me demanding and I will show you how it's done. "Sure" I replied. "Let's get it done."

And so it was. I managed to get the assignment I was dreaming of—my favorite subject, surgery; my favorite professor, Dr. Tountas; and my favorite second surgical service. The vast majority of the surgeons on the second surgical service were trained in the United States, United Kingdom or Germany. I was very impressed with the knowledge of the surgical stuff and the leadership of Dr. Tountas, in keeping everybody on their toes from the last student to his top surgeons. I felt so stimulated, I could not find enough surgical textbooks or sources of information to devour. I was completely in synchrony with the no-nonsense attitude of the professor when addressing common sense surgical problems.

As students, we were assigned patients at the time they were admitted to the Hospital. We had to study every patient, to the smallest detail, and be familiar with the relevant knowledge regarding the diagnosis, anatomy, pathology, physiology, treatment and natural course of every patient's condition. During rounds we had to present each patient assigned to us to the professor and his entourage and answer many questions relevant to the different facets of the patient's diagnosis, supporting basic science, and plan of treatment. I was always ready for his questions and looked forward to my presentations.

One of the patients I was taking care of, was a patient in his fifties with concussion, sustained in a car accident, resulting in head injury. He presented with the typical symptoms associated with his condition, which are transient loss of consciousness, loss of recent memory, dizziness and headache. During the rounds, the professor asked several questions which I answered without any problem.

He then came up with another question. "Would you do a spinal tap on a patient with a head injury, when you suspect intracranial hemorrhage?"

"No sir," I replied. "Because the bleeding causes increased intracranial pressure, and a spinal tap will cause pressure on the tonsils towards the spinal canal, which could result in death."

That is when one of the residents made a total fool of himself, reacting to my answer. He laughed aloud and then commented, "What do the tonsils have to do with the brain?" Dr. Tountas gave him a dirty look and then scolded him. "We are talking about the tonsils that are a part of the cerebellum you ignorant fool."

The rotation in surgery had given me an additional push to excel. I felt I was now in complete command of my professional development, and that my accumulation of knowledge was on the right tract to make me a good doctor. One of my patients, an older, malnourished lady, had a colon malignancy, and needed a blood specimen for laboratory testing. I was asked to draw blood from her. I checked the veins of her arm and I was pleased to see the biggest veins I had ever encounter. This is going to be easy, I thought to myself. The lady was very thin, so the veins were sticking out, the size of my pinky! I placed a tourniquet cleaned the skin with an alcohol swab, got the syringe with the needle in my hand and penetrated the skin on top of the vein and pushed it to enter the vein.

To my surprise the needle did not go in. Instead of penetrating the vein it pushed it away. I tried again and again to get in the vein, but it appeared that the vein had its own mind. It was moving away without penetration every time I tried to engage it. Frustrated by my failure, I pulled the needle out and tried to figure out what was preventing me from successfully accessing the vein. Why was the vein moving away? That was the question. I manipulated the vein with my finger, and I could move its position on the arm for a couple of centimeters. It is like a dog on a long leash I reasoned. You have to shorten the leash so that the dog cannot move. The connective tissue is too loose, and it renders the vein very mobile, like a moving target. I have to immobilize the vein before I even penetrate the skin. I then try to pull the skin on both sides of the vein, by positioning my left hand on the back side of the patient's forearm and pulling the skin away from both sides of the vein with my hand on the one side and my fingers on the other, and checked the vain mobility with my right index finger.

It was immobilized from side to side but not well enough up and down. That was corrected by stretching her skin towards the hand in addition to the above maneuver. The vein was now completely fixed in position to allow easy access. I tried again to draw blood and like magic the needle went in the vein and brought a big smile on my face. I had just developed my own method of accessing the veins successfully for blood drawing, administration of IV medication or starting IV access for fluid infusion. I carried this method throughout my career and demonstrated it to many medical students, interns and nurses over the years.

I received a letter from John, who was in Cyprus for summer recess, letting me know that he was going back to Milan to continue his studies. He was taking a boat to Piraeus, then to Brindisi Italy, and from there, by train, to Milan. The name of the boat was Pegasus and was scheduled to stay in Piraeus for several hours, so he wanted to see me if I could meet him by the boat. I wrote back that I will be there and made sure that I was not on duty at the psychiatric hospital that day. I took off a couple of hours earlier than usual from the university hospital and took the train from Athens to Piraeus. I walked around the port until I spotted the Pegasus and found a bench nearby, sat down and waited.

An American couple stopped by and asked me for directions to Tourkolimano, an area of Piraeus famous for the seafood restaurants. We struck a conversation and they said they were very interested in History. Their name was Goldstein, and they were surprised that I could pronounce it correctly. I told them I had a classmate by that name when I was a student at English School in Nicosia, Cyprus. I gave them the directions they wanted, and they went on their way. A few minutes later I saw John disembarking. I rushed to him to welcome him. We sat down at a coffee shop and talked and talked. First, I thanked him for his help that carried me over my difficult times. I told him that now I was in good shape financially since I had a job that I enjoyed, and that will take me through my studies. I boasted about how much I enjoyed my rotation at the surgical service and how good my performance was.

He told me he had a talk with Stavros about me, and that Stavros gave him a check for 60 Cyprus pounds to give me. I refused to accept it.

"John," I told him, "I will never again allow myself and my studies to become dependent on Stavros's mood or decisions. I have found my own pathway to success, and I will not allow Stavros to have anything to do with it. You keep the check, and let Stavros know that I don't want and don't need his money, his support or anything else from him. I am self-sufficient and I intent to stay like that."

Decades later John had told me that Stavros had told him at the time that he just wanted to teach me who the boss was, and that, after I learned my lesson, he intended to once again start providing funds for my studies. Well, my sentiment is that he did teach me that he was the boss, but he also taught me to depend solely on myself, if I wanted to finish my studies. I enjoyed seeing John again. He left for Brindisi, Italy and I took the train back to Athens.

My good performance in patient care did not go unnoticed by Dr. Tountas. I was lucky enough to see him perform the first kidney transplant in Athens. I was then asked by Dr. Tountas, together with three other students to "baby sit" the patient in shifts, for a week, measuring and recording the urine output and monitoring his vital signs every hour. The professor did not want to leave anything to chance. He was doing research relating to kidney transplantation in the animal lab for years, and I was lucky enough not only to be there when he did the first kidney transplant in Athens, but also to be a member of the team that took care of the transplant recipient. That made me very happy and proud.

I knew then that I was going to be a surgeon. I liked and enjoyed the excitement that comes from the surgical treatment, which is definitive most of the times. For example, when the patient has appendicitis, you take the appendix out and he is cured. The same situation applies to a plethora of other surgical problems.

The story is different in internal medicine conditions, such as heart failure. The patients are admitted with acute heart failure and they are in a really bad shape. You treat them, they get well, and you send them home, only to return a few days later with the same symptoms. That is something that did not appeal to me. Internal Medicine was the next three-month rotation of my senior year. It went by fast, without any significant events.

I finally reached the final rotation of my student career: Pediatrics. That was a specialty very dear to me, enjoying the cuteness of the children and their innocent remarks and reactions to my questions. I immensely enjoyed the three months I spent at the "Ayia Sophia" General Children's Hospital, though I came across an unfortunate situation that made me very sad. A four-year-old, an only child, beautiful, cute, smart girl was admitted to the hospital with anemia. A workup revealed that she had Acute Lymphocytic Leukemia, and she needed blood transfusions. I volunteered, together with another student, to donate blood for this little angel. She received the transfusions and many more, but her condition continued to deteriorate, and she finally died. I was in shock. I cried for her death, and I cried for her parents who lost the most precious part of their lives. I could not imagine their grief, and state of mind for their loss. This made me think how fragile life is and, at times, how limited our power is to affect events.

I found out that, despite my mental toughness, there was something I had great difficulty coping with: the death of a child, a situation that unfortunately I had to face two more times in later years during my practice. Before donating blood, I had to answer a questionnaire to make sure I did not have any conditions that would disqualify me as a donor. I mentioned the anemia I suffered as a child from consuming broad beans (favism). The pediatrician checked my blood for favism and the results showed that I had a severe deficiency of G-6-PD, (Glucose-6-Phosphoro Dehydrogenase), a red blood cell enzyme, something that was expected since I had a history of getting sick as a child after eating broad beans. The deficiency affects about 3% of the population.

When I had my blood drawn the pediatrician asked me to take a deep breath and hold it. I did, and I hardly felt the needle when I was stuck. So, I learned another thing that I applied in my practice for the rest of my career, which is that you hardly feel the needle if you take a deep breath and hold it, right before you are stuck with the needle.

I completed my senior year of medical school in June of 1969. I had no problem passing all my final exams, and I was eager to go back home to Cyprus. I missed my family so much. I had not seen them for two years so I could not wait to run back home. I did not even stay for the swearing in ceremony, to take the oath of medicine. I had to do that in a private ceremony with two other graduates in September, given by the Dean of the Medical School, Dr. Pantazis.

Hippocratic Oath

While in the senior year, I heard a lot of buzz about an exam you could take, if you wanted to continue your studies in the United States. The exam was called ECFMG (Educational Council for Foreign Medical Graduates) and would recognize the MD diploma as equivalent a diploma from an American medical school. I asked a student that had taken the test where I could find information and what I could expect. At first, he discouraged me, telling me that it was extremely difficult to pass. But then he told me that I could find all the information I needed at the Greek American Institute, in downtown Athens.

The exam was given in the summer and it was also administered in Cyprus, so I applied to take it there. I felt very confident about the level of my medical knowledge, and my command of the English terminology, since, in parallel to the Greek textbooks I used many English textbooks. I really felt very comfortable about my ability to understand and answer the questions. After all, the vast majority of the medical terms had a Greek origin, a fact that, as a Greek scholar, gave me an advantage.

Graduation and Returning to Cyprus as a Doctor

As soon as I finished my final exams of medical school, I took the boat back to Cyprus. I bought a ticket for the deck accommodations, since that was the only thing I could afford. It was a 36-hour journey from Piraeus to the port of Limassol. As the boat was going through the Aegean Sea, I was standing on the deck, holding onto the rail and thinking about the journey of my life, the difficulties I encountered, and how I was able to overcome all the obstacles and impediments to my success. Although I had difficulty accepting the betrayal by my eldest brother Stavros, I could not stop loving him. I decided I was not even going to bring up our disagreements when I saw him. After all, continuing the feud will not serve any purpose. What mattered most is the fact that I reached my goal, despite the difficulties I faced. I was a doctor now!

As the boat was moving and the sea breeze was caressing my face, I felt content with my achievements, and felt vindicated for not picking a fight with Stavros, when he left me hanging at the most critical point of my studies. It was over now. I was a doctor. Yes, I sacrificed a lot, but all the sacrifices and hard work made my victory ever so much sweeter.

I only had one huge regret: My father was not around to see his dream for me fulfilled. I found solace in the thought that he is looking at me from up there, in heaven, with a big smile on his face, filled with pride that I lived up to his standards and used his teachings to guide me to success. With that thought I took the blanket out of my suitcase, spread it open on the deck and laid down. When I woke up the boat had already docked in the port of Limassol. I was back in Cyprus.

I went back home and joined my family that I always loved dearly and had missed so much. I was so glad to see my mother and give her a big hug. She had kept me informed of what was going on with the family when I was in Athens. I checked her and found that she had a high blood pressure. I bought medication for her condition, gave it to her, and instructed her how to take it.

"Did the doctor give you these pills?" she asked. I smiled. "Mamma, I am the doctor," I replied, and that put a big smile on her face. She did not get used to the idea that now there was a doctor in the family. She also had Parkinson's disease and I had her come to Athens a couple of years earlier for evaluation. I had taken her to my professor of neurology for evaluation, and we also saw a neurosurgeon who talked to her about a procedure that could improve her condition. She declined the surgical treatment, but her condition remained stable on medication.

With everybody back home it was like old times again. There was a pressing problem that I had to address. I had no money left. Whatever little I had saved was drained and I needed to find a loan to help me out until I returned to Athens and found work. I took the ECFMG examination, on Sept. 10, 1969 in Nicosia, and the results would not be out for a couple of months. My future was totally dependent on the outcome of the ECFMG exams. If I passed it, then a big door opens up to go to the United States for specialization. If I failed, then I had to look for a surgical program in Greece or the UK. Of the doctors that took the ECFMG exam, only one third received a passing grade, so the odds were against me, but I still was very confident and hopeful that I was going to succeed. When I took the exam, I found it relatively easy. The only problem I had, was that I was not familiar with the multiple-choice questions format and ran out of time before I answered all the questions.

Nevertheless, the wide spectrum of medical science taught at Athens University Medical School had prepared me well, and I felt that I was ready for bigger and better things. I had to wait for a couple of months for the results and at the time I urgently needed funds to carry me over. First I went to my godparents and asked them for a loan. I explained the situation that I finished my studies and there was a possibility I would be going to America, but until then I needed to get a loan. I reassured them that their money was secure, and I was going to return every penny they loaned me with interest. I knew they were well to do and if they wanted, they could help me out.

"Unfortunately, we don't have any money" my godmother said. I knew that her assertion was not true, but I did not press the matter. I got the message. I had always been on very good terms with them and I was not about to spoil the relationship. They had no children and they may have been very careful with their money, which they will need for their retirement. I respected their decision, thanked them for their consideration and changed the subject.

Stavros' part of his business was to act as an agent for private loans, so I went to his office to see him, and asked him if he had any loans available. First, he asked me if I wanted any money to get by. I was penny less, but too proud to accept his money, so I told him that I was fine. Then he presented a ledger with my account, which indicated that he had paid me a total of 3,000 pounds. It included all the money he gave me to buy some clothes after I worked for him every summer.

I made a clear statement that I did not receive some of the money that was included in his ledger, but that was irrelevant now. Finally, he answered my question telling me that a client of his, Mr. Meletiou, whom I also knew, had 500 pounds to lend. He said he would ask him if he was willing to lend it to me and let me know.

Even if Mr. Meletiou did agree to let me the money, it would take some time and I was desperate for some funds now. I went to a cousin of mine, Tooulis, and asked him for a loan of 100 Cyprus pounds for a short term.

"Why don't you ask Stavros?" he said. I explained that I had a misunderstanding with Stavros, and I did not want to ask him for anything.

He gave me 100 pounds without any further ado and took me out of the bind.

That August, Anastasia was in her ninth month of pregnancy. She was due the end of the month, but Angelos, her husband left for the United States around Aug. 25, for post-graduate studies. She was going to follow him after he settled down. He was going to live with his cousin Christos in Dumont, New Jersey. The other cousin of Angelos, Evris, Christos' brother, had established a factory manufacturing filo dough and promised Angelos a job. Since Angelos left already, I was standing by to take Anastasia to the private clinic for delivery when she went into labor. She delivered on Aug. 30th, 1969. I went to a public phone booth to call Stavros with the news. I placed the coin in the slot and the dial tone came on. I dialed his number; the phone rang a few times and his wife Dina answered.

"Hello," she said, and kept repeating it while I was talking to her about Anastasias's new baby. She then hung up. I tried again, and the same thing happened. I did not know what to make of that. I then looked carefully at the instructions of using the phone, right in front of my eyes.

"After the party you are calling answers the phone, press button 'A' to complete the connection." I called again, and this time Stavros answered the phone. I pressed the "A" button and told him that Anastasia had a baby boy. He did not sound interested. If anything, he appeared irritated. It did not occur to me that I should have explained why Dina did not hear me say anything.

A few days later I received a call from Stavros telling me that Mr. Meletiou agreed to loan me the 500 pounds and that I could go to his office that evening to take care of the paperwork. That evening, I asked my mother to come with me and headed for Stavros's office, to sign the papers for the loan. His office was actually a four-bedroom apartment on the second floor of a building, across the street from the soccer stadium in the heart of Nicosia. The access to the apartment was from the side street, but he built a staircase on the Evagoras Avenue side, the main road,, to the balcony of the living room which he converted to his office. He maintained his residence there too, converting the apartment into a home office combination. He had that imagination and ability to think outside the box. I don't know who else would think to build a new staircase to an apartment and convert it into a prime office space!

We went in through the Evagoras Avenue access and climbed up to the office through the staircase. Stavros was sitting at his desk doing some paperwork. He welcomed us and asked us to have a seat, close to his desk. We did, as we went through the niceties, we expected to go through the process of the loan signing agreement.

Instead of that, Stavros said, "George can you explain to me why you ignore and despise my wife?"

"Who says I do!" I replied.

"You passed by her the other day and did not say hello," he said.

I did not remember such a thing. "I have no reason to ignore her or despise her, but if that was the case, then it is because I did not see her and did not notice her. I will always say 'hello' because that is the appropriate thing to do!"

I added. "I may not seek any advice from Dina or ask for any advice from her about any problem of mine, but I will always treat her with the appropriate respect!"

It did not end there. "Then why did you refuse to talk to her when you called to tell me that Anastasia had a baby?"

Oh! That's what it was all about. I realized I had made a big mistake by not explaining to Stavros when I talked to him on the phone the reason that Dina could not hear me. "This was the first time I used a public phone," I said, "and if you are familiar with the system, then you would know that the circuit is not complete until you press the appropriate button, after the person you are calling answers the phone. I was talking but the circuit was not complete! When I realized what happened I called back and pressed the button to complete the circuit. That is when you answered the phone. I am sorry, but I should have explained it then, when I called."

"You are finding excuses," he insisted in an aggressive, angry and disrespectful voice. "I still believe that you are not treating Dina with the proper respect."

I got irritated after all that I went through because of his refusal to live up to his promises at the most critical point of my studies. I was not about to sit there and allow him to step all over me, so I reacted in kind.

"Stavros, if you really believe that, then you are a typical example of a paranoid person. I am not in the mood and did not come here to have a fight or an argument!"

I then turned to my mother as I stood up. "Mamma, let's go home."

Stavros retreated. "No, no! Have a seat. Let's do the loan. I just wanted to let you know that I knew which rock I was going to trip on," using an old Cyprus saying, you use to indicate to somebody you know had betrayed you.

"Stavros," I answered, "on this rock, you did not trip! If you hurt your foot, it is because you kicked this rock!"

He did not respond. I sat down and we proceeded with finishing the paperwork of the loan. Mr. Meletiou showed up a few minutes later, and we concluded the transaction. Evidently Stavros asked us to be there earlier than he had told Mr. Meletiou, so that he had the opportunity to scold me for my behavior. Anyway, the loan was secured, and I had 500 pounds in my pocket, but not for long.

The next day I called my cousin Tooulis and asked him to pass by my house when he came to Nicosia, so I could repay him for the money he gave me. He lived in Karavas but traveled frequently to Nicosia for business. He came to my house the next day. He asked me to give him a medical examination, which I did. I then paid him the 100 pounds I had borrowed from him a couple of weeks earlier.

The next day I went to Karavas and visited Uncle John, my mother's brother. His son in law was a dentist that did some dental work for my mother, for which he was not paid as yet. Uncle John was complaining about it in public, while sitting in a coffee shop in the village. I thought that his behavior was inappropriate, so I wanted to put an end to it.

"Hello uncle John. My mother owes you some money, and I came to pay it. How much does she owe you?" I asked.

"Seventy pounds," he said.

I counted seventy pounds, gave it to him, asked for, and received a receipt that my mother's bill was paid in full. He asked me to stay for coffee, but I declined. I was not pleased with the way he treated my mother, his own younger sister and a widow, and I was not in the mood to sit down and sharing anything with him.

I went back to the house where I was born and relived the memories I had there. I remembered my Yiayia, who died in 1954, and all of the love she poured over me when she was alive. I recalled the good care she gave me and the sips of wine she treated me to, at dinner. I walked in the orchard and remembered climbing the lemon trees, the plum and orange trees. I climbed on a plum tree and collected some yellow plums. They were as delicious as I had remembered.

I went back to Nicosia. Anastasia had received a message from Angelos who was in the states, that he needed 165 pounds for his tuition. His cousin Christos was in Cyprus visiting, so he was going to come over to get the money and give it to Angelos. After giving Christos the 165 pounds for Angelos I was left with 165 pounds out of the 500 pounds that I borrowed. I gave my mother fifty pounds, but she was very reluctant to accept it.

"You need it more than I do my son," she said. That was a typical reaction of hers. She had always lived for her children and always gave us all she had, and more. She would deprive herself of everything so that we did not miss anything. Always praying for us, she never thought about herself, and always considered our needs, and that is all that mattered to her.

"Mamma," I responded. "I am a doctor now. I can find a job easily when I go back to Athens. I have enough to last me until then, and I am going to make a lot of money. From now on you will never have to wait for anybody's generosity, because I will make sure you will always have plenty of money for all your needs."

Her only income was from the sale of her orchard's lemon crop, but that was hardly enough for her basic needs. Stavros was the one who was handling that income and he would give her some money at times. She had no pension or other steady income on which she could rely, and I believed that this was very unfair after she worked so hard all her life and gave so much to all of us.

Now she had a pension plan—me—and the 50 pounds was the first installment. She accepted the money and thanked me from the bottom of her heart. I had a feeling that the 50 pounds did not mean much for her, but the respect with which I treated her meant the world.

Before I left, my mother wanted to transfer ownership of her house in Karavas to me, and give ownership of another piece of property she had by the main road to John and give the third property, a lemon orchard near the family house, to Theodora. We were her children that were still single. I did not accept her gift because I thought that it was better for John to own the family home, because he was on good terms with everyone, and still lived in Cyprus. I figured with John as the owner, everyone could visit and enjoy it.

So, she gave me the one-acre property by the main road, with the thought that someday I could built a clinic on that parcel of land. We went to the Land and Surveyors Departments, where the transfers of the titles were executed.

I went back to Athens in September of 1969. The first thing I did was to go to the medical School secretary and find out when I could take the "Oath of Hippocrates" to make my graduation official and join the ranks of medical professionals.

A week later I took the oath with two other graduates. Dr. Pantazis, the dean of the medical school, presided. It was just a humble ceremony, but it was charged with a great feeling of accomplishment. All the prerequisites for a stellar career and a promising future were met. I only had to take the opportunity that my graduation from medical school had given me and make the best of it.

My plan was to find a job and wait for the ECFMG examination results, which would determine my whole career and future. If I passed the examination, then it was America for me. If I failed, then I would have to do my specialty in Greece or the UK.

I saw a classified ad in the newspaper that said, "Doctor needed for the Tsagaris Hospital of Chest Diseases in Melissia." I called and went for an interview.

"You will work five days a week and you will be on call every other night and every other weekend, which you will have to spend in the hospital," Mr. Tsagaris, the administrator and owner of the Hospital, said as he offered me the Job. "The salary will be 3,000 drachmas a month, with a thirteenth salary for Christmas." That sounded good to me. We shook hands and I started work the next day.

The hospital was in a beautiful location in a suburb north of Athens and at a higher elevation. There were two internists, a female, Dr. Khoure, a male Dr. George Sakellarides, and a thoracic surgeon, Dr. Charonis on the staff. There was also another doctor who only worked three nights a week and every other weekend, just covering emergencies. The patient population consisted of lung tuberculosis patients, but there were also some with non-pulmonary diseases. I was very interested in pulmonary medicine, and took the opportunity to examine every patient, and listen to each patient's lungs. I became very good at locating any tuberculosis cavities of the lungs, by auscultation alone, and confirmed my clinical findings by an x-ray. There were one to two chest operations per week, resecting a badly infected lobe of the lung, and sometimes the indication for surgery was lung cancer.

Dr. Charonis was a chest surgeon who was trained at Kings County Hospital in Brooklyn, New York. I assisted him with every operation he performed, and I enjoyed participating in the surgical procedures.

The new academic year was about to start and since I anticipated passing the ECFMG exam and going to the USA, I thought that it will be prudent to find another student to share an apartment with Theodora. We had no problem finding another female student to stay with my sister and share the rent expenses. I also found a second job at a small private hospital in Psychico, another suburb of Athens. I worked there two to three nights a week and every other weekend. I rarely had a day and/or a night off, which I spend in an attic I had rented in Exarcheia, located at the Center of Athens. The attic was a very small room. It had a tiny window and its only access was through a small door in the corridor of the mansion, by using a wooden ladder stored in the corridor nearby.

After I climbed into my room, I pulled the ladder up and stored it in the room so no one would take it away and leave me stuck in my room. It was not the best of accommodations, but the price was right—300 drachmas, equivalent to $10 a month, was easily met, since Theodora's apartment rent was now shared with another girl, her roommate. Besides this was a temporary arrangement until I heard from the ECFMG about my examination results.

I often called my brother Stavros in Cyprus to find out if he received the results, because I had given my Nicosia home address as my mailing address for the results of the exam. Finally, when I asked him if the results were in, he said: "Yes! Congratulations! You got a 70!"

I did not know what to say. That meant that I fell into the "two thirds category" of the candidates that failed, since only one third of those taking the exam were successful.

"A 75 and up is the passing grade," I replied.

"Ha! Ha! I know! You got a 78! I was just kidding."

Stavros was always a prankster, but this was a step too far. I did not appreciate the joke about something on which my entire future depended. I thanked him anyway and asked him to mail the letter from ECFMG to me in Athens and ended the conversation.

Part 3: Life in America

Medical Internship and Residency

Deciding on a Program

So, with that, the pathway of my career and my future was drawn. I received the letter from ECFMG, which Stavros forwarded to me in mid November 1969. It certified that I passed the ECFMG exam and the English test that was given on Sept. 10 and had fulfilled all the obligations, with copies of my medical school diploma. I qualified for a Residency Program of the United States as either an intern or a resident. This was a dream come true for me. Now I had to find out about the steps I needed to take in order to reach my destination—the United States of America!

I asked Dr. Charonis for guidance. He explained that I would start my training as an intern for one year, followed by four years of surgical residency. I can do a rotating or straight surgical internship. There is a book listing all the internships and residencies available in the United States, and the Greek American Institute in Athens, has copies of this directory available to the public. The Greek American Institute was located close to the Athens University offices, in the center of Athens, an easy access location by bus.

Every opportunity I had, I went to the Greek American Institute and went through the Directory of Internships and Residencies. I read about the system of training in the different specialties, and what is expected from every candidate. I made copies of my medical school diploma, my high school diploma and the letter from the ECFMG stating that I completed the qualifying examination successfully. I had the Greek diplomas translated to English, at the Goethe Institute, which was a recognized translation service by the American Institutions. I started researching the training programs in the New Jersey, New York and Pennsylvania region, where I had many relatives.

There were programs that offered internships starting on Jan. 1, and those were the programs that interested me. I could not wait to fly to America and fulfill my own American Dream. I wanted to feel the challenge of meeting the demands of the specialization and continue my journey of becoming a surgeon.

I picked about 20 programs and sent copies of my documents, accompanied by the official translations and a letter applying for a rotating internship spot starting Jan. 1, 1970. The rotating internship included rotation in four specialties, three months each. They were: Internal Medicine, Surgery, Obstetrics and Gynecology and Pediatrics. I received some responses that were negative, some positive responses offering me a position, and some, like Kings county Hospital, did not respond at all.

I accepted a position at Christ Hospital on Palisades Avenue in Jersey City starting Jan. 1, 1970 with an annual salary of $9,000 that included accommodations at a hospital-owned apartment and a plane ticket to America. The hospital was close enough to Dumont, where my brother in law, Angelos, was staying, so everything seemed to be coming together on my terms.

I wrote a letter of acceptance to the administrator, Albert O. Davidson, informing him of my decision to join Christ Hospital's internship program. It was already December, so I requested that they send me the airplane ticket as soon as possible. I needed the letter of employment, so that I could get the necessary medical exam and exchange visitor's visa from the American Consulate.

I don't know what happened, but the ticket did not arrive until after the holidays. I fulfilled the requirements and received the visa, but the earliest day I could leave Greece for New York's Kennedy Airport was Jan. 6. I was scheduled to fly from Athens to Amsterdam with KLM, and then from there, to JFK airport.

I arrived in Amsterdam as scheduled but there was a snowstorm on Jan. 6 and the flight to JFK was cancelled and rescheduled for Jan. 7. Passengers were transferred to a local Hilton Hotel. I was given a room that was very cold. I had never stayed in a hotel before, so I did not complain. I just huddled under the covers and slept like a log.

The next day they took us back to the airport, and after a short delay we departed for our final destination.

Welcome to New York

We arrived at JFK in the evening of Jan. 7, 1970. "Welcome to JFK in New York," the pilot announced. "The temperature is 19 degrees, and the skies are clear."

Nice temperatures, I thought. I did not expect this balmy weather. I expected it to be much colder. The passengers were instructed to get off the plane and onto the tarmac, and head for the terminal. Upon exiting, the frigid cold caught my breath! This cannot be 19 degrees! Unless…unless the pilot was talking about Fahrenheit! Yes! That meant it was actually 7 degrees centigrade below freezing! I bundled up and hurried to the terminal.

The next thing was passport control, luggage retrieval and customs. That went by fast and I finally was in the public area of the terminal. I looked around and noticed a fellow holding a sign with my name. I approached him and introduced myself.

"Hi! I am Dr. George Christoudias and I think you are waiting for me!"

"Yes! My name is Sal, and I came to pick you up!"

He helped me with my luggage, and we walked to his ambulance! Yes, Sal came with a Christ Hospital ambulance! We got in and headed outside the airport.

"Do you mind if I go visit my mother? She lives near the airport," Sal asked.

"I have no objection," I replied.

We arrived at his mother's house in less than five minutes. He asked me to go in with him, but I declined. I preferred to wait in the ambulance. Sal only spent a few minutes visiting his mother and then we headed for Jersey City. I had no idea where we were and what route we were taking. Sal was kind enough to inform me about the area we were traveling.

"This is Queens, where the airport is. It is one of the five boroughs of New York City. The other four are Manhattan, Brooklyn, the Bronx, and Staten Island."

We continued talking about the Hospital and our families as we reached the next borough.

"This is Brooklyn," he informed me, and later, "This is Manhattan, the richest borough."

As we passed through the streets of Manhattan, I was stunned by the mountains of garbage, which was jammed up on the sidewalks.

"What happened here," I asked.

"Oh! The sanitation workers are on strike!" Sal replied.

I was amazed that New York City looked like a garbage dump. In my mind I expected a clean, shining city, the financial and cultural capital of the world. Of course, it was night and I could not see and appreciate everything New York City had to offer.

We went through the Holland tunnel and arrived at the hospital shortly thereafter. Sal took me to my apartment, on the second floor of an older red brick building across the street from Christ Hospital. I was going to share the two-bedroom apartment with Dr. Oscar Isidoro, a Filipino intern, whom I met for the first time when he answered the door. We introduced ourselves to each other, and talked about our lives, families and plans.

He told me that he had recently got married, but his wife, Luz, stayed back waiting for her visa to be issued. After we said our good-nights, I went to my room and got in bed. I slept well but at about 1 a.m. I was fully awake. I had hardly slept four hours, and I could not figure out why I was not sleepy anymore. I thought it could be because I was so excited that I was in America. I had never taken such a long trip, and the term "jet lag" was not invented yet, or, if it were invented, I was simply not aware of it.

I read until Oscar woke up and we both walked across the street to Christ Hospital. Everything outside was covered by several inches of snow, which looked so pretty. I met with Dr. Kawaja, the resident in charge of the intern schedule. She briefed me on the hospital rules and regulations and took me on an orientation tour around the hospital. The on-call schedule showed that I was on duty the first day. In addition to covering the inpatient emergencies overnight at regular dates, I was expected to staff the emergency room for 24 hours every few days. After the ER coverage we were not allowed to leave the hospital grounds, because we were then on ambulance call. Ambulance call meant that we had to go with the ambulance when they had to pick up or transfer a very sick patient.

A Gynecologist, Dr. Chary Sy, was in charge of the interns along with another gynecologist Dr. Fenimore, who was the director of the interns and residents' program. I met them both that day as I was assigned to the OB-GYN department for the first rotation of my internship.

Our duties as interns included taking patient history and doing the physical examination of every new admission. We documented all the findings in what is known as a "history and physical." We also had to secure intravenous access for iv fluid administration and blood transfusions and address any and all patient problems that presented during our watch, such as pain, bleeding, insomnia, high or low blood pressure, or any other problem of concern. We also had to assist in deliveries and any gynecological operations. I participated in numerous hysterectomies, which were performed by gynecologists or general practitioners. After a few days I was trusted to perform a delivery under the supervision of the obstetrician. I delivered a total of 21 babies, without any complication.

One of my priorities was to get in touch with Anastasia's husband Angelos, who was attending Fairleigh Dickinson University for post-graduate studies. He lived in Dumont, in Bergen County, New Jersey and worked at his cousin Evris' phyllo dough factory, which was also in Dumont. I called him and he came with Evris's brother-in-law, John Koufoudakis. They picked me up after work, the first time I was off, two days after I arrived in America.

We went to a diner for dinner and talked about his studies and his job, my trip and my plans. The next time I was off was on Sunday, so I went with Angelos and John to visit my cousin, Aunt Evgenia's son, Costas Kilaras at his diner on Hillside Avenue, in Queens New York. I knew Costas from the time he was in Cyprus, before he immigrated to America. He was a very pleasant, gentle and happy person who appeared to be very pleased that there was now a doctor in the family. He treated us to lunch and asked me about the rest of my brothers and sisters.

I told him that John and Theodora were still studying, and that I needed a loan because I wanted to help them until they graduate. He did not hesitate.

"How much do you need?" he said. I asked him for $500. He asked me to go with him to his office, where he counted out $500 and handed it to me.

"Let's write an agreement that shows that you loaned me this money," I suggested.

He smiled. "I know who you are," he replied. "No written agreement is needed. I trust you."

It was a good feeling to be trusted and respected, but I wanted to reinforce his trust.

"I thank you very much Costa! I will repay you as soon as I can, and definitely within a few months," I responded, expressing my gratitude. Sure enough, I was able to repay Costas about four months later, and reiterated my appreciation and gratitude to him.

The next day I went to the post office and bought three money orders. After finishing work, I sat down and wrote four letters. One to my mother, informing her that I arrived well, and everything was working out. I also included a money order for $150, asking her to use the money as she pleases. The second letter and $150 money order, I sent to John, telling him that from now on I will gladly be supporting him until he graduates from the Milan Polytechnic. I also wrote a letter to Dora, by which I reinforced my commitment to help her finish her studies and included the third $150 mail order.

Finally, the last letter I sent, was to Stavros, thanking him for everything he did for the family since our father's death, and letting him know that I was committed to take the responsibility of helping John and Theodora until they graduate, and also support my mother forever, thereby taking this "burden" off his shoulders. In other words, I was taking the control and responsibility for the family.

I was very happy that finally I was able to help John, Theodora and especially my mother, who had sacrificed so much for all of us. About five days later I received a letter from Stavros, stating that he had already done enough for the family, and it was now my turn to help John, because he had no intention of sending any more money to him. His letter came before I received my first paycheck! He did not mention Theodora because I was already helping her since he cut me off, before I started my senior year in medical school.

I am sure that Stavros received my letter at about the same time that I got his. My only regret was that I was not there to see his face when he found out that he did not have to officially go on record, that he openly betrayed his commitment to help John, since I offered on my own volition to help out.

A couple of weeks after I arrived, I traveled to Washington DC with Angelos and John Koufoudakis, and visited Angelos' cousin Kyriakos and his lovely wife Barbara. We went around and had the chance to see and admire the Capitol, passed outside the White House and visited the Smithsonian Museum. I found everything very impressive, realizing that I was in the Center of the World Power at a level never seen before.

Interning in Jersey City, New Jersey at Christ Hospital

The ground was covered by snow since I arrived in New Jersey, and it kept snowing enough to keep the ground hidden until March. It was also very cold and every time I tried to open a car door the static electricity would create a spark accompanied with a stinging sensation on my finger as it came in touch with the car door handle. It was a painful and unpleasant feeling and I did not like it at all. I kept thinking I had to find a way to eliminate that jolt from static electricity.

I thought about it and figured it out. My thought process went as follows: I am sure the amount of energy of the static electricity is negligible, but since the entire energy enters the body at a tiny point of a finger that came close to the metal, it becomes significant enough to cause pain. The only way to avoid the pain is to have whatever energy enters the skin distributed to a wider surface. This could be accomplished by holding a metal object, a key in this instance, before touching the metal object to the car door handle, transferring the static electricity energy to the entire area of the skin that was in contact with the metal object (key). I tried it and it worked! When touching the key to the door handle, I could see and hear the spark of the static electricity but did not feel anything else. Problem solved!

I was one of 10 new interns hired by Christ Hospital in January 1970. There was a special report about the new hires published on Feb. 4, 1970, in the *Hudson Dispatch*, a Union City newspaper that is now closed. The newspaper account indicated that the 10 new interns were: Dr. George C Christoudias, from Cyprus; Dr. Hoan Seng Tan and his wife Dr. Lien K. P. Oex-Tan from Indonesia; Dr Leo Fuentes and his wife Felma P. Jiminez-Fuentes, from the Philippines; Dr. Oscar O. Isidoro, from the Philippines; Dr. Sultan Mohammad, from west Pakistan; Dr Naheed Afzal from Pakistan; Dr Florante A. Novicio, from the Philippines; and Dr. Mukhtar Ahmad Malik from west Pakistan. At that time there was east and west Pakistan, that later were renamed Bangladesh (East Pakistan) and Pakistan (West Pakistan).

On Feb. 5, an official reception for the new interns was organized. The administrator, Mr. Albert O. Davidson, stressed the fact that despite the differences in the countries that we all came from with the United States, we were all joined by a lot of similarities and a common goal of providing quality healthcare to people. The director of the exchange program, Dr. Fenimore was present along with the administrator of the program, Dr. Chary Sy. The assistant administrator, Mr. Lacey, was also there, as well as the lovely librarian, Mrs. Lynch. It was a nice event that gave everyone the opportunity to get acquainted with the people we were going to be working and dealing with during our 12-month internship.

As all of the interns got acquainted with each other, I had this not-so-great idea to form a social club, so we could study and do clinical presentations to advance our studies, like a journal club. We had a meeting in the library area, and we formed an entity that we named "Christ Hospital Interns' Organization." We even had elections and I was elected president. We assigned reading material and I thought that everything was fine until a Greek American neurosurgeon, Dr. Sam Critides, who was a member of the Christ Hospital Medical Staff, called me a few weeks later, and told me that he wanted to talk to me. We met in the Hospital and he appeared very concerned. He asked me why we formed a union, what our intentions were, and informed me that the administration was very upset with the interns' activities of unionizing!

I was taken aback. I had no idea that the social club that we formed was conceived to be a union, that caused such a problem. It did not make any sense. My answer was very simple. "Dr. Critides," I said, "there is a huge misunderstanding. What we formed is nothing more than a journal club, to advance our studies. We are here but for 12 months. We all know what we signed up for, and we have no time or interest in changing the terms of our internship contract, or anything else for that matter. I appreciate very much that you made me aware of the trouble I unintentionally caused, but unionizing is not in my, or anybody else's, agenda. My main concern, as is every interns concern about the program, is to find a residency position in a decent program. Please assure the administration that they don't have to worry about this "perceived" problem anymore, because as of this moment our "organization" is dissolved. We can further our studies without it."

This was an honest presentation of the facts, and I am sure he appreciated it as such. I guess this was the time of Unions aggressive stands in the United States, and no employer wanted to deal with such problems.

Dr. Sam Critides was a fine neurosurgeon and a real Gentleman. He asked me what specialty I wanted to pursue, and I told him I was interested in Thoracic Surgery. I told him that I had heard the Kings County Medical Center's program was very good, and that I had asked them for an application form before I came to the States, but they did not even respond to me.

He smiled. "The word around is that you are a very good doctor. Your bedside manners, your knowledge and patient management are exceptional! The director of Thoracic Surgery at Kings County Medical Center, State university of New York, Downstate Medical Center Dr. Stuckey, was my classmate and he is a good friend of mine. I will be very happy to send him a note about you securing a position at that program."

I was stunned! This was an act of kindness and care beyond anything I could have dreamed of happening to me. This kind man was willing to help me and opened the door for me, to my dream residency, and I did not even ask him to do it. This had never happened to me before. I could not thank him enough and I made sure that I communicated to him how grateful I was for his gesture, and how that was going to define my career and my future.

"Sir, I will not let you down," I said. "I will make sure I do my best and I will make you proud of me."

Our earlier misunderstanding was ironed out and eliminated, and it was a smooth sailing after that.

I could not believe that I could be given the opportunity to secure a position in one of the top residency programs in America. Of course, getting into the residency program at KCMC, SUNY-DMC, did not in any way guarantee that I would remain in the program, nor that I would graduate from it. This was a "Pyramid" Program, meaning that there were many more positions for interns and first year residents that were positions for chief residents, who will graduate. So, the first hurdle was to be accepted in the program. Then every year there would be an evaluation of my performance, and that of all the residents, to decide if I could advance to the next level, until I reached the Chief Resident level, after 5 years, at which time I could graduate as a fully trained surgeon. But that was just fine with me. The only thing I needed was that opportunity to show who I was and what I could achieve. It appeared that the opportunity I was looking for was on the horizon.

I sent a letter to KCMC, SUNY-DMC asking for a residency application form. I was called for an interview in June of 1970. I saw Dr. Sawyer, a vascular Surgeon and Dr. Stuckey, the director of thoracic surgery. The interview went well, and I just had to wait for their decision.

In the meantime, my life as an intern continued—hard work, plenty surgery assistance, which I loved, and continuous study.

A couple of weeks after the fiasco of the "organization," which was misunderstood as a unionization, there was an interesting, though disturbing, incident. The intern Dr. Leo Fuentes had just finished a 24-hour shift and went to his apartment across the street from the hospital on a Sunday morning. Later that day he was called to go on an ambulance call, but did not respond fast enough, stating that he was too tired. The assistant administrator, Mr. Lacey was notified, and he called Dr. Fuentes telling him that if he didn't "show up right now," he will be fired. The argument escalated and Mr. Lacey proceeded to fire him. This was not a good thing, and I believed that the confrontation was unnecessary.

That Sunday I was at my cousin Peter's house in Spring Valley, New York. Peter Kilaras was aunt Eugenia's son, Costas Kilaras older brother. He was married to Sotera Klostris, also from Karavas, a terrific cook. They Had 3 beautiful daughters, Soula, Jenny and Antonia. I spent the day with them, and I heard the events about Dr. Leo Fuentes from Dr. Tan, when I got back to my apartment that evening. I was not sure that I should get involved, but then I thought that these actions were not good for any party, and I believed the problem could be addressed effectively by common sense.

The next day I went to the administrator's office and asked to see him and discuss the situation. The administrator, Albert O. Davidson, was very welcoming, and invited me into his office. I explained to him that I was not there as anybody's representative, or at anybody's request. I was there on my own initiative, in an attempt to help solve an unnecessary complication.

"I cannot talk about Dr. Fuentes decision to refuse to go to the ambulance call; personally, I would have not acted in that manner. At the same time, I don't think that Mr. Lacey's threats and subsequent firing of Dr. Fuentes was the appropriate course of action. You know that doctors don't grow on trees! It takes a lot of hard work, sacrifices and dedication to get to the point where we are as interns. After graduation from medical school we had to pass the qualifying ECFMG examination before we could get recognized as doctors by the American system and become eligible for a position in an internship or residency program. All these, I believe, have earned each and every one of the doctors a basic level of respect. Talking to them in a demeaning or threatening manner, is something I don't feel is the appropriate way of dealing with them. We need each other and we should act accordingly. Dr. Leo Fuentes's wife is also an intern at Christ Hospital. If Dr. Leo goes, the hospital will lose two interns, which I don't think is a desirable outcome. I suggest that you consider putting a hold on the firing of Dr. Fuentes and reset the way we interact with each other."

He listened to me carefully before responding. "That son of a gun has a short fuse that causes problems," he said referring to Mr. Lacey. I remember his words vividly because that was the first time I had ever heard the phrase "son of a gun."

He continued: "I think your suggestion is fair and wise, and I will go along with it. I will cancel the firing of Dr. Fuentes. You can tell him he can come back to work."

Mr. Davidson was a real gentleman, and a very wise and good administrator, and I was elated about his positive response to my request. This incident did not have any direct effect on my job or my relationship with the hospital or the interns, but it felt good that my intervention was helpful to both the hospital and the intern. I went to Dr. Fuentes and told him that I talked to the administrator, who agreed to cancel his dismissal, so he could return back to work, which he did.

Dr. Oscar Isidoro's wife Luz came from the Philippines, so I had to move into a new apartment. Dr. Isidoro was a nice man and the times we shared the same apartment were interesting. There were a lot of Philippino nurses at Christ Hospital, so I asked Oscar to teach me some common Philippine words. I wanted to learn how to say, "good morning" and he told me "halikan mo ako". When making my rounds, every time I saw a Filipino nurse, I greeted them with what I thought was "good morning" in their language. The response was strange. They would giggle and look at me like I had three heads! I could not figure out why they were acting so strange until one of them told me: "Later."

"Later what?" I said.

She laughed. "Do you know what 'halikan mo ako' means?"

"Yes," I said. "It means good morning."

She laughed even louder. "It means kiss me," she said with some satisfaction.

I took her up on that and discovered she was a superb kisser.

My first "affair" happened with a beautiful nurse. I was called to evaluate a patient on her unit. When I got to the unit, she looked at me. "What can I do for you honey?"

"Don't call me honey," I said, "because I come from a hot climate and catch on fire very easily!"

"Oh honey! That's what I am looking for," she replied.

Those words led to my first affair in the States. And it lasted for a while. Many followed and helped to make life feel complete, though I did not have much time to devote on the development of a serious relationship.

Several months after my arrival, I bought my first car from the Ford dealership about a 10-minute drive from the Hospital. It was a used 1967 blue metallic Ford Mustang. I paid $1,600 with two-year financing from the dealer. I was feeling quite happy that I was able to spend some money on myself and still be able to help my mother, my brother John and my sister Theodora. The hard work and tough times I went through were finally paying off and were providing the expected rewards.

On the professional side, the hospital was participating in a two-way, radio transmitted educational program with Albany Medical Center once a week. All interns had to attend. It was a stimulating program with a lot of information about the progress and innovations in patient care.

One such innovation was the "subclavian stick" for intravenous access. This method involved the insertion of a long needle into the large vein under the collarbone, medically known as the clavicle. Using a needle as a guide to find the vein, a long catheter was threaded through it into the vein. The needle was then removed, and the catheter was secured in place with a suture. The catheter could then be used for drawing blood, administering intravenous fluids, infusing blood or administering medications as needed. Of course, this was a special technique and precautions had to be made to minimize the possibility of complications, such as collapse of the lung, bleeding, penetration of the subclavian artery instead of the vein and infection.

This method was very appealing to me, especially for patients without visible or palpable peripheral veins. Not being able to find a vein for access was common, especially in overweight patients and those who were hospitalized for a prolonged period of time. That problem presented a real challenge for anyone who needed to draw blood or secure intravenous access.

The first opportunity to use the method presented itself with an overweight patient who needed to have blood drawn for lab work and also needed intravenous access for fluid administration. All attempts to find a vein had failed. The usual remaining option was to do a "cut down" under local anesthesia. That procedure involved making a small incision on the arm over the area of the vein, then locate the vein and insert the catheter.

The new subclavian stick approach did not require an incision and it was faster and less painful. I offered it to the patient instead of the "cut down." I explained to him that this was a new method and told him about the possible but unlikely complications.

I followed the directions and recommendations of the technique and I was able to access the subclavian vein on the first try. From then on, I became the specialist for vein access at Christ Hospital. I was called upon whenever there was a patient with "no good veins", to insert a "subclavian central venous catheter" as it was called, because the tip of the catheter was located in the big, central vein (Superior Vena Cava), close to the heart.

I enjoyed a good reputation with the medical staff, being complimented about my surgical skills assisting in the operating room, my competent patient management, and my wide spectrum of medical knowledge. Many Attending physicians allowed me to do small procedures under their supervision, such as a needle biopsy of the liver.

Dr. Frank, a medical Attending, showed me the biopsy needle, which was several inches long. He explained how to use it and the location and angle needed to insert it into the liver, to get a core of tissue for the biopsy. He then gave me the needle.

"Go ahead," he said, "get the biopsy.

I prepared the skin as per protocol, Inserted the long needle and maneuvered it accordingly to separate the core inside the needle from the liver. The result was a beautifully shaped intact core, perfect for the biopsy.

"Beginner's luck," exclaimed Dr. Frank. "Very often you have to try more than once to get a decent core."

I knew that I had the talent, the skills and the abilities I was born with, but I was not about to argue with Dr. Frank.

"Thank you, sir. I think it's because I have a good teacher that explained everything very well," I said pointing at him.

It was a true and accurate statement. I remembered the first time I had sutured a laceration in the emergency room in Athens. I was a medical student at the time, doing my surgical rotation in my senior year. The ER surgeon showed me how to tie surgical knots. A patient came in with a hand laceration and the surgeon asked me to stitch it under his supervision. I cleaned the wound as per the protocol and suture-repaired the laceration with interrupted sutures.

When I finished applying the dressing, the surgeon looked at me. "Are you sure you have not done this before"? He asked. I knew then that God, nature, and my parents had blessed me with the inherent abilities and talent to be a skillful surgeon, and that I could help a lot of patients, something I never allowed myself to forget throughout my career.

Another memorable event happened while I was on ER duty at Christ Hospital. It involved a patient in his 30s, who sustained severe injuries when a car he was working under, fell on him causing a crushing injury to his abdomen. He was brought to the ER in shock. He had a very rapid heart rate and barely detectable blood pressure, indicating severe blood loss. I immediately started an IV and sent a blood specimen for type and cross mach. I infused normal saline at a rapid rate, requested, received and transfused "O" negative blood.

At the same time the surgeon on call was notified and the operating room was informed. In a few minutes, the patient's blood pressure was better with a stronger, though still fast, heart rate. This was the first time that I was faced with an acute, severe, life-threatening situation alone. I did all the right things in patient management, resulting in stabilization of the patient in preparation for surgical intervention. That made me proud and served my confidence and self-esteem well.

The surgeon on call responded fast and the patient was taken to the operating room for emergency surgery. The attending surgeon presented the patient at the M and M (Morbidity and Mortality) conference a week later and in his presentation, he commented the "intern's management" of the patient in the emergency room, which saved the patient's life. Though he did not mention me by name, I was surprised for the credit he gave me because I thought that I did not do anything more than what I was supposed to do.

I learned a lot of things during my internship. A patient taught me one of the most important lessons in life, I ever learned. She was a lovely lady in her early 40s who had been operated on by general practitioner Dr. Miller and I was his assistant for the operation. She had multiple cancer tumors all over the abdomen, which originated from the ovaries. At the time, nothing could be done surgically, or medically to save her life.

I went to visit her the next day and try to give her courage. I entered her room and greeted her. "Good morning Mrs. Johnson. How are you today?"

"Oh, I am OK," she said.

"Your operation went well. You are going to be OK," I told her.

"No, I will not," she responded calmly. "I know I have end stage ovarian cancer, and nothing can be done about it. Dr. Miller talked to me and explained my condition. I know I am dying, but I am at peace with myself. That's life; sooner or later it always leads to death. For me, it is just going to be sooner."

I was taken aback because that's an answer I never anticipated. What a stoic position that lifted this lovely lady into a cloud of serenity and acceptance of her fate and the terrible news she received. I just realized that in my effort to comfort her I was just plainly and simply lying to her.

I remembered my father who suffered terribly for months before he died from advanced colon cancer when he was a mere 53 years old. At the time, neither I, nor anybody else had the decency or courage to tell him the truth. We thought that we were "protecting" him by hiding the information from him. We never gave him the opportunity to decide for himself how he wanted to arrange his affairs before the end arrived. I thought of the times he called for me in the middle of the night, and I was afraid to go to him. It's something I regret to this very day, because I did not know what to tell him or how to deal with the situation. I did not know what to do to lessen his pain. I did not have a clue on how to comfort him.

This lovely lady woke me up. I could only imagine how different things would have been if we were honest with my father about his condition towards the end of his life. I was so moved by this patient's demeanor and calmness. I felt embarrassed for lying to her, despite my good intentions. I admired her courage and told her that, as I desperately and unsuccessfully tried to hold back my tears.

This incident was engraved deeply in my memory and I think of that lovely lady very often. I don't think she ever realized how much of an influence she had on me personally, and on my career as a cancer surgeon in general. She surely shook me up so violently, so that from then on, I always told every patient the absolute truth about their condition and the prognosis, with just one exception. That was when, before the operation, the patient instructed me not to tell them what I found.

Typically, in that instance they would tell me, "Doctor, I do not want to know what you find when you operate on me. Just talk to my family."

In that case I respected their wishes and did not discuss any bad news with them. At times, during my career, the patient's family requested that I hide a bad diagnosis from the patient, and I refused to honor any such request. I explained to the family that patients do better when they know what is wrong with them. " I know that your request is made because you want to protect your loved one, but It is better for the patient to know the truth, and it is better for you", I would tell the family.

One thing that I was careful about was the timing of providing the information to the patient. I always waited a few days after surgery, when the patient recovered sufficiently, before proceeding to any discussion about their condition, unless the patient specifically asked me for the information earlier.

Discussing bad news with a patient was always the most difficult part of my job as a cancer surgeon. I always made sure that I presented the findings and their condition in a thoughtful way, with empathy and compassion, as if the patients were part of my family. The vast majority of the patients accepted the difficult situation with dignity and strength, as I assured them that I will always be there for them to answer any questions that might arise. I assured them I would help them deal with any problems that presented or decisions that had to be made in the course of their disease. This is a pledge and a promise I made sure I kept all the times with all my patients throughout my career.

I enjoyed my year at Christ Hospital. In general people were kind and considerate, though the work was hard and the hours, at times, too long. That was five decades ago but I remember very vividly a time that I had worked for 36 hours straight and had not eaten a meal for a whole day. When I finished from work at 6 p.m., I was exhausted but not as much as I was famished. There was a pizza place on Palisades Avenue next to Christ Hospital. I went there, bought a large pie for $2 and a 2-liter bottle of Coca-Cola and walked to my apartment across the street. I devoured the whole pie and the entire 2 liters of Coke. It was so delicious, that I can still taste it to this day! I then went to bed in complete "food coma." I slept through the night. I got up the next morning, took a shower, changed and walked across the street to continue my mission.

My brother in law Angelos had told me about a deli on Baldwin Avenue, a few blocks from the hospital that belonged to two people from Cyprus—Andy Michael and Chris Hadjiyerou. One day after work I walked there and introduced myself. It turned out that Andy's cousin, Stavros Christodoulou, was my classmate in the elementary school!

I ordered a roast beef sandwich and a bottle of coke, sat down on a milk carton and enjoyed it. I used to visit the deli frequently, especially when I was hungry and had an appetite to talk to somebody in Cyprus dialect, which is similar to the ancient Greek language. Andy Michael's family lived close to my sister in Teaneck. I met his family and we remained friends all my life. They are nice people and we treated each other like family. Andy lived a long life and died in 2019 at the age of 87.

The Next Step—Residency

Time quickly passed and I got accustomed to the rapid pace, though it was far from routine. Though I had applied to several programs for a surgical residency, I eagerly waited for a response from Kings County Hospital, Downstate Medical Center. The letter finally arrived in late fall. I nervously looked at the envelope. The secret of my future, my career and my success were sealed in that envelope, waiting to come out and reveal itself. I nervously opened the envelope, and pulled out the letter:

> "*We are pleased to inform you that you are accepted in the residency program of KCH-DMC. Please report at the Medical*

Staff Office on Dec. 7, 1970 between 9 and 10 a.m. for orientation, ID card and uniforms.

Signed, Zena Budris, Medical Staff secretary."

I was so happy! My dream was coming to fruition and transformed from imagination to flesh and bone reality. I just could not wait for "Pearl Harbor Day" to come. Dec. 7, 1970 finally arrived, and with it, several inches of snow dropped down from the sky and covered the entire region. When I asked for a day off to go to Kings County Hospital, the director of the program granted my request, but commented that it would be a treacherous drive to Brooklyn since so much snow was expected. I had been waiting for this day for too long, and no amount of snow or storm was going to keep me away. I started early and despite the accumulation of several inches of snow I arrived at the hospital on time. I found my way to the medical staff office, but nobody was there. They took the day off, because of the heavy snow.

I went to the department of surgery office and asked the secretary what I should do. They had a surgical resident take me around and show me the different surgical units, the ER departments for adults and the ones for children. I was also shown the house staff building where I would be staying. It was a massive conglomerate of different buildings covering 16 city blocks, with a 3,000-bed capacity. It was very impressive indeed. They also gave me a map as a guide to the different departments and buildings. The rest of the process would be completed when I reported for work in January. I got in my 1967 ford Mustang and drove back to my base at Christ Hospital, very carefully and very slowly through the heavy snow.

The rest of the days flew by and I was ready and eager to step up to the next level of my training. The events of my first year in the United States rolled through my mind like a movie. I revisited all the experiences of the year that went by and separated them into two categories: professional and personal.

At the professional level the event that stood out above all was the help I received from Dr. Critides to secure a spot at the residency program of my dreams. I felt so much gratitude. I was also very happy with the opportunity I had to learn new things in all specialties and assist in a great number of operations. Many surgeons allowed me to do small procedures, as they were as happy with me as I was with their generosity and willingness to teach me their surgical techniques. The surgical procedures were done either by the general practitioners or fully trained surgeons. Dr. Miller, a general practitioner, was doing more operations than anyone else. The fully trained surgeons that stood out were Dr. Morrow, Dr. Judy, Dr. Variano, Dr. Reyes, Dr. Arago and Dr. Lieberson.

The Strange, Unsettling Case of Dr. Mario Jascalevich

Of the many surgeons I became acquainted with, the fastest surgeon was Dr. Mario Jascalevich from Argentina. He ended up being charged in 1976 of murdering at least five patients in 1966 at Riverdell Hospital in Oradell, New Jersey while he was chief of surgery. He reportedly injected them with curare, a deadly Indian paralyzing agent that kills unless the patient is placed on a respirator.

The case unfolded following the suspicious deaths of several patients that were treated by other surgeons. Dr. Jascalevich's locker was searched and 18 vials of curare were discovered. The Bergen County District Attorney did not proceed with an indictment at the time (1966), because he did not think there was enough evidence for a conviction.

In January of 1976, however, the New York Times did their own investigation after an anonymous letter alleged that the Chief of Surgery at Riverdell Hospital in Oradell NJ was responsible for the deaths of several patients of other surgeons. There was enough evidence to proceed with a report about the alleged suspicious deaths caused by "Dr. X," as he was known in the media. Dr. Jascalevich was initially not exposed since the Bergen County DA had not proceeded with an indictment when this problem first surfaced in 1966.

Four months after the case was reopened in January 1976, Dr. Jascalevich's identity was revealed when he was indicted for the deaths of five patients. By then I was a chief resident and was shocked when I heard this "jaw dropping" news. I remembered him as a good and competent surgeon, and I could not imagine him killing other doctors' patients in order destroy their reputation and enhance his. It was stunning and sickening!

The 1978 verdict found him not guilty. After reading all of the reports, I concluded he was most likely guilty as charged. He ended up returning to Argentina where he died in 1984 at the age of 57.

During the time I operated with him at Christ Hospital, I had absolutely no idea, who he really was or what he had done. My understanding of my profession was always that it is not a job, but a calling to serve humanity by saving lives, not taking them away for any reason or excuse.

Defining Moments at Christ Hospital

During my internship at Christ Hospital, there were several patients who taught me valuable lessons. The first was from Mrs. Johnson, who told me she knew that she had end stage cancer and was aware that she was going to die "sooner rather than later." Another was the saddest and most heart-breaking moment of my internship—the death of an angelic 3-year-old girl who died in the hospital from pneumonia when I was rotating in pediatrics. I always had trouble coping with the death of any child, from whatever cause. I always believed, that there was a special place for them in heaven, where there is no pain or suffering, but the thought failed to soothe my sadness.

Then there was the kindness of Mrs. Lynch, the librarian. I asked her for instructions on how to go to New York. She was kind enough to ask Janette, a student nurse, to go with me to the city. Janette was a sweet girl and showed me where to get the bus to Journal Square and from there, the train to 42nd street in New York City. We walked around and found a Greek restaurant, called "Paradise," where we had a delicious dinner. It was my pleasure to treat Janette for her kindness and willingness to show me around.

The area was buzzing with all sorts of activities that could satisfy everybody's imagination, likes and desires. We walked around for a little longer and then returned to Jersey City. I thanked Janette for her kindness, and we went our own way.

I went back to Times Square often, because among other things, there was a Greek gift store where I could find newspapers from Greece and keep in touch with what was going on in my old country. One time, after getting the Greek papers, I saw a barbershop on my way to the train, so I went in for a haircut. The barber didn't know a word of English, so it was challenging to explain to him how I wanted my hair cut. I tried using my Italian but he did not understand either. I looked around, and after I showed him one of the pictures in his barbershop, he understood what I wanted.

Did I say, "he didn't know a word in English"? Actually, he did. He said "OK." So, he started cutting my hair and I started reading through the Greek newspaper. At one point somebody else walked in the shop and addressed the barber in Greek: Yasou Mitso! Pos Ise? ("I salute you Mitso. How are you"?).

I said to him in Greek, "You are Greek, and you were torturing me all this time trying to communicate with you?"

He was more surprised than I was. "I did not know that you are Greek," he said.

"Don't you see my newspaper? Did you think I was an Italian reading a Greek Newspaper, or what?" I said.

We both had a good laugh and from then on, his mouth moved faster than his scissors until the haircut was finished.

An important event that year was the May 1970 arrival of my sister Anastasia and her nine-month-old son Christos to join her husband Angelos, who was still a graduate student at Fairleigh Dickinson University and still working for his cousin in the phyllo dough factory in Dumont. He shared an apartment on Fort Lee Road in Teaneck, New Jersey. The apartment was about a 20-minute drive from Christ Hospital but was an hour by bus on the Red and Tan line. I did not get a car until a couple of months after Anastasia came to America. But regardless of the time it took to get there, I visited her often and enjoyed her homemade Cyprus cuisine and delicacies.

Dr. Hoan Tan and his wife Lian Oex Tan, both interns at Christ Hospital, were a very polite and gentle couple. In the Summer of 1970, they told me that they were planning to go to Allentown Pennsylvania to visit a friend and they invited me to join them. We drove for about two hours to Allentown and reached their friend's farm. It so happened that a cow was giving birth. Since I had finished my OB rotation with 21 deliveries under my belt, I promptly volunteered to help out. This was the first and only time that I saw or assisted in a calf's delivery, so in my resume about my internship, I could say that I delivered 21 babies and one calf!

My rotating internship year at Christ Hospital was interesting, fulfilling and rewarding. I enjoyed meeting so many new people, who in general, were kind and welcoming. I learned quite a lot, not only relating to medicine, but also about the culture, way of life and customs in the United States, and more specifically New Jersey. The rotating internship had fully met my hopes and expectations. Those experiences and memories have stayed with me through my entire life.

After finishing work on Dec. 31, 1970, I packed up my few belongings and drove to my sister Anastasia's place in Teaneck. It was a chance to spend New Year's Day with my family and rest for a day before reporting for work at KCH-DMC to continue my training.

My Residency at Kings County Hospital

On Jan. 2, I got up early and headed to my new home: Kings County Hospital Center. I arrived early and waited outside the medical staff office until the secretary and other personnel came in. I went through the routine process of getting a photo ID, six pairs of white uniforms and my lodging room keys for the medical staff building where all the interns were staying. There was a dining room on the ground floor with tables covered with white tablecloths, where the doctors were served three generous meals a day.

After the processing routine, the secretary referred me to Dr. Donald Klotz, a pediatric surgeon in charge of the work schedule for surgical interns and residents. There were over 100 of us. He was a very tall, kind, soft-spoken gentleman, who informed me that I was assigned to the surgical service at the State University Hospital, across the street from the Kings County Hospital. He explained to me that the schedule entailed reporting to the assigned unit at between 6:30 and 7 a.m.

When I was on call, I stayed on duty for 36 hours, finishing the next day between 5 and 6 p.m. I would be on call every other day and every other weekend. When we were on call on a Friday, we would work overnight until Saturday at Noon and have the rest of the weekend off. There was no specific number of hours that we had to work and no limit to the work hours per week either. I knew that the schedule was going to be tough, but I was wholly prepared for it.

I thanked Dr. Klotz for his help, and I walked across the street to the University Hospital, where I joined my assigned surgical team. I was given the list of the scat work that had to be completed and got to work. The difficulty I faced was the lack of familiarity with the unit. I did not know where anything was, and the nurses did not show any interest in helping me find that out. I was taken aback by the indifference of the University Hospital Surgical Service nurses, whose demeanor and interest was so different than that, at Christ Hospital, or any other hospital I had worked at in Greece, where the nurses were always there, ready to help out and assist me.

The other element that made my job difficult was that I had to answer to each and every attending surgeon about the patients and I was the only intern assigned to scat work. I had no time for lunch or dinner when I was on duty, and by the time I finished my 36-hour shift I was exhausted. It was customary that all the scat work was assigned to the interns. When I finished my internship, the "internship" category was eliminated, and all the staff became PGY (Post Graduate Year) indicating the years spent in training. The final year before graduation was the "Chief Resident" year.

One of my worse days at the University Hospital illustrates the nurses' disinterest. It was a hectic day, a really bad hectic day, and every resident was in the operating room. I alone was left in the unit to do the scat work—draw patients' bloods for lab work, change dressings, clean and irrigate infected wounds, start IVs and address all and every problem that needed immediate attention. During the day there was decent response by the nurses when I requested help. But when the evening shift showed up, that wasn't the case.

That particularly hectic day I was so busy that I had no time for food; there was no such thing as a lunch or dinner hour or even a coffee break, or any other break for that matter. One of the patients needed a vein access. He was an overweight man in his 50s who needed IV fluids and IV antibiotics. He had no peripheral veins and all attempts for access failed. During our team's evening rounds the chief resident instructed me to do a cut down on that patient. It was already about 9 p.m. and I had just finished all of my scat work. The nurses were sitting on their fat asses, talking their tongues out at the nursing station. I asked them to get me a cut-down set of instruments, betadine antiseptic solution and size 7.5 sterile gloves in. Not a single nurse moved from her chair! They stayed on their fat asses, yes, they were fat, and gave me directions on how to find the material I requested.

"It's in the utility room, second door on your right, down the hall," one of them said and continued her conversation.

I was quite hungry and a little light-headed. I was upset with the unprofessional demeanor of the nurses, but I went and got what I needed for the cut-down. I brought a "mayo stand" (a portable metal table designed for medical procedures) and the cut-down items to the bedside and prepared the sterile set up to get started. I was wearing my surgical mask, hat and sterile surgical gloves and prepped the patient's right arm and injected local anesthetic in the area of the planned cut-down. I made an incision about an inch above the elbow level. I continued the dissection until I reached and exposed the cephalic vein, making sure that I did not cause any injury to the adjacent nerve or artery. I then inserted the catheter into the wound and into the vein. I then closed the wound with a plastic technique and secured the catheter in place with a silk suture. I used a sterile syringe with saline to make sure that I could draw blood through the catheter. I flushed the catheter with heparin and connected it to the IV solution.

Due to the obesity of the patient I had to proceed very slowly. It took a long time before I identified the cephalic vein and inserted the catheter. I was not feeling well and started getting nausea, which got worse as time went by. I managed to put the dressing on the wound before I let my system express itself with a bout of vomiting into the garbage can at the patient's bedside. I cleaned up, placed the sharps (needles and disposable scalpel blades) in the proper container and then took the instruments and the mayo stand to the nursing station.

"I am done," I told the bunch of lazy nurses, "but I got sick and threw up. Is there a cup of tea I can have?" I asked. I had hoped that somebody would volunteer to get up and get me a cup of tea but instead one of them pointed to a door.

"There is some in the break room, in the cabinet on your left."

I found my way to the break room, and yes there were some tea bags in "the cabinet on my left." There were cups and hot water there too, so I made myself a cup of tea and sat down for a few minutes. It was very soothing, and my nausea went away. The three teaspoons of sugar I had put in the tea made me feel a little better. I then finished writing my notes on every patient I attended, and I addressed other problems, such as replacing NG (nasogastric) tubes on patients who pulled them out, drawing blood from patients that needed lab work done and starting IV accesses on patients whose IVs were infiltrated.

I got done at midnight and walked to my room at the medical staff building, my beeper at my side. I got beeped several times for infiltrated IVs, patients vomiting, NG tubes pulled out by the patients, or others needing a sleeping pill. I had to walk back and forth to the unit from my room several times that night, which was the proper cap for a hellish day.

I got up at 6 a.m. and went to the dining room. I had two fried eggs with several strips of crispy bacon and three bananas, making up for the starvation of the previous day. The morning rounds started at 7 a.m. and I was there. As usual we saw every patient, discussed their problems and made decisions about their treatments or care.

A first-year resident on our team, Dr. Chris, was also from Cyprus. He told me that he was sponsored by the Cyprus Government to come to America and specialize in pathology in order to fill a void at Nicosia

General Hospital. He said he had changed his mind and intended to study neurosurgery instead and stay in America.

The two months that I spent on surgical service went by, but not fast enough for me. It was a bad experience, but I did not complain at all to anyone. It did not appear appropriate to start my internship with complaints about the nursing staff, which was the only thing that I was really upset about. It was hard work, but that was something I could handle.

My next assignment was pediatric surgery, covering services for both Kings County Hospital and University Hospital. There were only two attending surgeons: The director of Pediatric surgery, Dr. Peter Kottmeier, and Dr. Donald Klotz whom I had met already on my first day I joined the program. There was also a fellow in pediatric surgery, a chief resident, two other residents and me as the intern. The small team made the service tight and orderly while also being a unique learning experience. And the nursing staff was superb! They were extremely professional, knowledgeable, kind and eager to assist the medical staff. They also actively participated in patient care. There was a huge difference between the nursing staff at the University Hospital General Surgery Service and the Pediatric Surgical Services of both the Kings County and University Hospitals. I was so happy that I finally found myself in a learning, caring environment with all the right people.

Dr. Kottmeier was a knowledgeable pediatric surgeon and an excellent teacher who used a lot of irony and sarcasm during his interactions with interns and residents. One time when I was on duty, I was called late at night to start an intravenous access on an eight-month-old infant. The only vein I could find was on the scalp—common for infants—and started an IV without any difficulty. The next day, like every other day, we made early rounds with the residents and Dr. Yurgen, the chief resident. I gave a report to the team about what happened during the night and we all went about the formal rounds at 7 a.m. with Dr. Kottmeier, which was about one hour before any scheduled surgery.

When we reached the infant that I had started a scalp IV the night before, Dr. Kottmeier turned to Dr. Yurgen.

"I see you found a vein on this patient. Who started the IV?" Dr. Kottmeier asked.

Dr. Yurgen pointed at me. "The intern did it," he replied.

Dr. Kottmeier was not kind to him. "You idiot! You assigned an intern to start an IV on an infant on whom nobody, not even the pediatrician, could find a vein yesterday?"

I guess Dr. Kottmeier expected Dr. Yurgen to come in himself and do the cut-down IV access at the infant's ankle. I was completely unaware of those facts. Evidently nobody could find a vein to start an IV the day before. The night shift came on and, unaware of what transpired, noticed that there were IV fluids ordered for the baby, but there was no IV access. The night nurse paged me and told me she needed an IV for this child, so I went and started one.

The IV was working fine so nothing else needed to be done. The rounds finished. For a reason I cannot explain, I felt the urge to mess with Dr. Yurgen. I walked close to him and whispered, "You know when I put the needle in that infant I got clear fluid back, not blood!" This would have indicated that the needle was not in the vein, but instead was in the central nervous system, or simply put, in the brain area.

He stepped back, and appeared very alarmed, and that's when I jumped back in. "Calm down Yurgen. I am only kidding!" He appeared upset but then smiled and laughed it off. He was a decent guy and was always nice to me.

I spent two months in pediatric surgery rotation, and I enjoyed it. Everyone was nice, knowledgeable and interested in teaching. But I mostly enjoyed it because I have special feelings towards children. I always took great pleasure seeing my nieces and nephews growing up and coming up with the sweetest comments to show their love. I also enjoyed the responses of the pediatric patients to the routine first question of Dr. Klotz.

"Are you a good boy (girl) or a bad boy (girl)?"

The answers would always crack me up. Sometimes the kid would just look down and not answer, sometimes the response was, "A good boy (girl)!" But not all "good boy/girl" were the same; some were stern, filled with confidence. Some "good boy/girl" responses were soft and shy, and some were loud and clear like a public announcement, as if the kid wanted the whole world to hear about it. There were also different variations in between the responses.

Of course, there were the other responses that were different in tone and expression. Some appeared apologetic while others were filled with confidence, as if the kids were proud of being "bad."

Dr. Klotz used this question to break the ice and put the kids at ease before he got started with medical questions. I could tell that he enjoyed the answers, as I did. After that, I used that routine question as my first question for all of my pediatric patients throughout my career.

There were a lot of big operations performed in pediatric surgery service, such as the correction of congenital abnormalities of the GI tract, like esophageal atresia; duplication of the small intestine, duodenal atresia; congenital abnormalities of the biliary system; and others. The most common operations were hernia repairs and circumcisions; there were days that we performed more than a dozen of them. They were done by the interns/residents under the supervision of the chief resident. There were also a lot of appendectomies performed, also by the interns/residents under supervision. The rotation in the pediatric surgery service was a great learning experience for me, for both theory and practice.

Most of the patients having circumcisions or hernia repairs stayed in the hospital for a day. Patients undergoing appendectomies or splenectomies could be hospitalized for several days. Patients who had surgery for congenital gastrointestinal abnormalities sometimes stayed for a few weeks. And then there was Teddy, who lived in the pediatric surgery ward of Kings County Hospital. This unfortunate eight-year-old boy had surgery to remove a brain tumor. The operation was successful but, in the process, he became blind and his family abandoned him. He was sort of adopted by the pediatric nurses and surgeons and he spent his life in the hospital. Contrary to expectations, he was always happy and was the heart and soul of the pediatric surgery unit. He was upbeat and sang his heart out.

Every time the surgical team got together to make patient rounds, we only had to say, "hello Teddy" to get a cheerful response from him.

"Hello!" he always responded before breaking out in song. "Let's get the show on the road, road partner" he would sing.

The thoughts that sprung in my mind the first time I heard his story and experienced his reaction on rounds were, "Blindness, brain tumor abandonment by his parents, so much suffering and so much misery. And yet so much love and attention by the nurses and doctors, with such a cheerful demonstration of contention and even possibly happiness! People who think they have problems should pay this angel a visit."

I could not hold back my tears when I first experienced this. Every time I was on the unit, I made sure I went to see Teddy and talk to him. He is still always in my heart and thoughts, though I don't know what happened to him, whether the brain tumor came back, or if he grew up free of cancer.

In addition to the work in the units, the interns also covered the pediatric surgery emergency room. We were assigned to pediatric ER coverage for 24-hour shifts. After that, we had to work in the pediatric surgery unit until 6 p.m. before finishing up for the 36-hour "day." Usually, after midnight, it was quiet and I could walk to the medical staff building to my room and get some sleep, save for some referrals by the pediatrics ER for acute appendicitis, in the middle of the night.

Most of the ER pediatric surgery patients were for soft tissue injuries, cuts, and broken bones, acute appendicitis and occasionally foreign body ingestions. For the most part, pediatric ER visits happened when children were awake. It was usually quiet after midnight. An exception was on Sept. 8, 1974. It was on this date that Evel Knievel attempted his famous jump over the Snake River Canyon using the Skycycle X-2, his own steam-powered rocket.

It was an impressive, although, unsuccessful stunt. It impressed a lot of people though, especially young kids. It was all over the news, and there was no household that did not hear about it. Many kids were so impressed by it, that they attempted to make jumps from the windows of their second and third floor apartments. Many hit the pavement and sustained severe head and abdominal injuries as well as broken bones.

On Sept. 9, the day after Knievel's jump, I was the doctor on duty covering pediatric surgery ER. By then I was a seasoned surgeon with nearly five years of intense surgical training and experience. That day was one of the busiest of my training. The copycats of Evel Knievel, silly little kids, all of a sudden thought that they had those super-human qualities that would allow them to fly from their apartments to the surrounding trees. They ended up on the pavements below, with severe injuries, which secured them a trip to the pediatric ER.

The ambulances kept bringing them in, and bringing them in, and bringing them in; I thought it would never end. I felt like I saw over 100 injured, foolish kids that day. Some were admitted for observation and/or treatment, but the majority were treated and released. Finally, I managed to treat everyone by 3 a.m. and went to my room to get some sleep. As soon as I entered, my beeper went on. I called the ER and they told me another kid came in with a bad head injury and abdominal pain. I went back and examined the patient, sent some labs and ordered some X-rays. There were no fractures, but the kid had a bad scalp laceration, had lost consciousness and also experienced abdominal pain. These findings indicated that the patient had a concussion and he might have intra-abdominal bleeding, both of which required admission for follow up testing and observation.

I sutured his scalp laceration, got his history, did a physical and then admitted the patient to the pediatric surgery unit. By then, it was already after 5 a.m. I walked back to my room and relaxed for about an hour before I went for breakfast and returned to the daily fast-paced routine.

That same month, I got sick while I was on duty, with high fever, muscle aches, fatigue and lack of appetite. I felt awful. They called me to see a patient in pediatric surgery unit. I dragged my feet to get there and took care of the problem. I then called the chief resident and explained to him that I was sick and asked him if he could take over so I could go to my room. His name was Dr. D. He was in the same year as me, but he was doing his chief residency in pediatric surgery, a specialty he intended to practice. I was stunned by his answer.

"No, I will not cover you! You are on call; figure it out," he said.

What an indifferent, callous and reckless answer that was! I stayed on and finished the on-duty assignments. But I never forgot his answer and never had any respect for him after that. I did not think he belonged in the medical profession.

Of interest is an event that happened 20 years later. We were both practicing in the same area, in New Jersey and we both had privileges at the same hospital. I was in solo practice, while Dr. D. was in a partnership with another surgeon. One night he called me at 1 a.m., and woke me up.

"George, I have to do an emergency surgery and need an assistant. Can you give me a hand?" This was the first time he called me to assist him.

The first thing that came to my mind was his answer to my request for coverage when I was sick. "Why don't you call your partner?" I asked.

"He is off," he answered.

"And what makes you think that I am not off?" I replied.

"I don't know," he said. "I need some help."

"I am sorry D.; I cannot help you. It is your responsibility. You figure it out!"

Sooner or later what you do in life will come back to bless you or curse you. There is a wise saying about this: "What goes around, comes around." How true!

After completing the pediatric surgery rotation of my six-month internship at KCH-DMC, I was assigned to one of the two surgical oncology services for tumors at Kings County Hospital. This was of special interest to me since our family had been hit so hard with my father's horrific death from colon cancer at the age of 53.

The tumor service dealt with gastrointestinal tumors as well as skin, breast, head and neck tumors and all soft tissue tumors. It also treated emergency general surgical conditions that were admitted through the adult ER. Dr. Bernard Gardner was the director of the well-run surgical oncology unit, and included regular conferences with the medical oncologists, radiologists, radiation oncologists and a pathologist. There were other attending faculty members on the service but the most knowledgeable and skillful one was Dr. Antonio Alfonso, a younger, gentle Philippine man who had a lot of knowledge, teaching abilities and skills. He also had a willingness to help any time anyone needed him.

My assignment to tumor surgery ended on June 30, 1971, and with that, so did the extension of my internship. As of July 1, I finished my internship and became an official resident or, as the new classification demanded, a PGY-2 or surgical trainee in the second "post graduate year". Two years down, four more to go, unless I decided to do a subspecialty.

A Visit to Cyprus

In July of 1971, I took my month vacation and went back to Cyprus to see my mother and the rest of the family. I had not been back for almost two years and I missed them immensely, especially my mother. I had been working every minute I was away, and I really needed some rest. I longed to sleep without waking up in the middle of the night to the sound of the phone or beeper. I left both behind in my room at Kings County Hospital.

The trip took 10 hours to Athens and over an hour and 20 minutes, to Nicosia Airport in Cyprus. I was so sleep-deprived that I slept most of the way to Greece. The plane landed in Nicosia Airport in the afternoon and my brother John and my sister Dora were there to pick me up. I was so happy to see them, as we hugged each other and exchanged niceties. We drove back to our house, about 10 minutes away, talking up a storm about our lives and activities.

Dora had just graduated from the school of fine arts in Athens. John had graduated from the Milan Polytechnic with a doctorate in civil engineering. He had entered into an agreement with our eldest brother Stavros, forming a land development company. John had actually written to me about it in January, when he graduated from the Milan Polytechnic and returned back to Cyprus. At that time, I advised him against such an agreement, because "Stavros had proven himself unpredictable."

But John went ahead with the agreement anyway. They were in the process of constructing an apartment complex and John was happy with the arrangement. His happiness made me happy too, though I still had reservations about Stavros and what his behavior might be in the long run.

When we arrived home, our mother was outside in front of the house waiting for us. I got out of the car and ran to her and gave her a big hug and told her how much I missed her and how happy I was to be back. She told me she missed me too, and she was happy to see me back home, but she really did not have to say anything. Her face was shining, radiating with happiness and joy from the moment she saw me. We talked about the old times, and I told them a lot of stories about my experiences in America. It was like old times, talking and teasing each other from the time I arrived and through the home cooked dinner and beyond until we went to bed.

The days swiftly went by, as I visited my high school friends and a lot of relatives. We took frequent trips to our village, and stayed in the family home where I was born, which was built in 1869 by my great grandfather Stavros Spanoudis. We went to "Mare Monte," the same beach we played and swam in when we were little kids. There were so many wonderful memories in this little paradise and I appreciated each one much more after spending so many years far away. My family had been living in that area for 100 generations, starting with the time Lapithos, the first known settlement, was established by the Spartan King Praxandros 3,000 years ago, after the end of the Trojan War.

Church of Saint Irene

Mare Monte Beach

Karavas Old Port

Overview of Karavas

I let my imagination wander deep into the past to the time the Spartans landed on the ground I was standing on. I was certain that the reason they chose that area for their first settlement was not just due to its natural beauty and spring, but also because of the easy access to the sea and hills. About 100 feet away from our family house, there was an accidental discovery of ancient artifacts, verifying the presence of inhabitants in the area in the distant past.

I found that I badly missed this paradise, but I found solace in the fact that it was only a temporary arrangement. I imagined I would return after my training and acquire a piece of land in a good location. I thought I might build a small hospital where I could have my practice and live for the rest of my life, like my ancestors did for the past 3,000 years. It felt so good to allow myself to slip into a cloud of imagination and daydreaming, something I never had the time or the luxury to do while I was wrapped up in the daily hectic schedule of my work. The serenity, tranquility and the natural beauty of the environment and the mesmerizing motion of the sea had a calming effect on me, letting my imagination expand to new dimensions.

I visited a lot of relatives, and among them, uncle Stavros, my mother's oldest brother. He had spent the 1920s to the mid 30s in Rockland County, New York, where he owned and operated a Nyack hotel. According to my uncle Christ, who was also in America, uncle Stavros was the first person to own a car in Rockland County.

Uncle Stavros returned to Karavas in 1935 and got married to Stavrini, a teacher, but they had no children. He was the only relative my mother had ever asked for a loan to help with our studies. His answer was stunning.

"Why did you send them to study? You should let them be masons and day workers, so they will make some money and bring some back to you too! I cannot help you"

My mother did not answer his question or his suggestion. She just thanked him and left. The pathway of the family was already been decided and etched in stone by our father. He left the leisurely life of Karavas and went to Nicosia to give us the opportunity of a better education. This was something he emphasized time after time when he was alive. That was one of the best decisions he ever made.

This time I visited Uncle Stavros to pay my respect, but I did not neglect to mention to him that I was a doctor, receiving my surgical training in one of the best medical Centers in the world. I also mentioned that John was a doctor in civil engineering and Dora had graduated from the Athens School of Fine Arts. I treated him with respect, but I wanted him to know that his youngest sister's family had reached the goals that our father had set, irrespective of other people's opinions. It did not bother me that he did not want to help us, but it bothered me a lot that he scolded my mother for letting her children pursue higher education.

In high school I developed a sincere and long-lasting friendship with three classmates: George Drakos, Nicos Polemidiotis and Stelios Papantoniou. We were all members of the resistance against the British and we held each other in high regard. They had all taken classical studies at the university of Athens, and all three were working as high school teachers and principals.

Nicos had founded his own school with another teacher from Karavas and I showed up unannounced to surprise him. We talked for a while and planned dinner with George and Stelios. We met at a tavern and enjoyed some delicious Cyprus food, accompanied with ice-cold refreshing Cyprus beer. Talking and remembering the old times was enjoyable, followed by the singing of popular Greek songs, like we did so many times in the past. Stelios and George had beautiful melodic voices and were great singers. Stelios, a priest's grandson, was a cantor in his church from a very young age and had the best voice of the bunch.

Nicos also had a good voice but I had a terrible one! We sang together anyway. As always, I kept my voice down, hoping my cacophony (literal translation: "bad voice") would be drowned out by the melody of my friends. Like old times, we had a nice get together before calling it a night. Time went by fast, before I had to say goodbye and head back to my training hub in Brooklyn, New York.

Second Year Residency at the Brooklyn VA Hospital —and Finding Love

Out of the 20-plus interns, only 12 of us advanced to the PGY-2 level of the general surgery program, with the rest going to subspecialties. In September 1971, I was assigned to the surgical service at the Brooklyn VA Hospital, which was an integral part of the DMC system. The first thing I noticed was the much less demanding schedule and the lighter volume of work. That was due, however, to the negligible number of emergency admissions and operations at the VA Hospital. The difference in the amount of work between the VA hospital and KCHC was so obvious, that the time I spent there seemed more like a vacation. We were on 36-hour shifts of duty every third day while at Kings County Hospital the 36-hour shifts were every second day. Also, we were on duty every second weekend at Kings County Hospital but at the VA, it was every third weekend. To top that, spending the night on duty at Kings County Hospital meant being up most of the night. At the VA, I usually got a good night's sleep and was rarely woken up for patient care or emergency admissions. It was like vacation! While on duty at the Brooklyn VA hospital, we were entitled to breakfast, lunch and dinner plus a midnight snack served from 10 p.m. to 12 p.m. in case we were up.

Despite the less hectic work, the elective operation caseload, was by no means any lighter than that of Kings County Hospital. We had several operations every day that were all scheduled routine, elective procedures. All patients were admitted at least one day before surgery and lab work, chest X-ray and Electrocardiogram (EKG) were done on admission and reviewed and recorded in the patient's chart. If any abnormalities were detected during the work up, they were addressed and corrected, making the patient fully prepared for a safe operation. This also allowed for a smooth progression of the procedures. The drama of having to order the preoperative lab work, X-rays and EKG, wait for the results, review the findings and address any abnormalities before an emergency operation, was a very rare occurrence at the VA hospital.

I was enjoying my rotation at the Brooklyn VA Hospital and then something happened. I got in the elevator heading to the surgical unit on the seventh floor and there she was! I saw an elegant, stunning, smashing, Asian beauty, a nurse, standing next to me in the elevator.

Though generally shy to initiate a conversation, I knew that this time I had to do it.

"Magandan gabi," I said, which means "good evening" in Tegalog, the Filipino language. She gave me a strange look, like she did not know what I was saying. It turned out she wasn't Filipino. As the elevator reached the seventh floor, I managed to squeeze in a quick "good evening" in English. She responded in kind but stayed on the elevator to a higher floor. This girl stuck in my mind. I had a feeling that she was going to play a significant role in my life.

A few days later while on duty, I went for dinner at the cafeteria. After I finished my meal and started to head back to my room to study, I saw her again! She was just coming in for dinner and carrying her tray looking for a table. For some reason I suddenly felt a strong craving for a cup of coffee! I got a cup and pulled a chair from the table across from her.

"Good evening," I said.

"Good evening," she responded.

We struck up a conversation and I found out that she was Chinese, her name was Sharon and she lived in the dorm on the hospital grounds. I asked her for her phone number, and she gave it to me without any obvious hesitation, which I found very encouraging. I was sure I was on the right track. She told me she was planning a Halloween party and if I was interested, it will cost $5. I gladly paid up and secured my reservation.

Sharon was working the night shift, so I called her the next afternoon. I was stunned by her looks, her delicate elegant features, the way she moved, the way she walked and the way she talked. I thought I was in love! During our conversation I mentioned that I had some friends in Philadelphia, Dr. Tan, whom I intended to visit. I invited her to come along and I was elated when she said yes! Before we went to Philadelphia, we took a trip to Bear Mountain in New York. While hiking we found a dead fox and took some pictures with it before returning to the lodge for lunch. We also visited West Point, where I gave her a driving lesson—her first— and let her drive my 1967 Mustang in the West Point parking lot.

Her Halloween party was a success, though Sharon got very upset when she realized one of her guests stole her prized vase. We enjoyed each other's company and spent a lot of time together. I introduced her to my sister and took her to several family gatherings at my cousin Peter's house in Spring Valley, New York. We went to Paradise Restaurant on 46th street, by the Times Square area and enjoyed some Greek food.

She introduced me to her best friend Lucy, who was a former classmate from her nursing school days. Lucy lived in Queens with her husband Ming and their two children Howard and Jenny. We went there often, and they taught me how to play mahjong. It actually took me over 25 years before I kept my promise to take Sharon to Philadelphia! When we finally went, it was to a plant and flower show.

In the meantime, I had moved out of Kings County Hospital's staff housing, which was only for PGY-1 doctors, to an apartment a few blocks away at 295 East 48th St. It was the lower level of a house, a sort of above-ground basement, with a separate entrance and a back door leading to a garden.

My professional life was no less significant than my love life. There were three surgical services at the Brooklyn VA Hospital: The General Surgery Service on Four East, the Vascular Surgery Service on Four West, and the Head and Neck Service on the seventh floor. The Chief of Surgery was Dr. Harry LeVeen, a brilliant thinker with a brainstorm of ideas for innovations, but who lacked surgical skills.

The attending surgeon of General Surgery Service was Dr. George Stergiopoulos, the most skillful and elegant surgeon of the whole DMC program. He was trained as a surgeon in Romania and had practiced in Romania and Greece for years before coming to America. His skills as a surgeon made him the best teacher of surgical techniques in the entire surgical program. He made everything look easy and enjoyed the admiration and respect of every resident surgeon lucky enough to rotate through his service.

The other super star at the VA was the attending surgeon of the Vascular Surgery Service, Dr. Carlos Diaz, whose superior skills and abilities were also respected and appreciated by all the surgical residents who scrubbed with him. I was fortunate to rotate in both general and vascular services at the VA Hospital and learn a lot about advanced surgical techniques from the great masters themselves, Dr. Stergiopoulos and Dr. Diaz.

I considered Dr. Stergiopoulos my mentor for all he taught me and for his help in supporting my progression and promotion all the way to my chief residency and graduation. The four months that I spent at the Brooklyn VA Hospital were very fruitful. The caseload of surgical cases with the associated opportunity to learn the best surgical skills from the masters was great, and meeting and hooking up with Sharon, made me very happy. On top of that there was an incident that had an effect on my career.

One day I was having lunch at the cafeteria and a couple of minutes later Dr. Harry LeVeen, The Chief of Surgery at the VA, came with his tray and sat right next to me. We started chatting and he asked me if I was interested in research, and more specifically, if I was interested in spending my research year in his lab.

"I am working on a new operation to treat ascites," he said. Ascites is a condition that results from liver cirrhosis and consists of the accumulation of large amounts of fluid in the abdomen. "I developed a system with a silastic valve and tube that will be used to transfer the fluid from the peritoneal cavity back to the circulation, where it came from.

I have already tried it and although it hasn't worked so far, I know the reason why it failed. I put one end of the tube in the peritoneal cavity and the other end in the saphenous vein in the thigh and didn't work. But I think that if we place the vascular end of the tube in the femoral vein it is going to do the job."

I carefully listened, before expressing my opinion: "Dr. LeVeen, it will never work".

He looked at me as if I had two heads. "Why?" he asked.

"It's very simple Dr. LeVeen. You are trying to drain fluid from the abdomen, a high-pressure area, to the vein in the lower extremity, which is an even higher-pressure area. That's against the laws of physics. It will never happen."

I could see a look of disbelief in his eyes. He was speechless, so I continued. "The only way you could make it work is to position the vascular end of the drainage tube in the superior vena cava in the chest, through the jugular vein, where there is negative pressure during the breathing cycle. Then you create a pressure gradient, which will trigger a flow of the fluid through the system, from the peritoneal cavity to the venous system."

I could see a sparkle in his eyes. "Will you do that and spend a year of research with me in the lab?"

I always had a special interest in research, if nothing else, just to challenge myself to achieve something special.

"I will be happy to spend my research year with you, Dr. Leveen," I replied.

That was settled, so I was scheduled to spend the year from July 1, 1972 to June 30, 1973, in the research lab to prove the concept of shunting the fluid from the peritoneal cavity to the vascular system and provide some relieve from the symptoms of ascites.

Residency at Kings County Hospital

I spent the first six months of 1972 at Kings County Hospital rotating in the emergency room, trauma, and tumor service. The ER at KCH is huge. It is divided into adult and pediatric divisions and there are more sections to accommodate the different conditions patients may present with.

The pediatric ER was on the ground floor of the B building, with multiple screening rooms, pediatric medical rooms and a large treatment room for surgical conditions, such as lacerations, soft tissue injuries, bone fractures, and other surgical problems, such as acute appendicitis, bleeding, abdominal pain and/or swelling, abscesses etc. The pediatric treatment room was managed by the pediatric surgery service, while the screening and medical pediatric rooms, were handled by the pediatricians.

After registration any new patients with an obvious injury were directed to the treatment room. The other patients were first evaluated in the screening room by a pediatrician, and depending on the patient's condition, they were either treated and released or sent to the other pediatricians, or to the treatment room for further evaluation and management.

The adult ER occupied the entire ground floor of the C building and also had several divisions. There were five screening exam rooms manned by five doctors who did the first patient evaluations following registration. If the patients had minor problems such as a cold, a headache, allergies, runny nose or any other condition that did not need any further work up, they were treated and released with a referral to the appropriate clinic for follow up, if necessary. There also were two large rooms, with 10 beds each, one for men and the other for women. Both were manned by medical residents and were reserved for patients with obvious serious medical conditions that needed further work up and treatment. From there, if the exam and work up showed a condition that needed in-hospital treatment, the patient was admitted; if the patient could be treated as an outpatient, he or she was given the necessary prescriptions and instructions, and discharged home.

When a surgical problem was suspected or diagnosed, the surgical resident on duty in the ER was called to evaluate the patient. If a surgical diagnosis was confirmed, such as acute appendicitis, bowel obstruction, acute cholecystitis, abscess etc., the patient was admitted to the surgical service on duty. If no surgical problem was identified, the surgical ER resident would make a note and sign off that patient's care.

The other unit of the ER was the asthma room where all the patients with acute bronchial asthma attack, and there were a lot of them, would be taken directly for evaluation and treatment. All the patients with lacerations, soft tissue trauma, car accident or other victims with multiple injuries, gunshot, or stab wounds and broken bones were taken directly to the treatment room for evaluation by the surgical team comprised of a PGY-1 and a more senior surgical resident.

In addition to all the Emergency Room divisions and units mentioned, there was a surgical intensive care unit (SICU) for life threatening injuries and conditions, such as gastrointestinal bleeding, car accident victims, stab wounds and gunshot wounds, and for any unstable surgical patients. Life-saving emergency care was initiated promptly in the SICU, with intravenous fluid infusions, and/or blood transfusions. Once the patient was stabilized, he or she would be taken to the operating room for emergency surgery or transferred to the regular SICU on the second floor for monitoring and treatment.

There was also a medical intensive care unit (MICU) in the ER for all life-threatening medical conditions, such as heart attacks, severe shortness of breath, multiple organ failure etc. Both the SICU and MICU were equipped with respirators, cardiac monitors and all the necessary medical equipment available at the time.

The ER assignment was always stimulating, interesting, instructive, demanding, and intellectually rewarding all at the same time. There was never a dull moment during my time there. Anything could happen in the KCHC ER, at any time, in many ways. Daily events were totally unpredictable. The variety of challenging, strange and unusual conditions of the patients brought to the ER were vast. Sooner or later, any condition that was in any surgical textbook would present itself there. There were so many conditions that I saw and experienced during my training, even when I was not on duty.

Challenging, Strange and Unusual Incidents

A young man walked into the ER with the handle of a butcher knife sticking out of the side of his head. The patient was immediately placed in a wheelchair and taken to the ER-ICU. The surgical resident attended to the patient immediately and asked him how it happened.

"I fell down onto a knife that was on the ground and that got in my head," the patient said.

No one believed him, but it was not relevant. There was no question that somebody tried to kill this fellow and used substantial force to put this knife through his head. The blade had actually gone through the brain and cranium on the other side of his head, and the point of the blade could be palpated under the skin.

A vein access was immediately established, and IV fluids started. The neurosurgical resident paged stat to come to the ER. IV antibiotics were also administered to fight infection and blood work and other work up initiated, preparing the patient for emergency surgery. The neurosurgical resident arrived, examined the patient, reviewed the lab reports and scheduled the patient for surgery.

The operation, under general anesthesia, consisted of craniotomy (opening the cranium up), establishing control of the arteries and veins that were cut by the blade and the knife removed. The reason that there was no significant bleeding while the knife was in the head, is because the knife was acting as a tamponade of the cut vessels. Had anybody pulled the blade out of the brain, there would have been massive bleeding inside the head, resulting in immediate death. It is amazing that this man walked in the ER by himself, with a knife in his head, but it is even more amazing that after surgery and treatment, he walked out of the hospital a few days later, with only a minor visual deficit as a result of the injury.

In the same category of events, a man came to the ER, registered and was directed to the screening area. He was seen by the Doctor, who asked him what his problem was.

"I have a nail in my head," the patient said. The doctor gave him a strange look, but the patient did not elaborate. The doctor asked him some more questions to complete the history, did a basic examination, recorded everything and referred him to the male room for a psychiatric consultation.

The psychiatric resident was called and he came and evaluated the patient. He admitted him to the G building, which housed the hospital's psychiatric department. A couple of days later, the patient became febrile and lethargic. An x-ray of his head was taken, and guess what showed up? A nail-shaped piece of metal was in his head. The neurosurgeon was called who transferred the patient to his unit and prepared him for surgery. The patient had a craniotomy under general anesthesia and the nail was removed. The area of the infection (meningitis, encephalitis) caused by the nail, was cleaned, and the patient was also treated with antibiotics. He also recovered fully and was discharged home, in a couple of weeks.

This incident may sound funny to some people, but in actuality, it was a pretty serious matter. The man came to the ER and he very explicitly told one doctor after another that he "had a nail in his head" and all of them labeled him as "psychotic" and locked him up in the psychiatric unit. Nobody bothered to confirm, or rule out his complaint, causing him additional complications with a worsening meningitis and encephalitis and rendering his recovery more difficult and prolonged. He might have been psychotic, but that in itself, doesn't imply that he is not capable of telling the truth.

Though I was not involved in this patient's evaluation or treatment, his story taught me a very valuable lesson that I carried with me throughout my career: "Always listen to the patient no matter how crazy you think his words are, even if you think that if you act on his words you may look foolish. I'd rather look foolish, than proven to be foolish!" This lesson served me well throughout my career.

Patients with stab wounds, gunshot wounds, slash wounds, car accident victims with multiple injuries and broken bones were a daily occurrence at KCHC-ER and every patient had his own story, cause and circumstances of injuries. The ER head nurse, Mitzie, was a smart, kind, tall, beautiful lady, with solid knowledge of what needed to be done, and how to organize and direct the nursing staff to carry out their duties effectively and efficiently. She was very helpful in guiding me, as she did with all the interns and residents, and helping me adjust to the frantic pace of the ER. There was always a pot of coffee to help everyone keep their eyes open after the long and hectic hours on duty. An exceptional member of the nursing staff was Sister Linda, a nun who treated every patient with a typical, true, unadulterated, Christian compassion. In general, the ER, like the rest of KCH was blessed with exceptional nursing talent, a huge contrast from the indifferent staff at the University Hospital's general surgery unit. There are several incidents I came across in the ER that got stuck in my mind forever.

One of the stranger things I had encountered was the result of a modern day "duel" between a man and his wife's lover. The wife was fooling around with this man, who had an overgrown lower lip, like it was Bubba's lip, in "Forest Gump." The husband found out about the affair and he confronted the wife's lover. An altercation ensued, and the husband had the terrible idea to attack and bite off a good chunk of the lover's lower lip. That ended up being a bad idea. While the husband was biting off the lover's lip, the lover in turn bit off a big chunk of the husband's nose. They were both brought to the ER in separate ambulances. The plastic surgery resident was called in for a consultation, and both of them were admitted for reconstructive surgery. When all was said and done, the "lover" wound up with a very good-looking, reduced size lower lip, while the husband got the short end of the stick again. He needed several operations to restore his amputated nose.

Another time, a police officer was brought in with a slash injury to his face, in front of his right ear. There was bleeding from a cut artery, which was pumping blood all over the place. Despite the alarming appearance of the blood gushing out, the temporal artery that was injured is a small caliber vessel and the amount of blood lost was not life threatening. I immediately applied pressure on the bleeding site with a sterile gauze, then asked the nurse to continue the pressure as I prepared the instrument tray and changed my gloves. Under aseptic conditions and local anesthesia, I identified the bleeding point and stopped it by clamping and tying the severed artery. I repaired the wound in a plastic fashion, and while I was finishing the repair, I was shooting questions to the wounded officer.

"How did this happen?" I asked him.

"A guy with a knife attacked me," he answered.

"Did they catch him?"

Just as I finished the question, two officers came in with a young man in handcuffs. His face was black and blue all over. The wounded officer looked at him and said with a calm voice, "That's him."

It was obvious to me that the guy who attacked the officer got caught and after the police officers gave him a piece of their mind and their fists, they brought him in for treatment. The officers said he "resisted arrest," which is not surprising, taking into consideration his attack on the bleeding officer I just treated.

Another memorable incident happened when a lady came into the ER accompanied by her husband. She had a laceration on her scalp that she said was caused by a fall. As usual, that day was very busy. As per protocol, the husband was asked to remain in the waiting room. Instead, he snuck into a cubicle and hid behind the separating curtain.

As I was evaluating his wife for a possible concussion, two officers walked in, one of them pushing a young man in a wheelchair. The young man was deranged and mumbling something that was difficult to understand. The police said that he was under arrest and he complained that during the arrest he was hurt, and his legs were paralyzed, so he could not walk. He was not in handcuffs. All of a sudden, he started shouting.

"You are making fun of me! You are laughing at me!" Then he jumped out of the wheelchair and ran to the cubicle behind the curtain. He loudly smacked the hiding husband on the side of the face. That was a typical reaction of a paranoid schizophrenic person. The actions of the husband revealed that the guy in the wheelchair suffered from a psychiatric problem but did not suffer from paralysis of his legs. The husband's actions also resulted in converting him from a "patient's family member" to a patient, since examination showed a rupture of the tympanic membrane (eardrum) of his left ear. That earned him the right to stay in the treatment room until the ENT Doctor came to evaluate him.

His wife was taken care off, discharged and directed to stay in the waiting room and she did. The wheelchair patient was admitted to the G building, which housed all the patients with psychiatric problems, and I proceeded to attend to the next patient on line.

One afternoon that I was on ER duty, a patient was brought to the treatment room with the distal phalanx—the part of a finger with the nail—detached and hanging with a sliver of skin bridging it to the rest of the finger. The patient was very upset about the accident and did not want to lose part of his index finger. He was a court stenographer and not having part of this index finger could affect his job.

I examined the finger very carefully and found the detached portion was dusky, which indicated inadequate circulation. I explained to the patient that I could try to save the distal phalanx by re-attaching it, but it was unlikely to survive. Most likely, I told him, it would become gangrenous and he would end up having to amputate that portion. He asked me to please try my best to save it, and that much I did.

I spent two hours cleaning the wound and reattaching the hanging portion to the remaining finger with multiple layers of sutures, using the skills that I developed after endless hours of practicing suturing and knot tying. I applied a splint to protect the wound, gave him a prescription for antibiotics, and pain medicine and sent him home. I instructed him to come daily to the ER so I could examine the wound and see if gangrene was setting in.

On the follow-up visits, the injured portion appeared to be still dusky, but not grossly gangrenous. Eventually after three weeks, the skin of the attached portion got loose at the suture line area. I lifted it up gently with a pair of forceps and it appeared to be pulling away from the underlying tissue, which was good-looking, healthy, new skin. I peeled off the old skin and a healthy distal phalanx emerged from underneath! The patient was very grateful and happy, just as I was. He wanted to pay me, but I told him that I would not accept any money and the good result was more than enough payment for me. He came back the next day and gave me a gift certificate for Macys. I took it but I don't even remember if I ever used it. I was serious when I told the patient that the good result was much more valuable to me than any payment.

Before my year of research, I was assigned to trauma service, which in a way was an extension of the ER. There were two trauma units, A and B, manned by two surgical resident teams. Each unit was headed by a respective Chief Resident functioning under the supervision of the director of the Trauma Service, Dr. Shaftan and his team of attending Surgeons. The other attending surgeons were mostly instructing and assisting the residents in patient care and surgical techniques.

Each of the trauma units admitted patients on alternate days, so the doctors of each team were on duty every day and every other night, alternating between 12-hour and 36-hour shifts. The unique characteristic of the trauma service was that in addition to the soft tissue injuries, such as stab wounds, gunshot wounds and blunt trauma, it also treated bone fractures, which is normally handled by orthopedics, a completely different specialty. Of all the bone fractures that came through the ER, the trauma service handled two thirds of them. Patients with broken bones were assigned by rotation, to unit A one day, unit B the next day and orthopedic service the day after. The days that the orthopedic residents handled the fractures were called "soft tissue days," indicating that the trauma service will treat everything except bone injuries. Elective bone operations, not related to trauma, were always done by the orthopedic surgery residents, and thus they were not a part of the Trauma service.

Every resident that worked in trauma service had to think and act fast while also being accurate; the patient's life often depended on it. At the time of my training, there were no advanced diagnostic tests, like CT scan and MRI, to assist us in making the right diagnosis. The only radiology test available was a plain X-ray, which was helpful in diagnosing bone fractures as well as detecting the presence of free air in the abdomen. When taking information on a trauma patient, the accident history and the physical examination were of paramount importance in diagnosing the condition and determining the course of action. The doctor's diagnostic skills were just as important as surgical techniques. A wrong diagnosis could lead to an unnecessary operation. Just as bad, failure to diagnose and operate on a surgical condition could have catastrophic consequences.

There was a test we used at that time to determine intra-abdominal injuries called "abdominal tap and lavage." The director of the KCHC Trauma Service, Dr. Shaftan, was instrumental in developing the technique, which required making a small cut above the patient's belly button under local anesthesia. Through a long needle, up to a liter of saline was then instilled into the abdomen. The abdominal fluid was then drained through the same route, giving us clues about the nature of the injury, if any. If the fluid was bloody, the diagnosis of bleeding was considered, necessitating an operation. If the fluid was clear, then the patient was admitted and placed under observation.

Other important diagnostic tools we used were vital signs (VS), heart rate, blood pressure, and breathing rate, which all had a story to tell. If VS were stable and normal, that was good news. Changes in blood pressure, heart rate and breathing parameters indicated that something was wrong. The blood's hemoglobin was also repeatedly measured; a progressive decrease in levels could indicate the presence of active bleeding, which needed to be addressed and stopped. Through the years of my training I encountered some memorable situations in trauma service.

It was a freezing, icy, February weekend in Brooklyn when I happened to be on duty for a 64-hour shift from Saturday morning until Monday night. The icy weather made this an extraordinarily long and busy shift. There were less stab wounds and gunshot injuries than usual; I guess not many people braved the freezing cold and icy conditions to go out. Those who did had a high probability of slipping and falling on the ice, and of those that fell many wound up with one or more broken bone.

Between Saturday and Monday mornings my trauma team was responsible for taking care of all the ER emergencies. There were 23 patients with fractures that I had to attend to. Most of them were ankle or wrist fractures. Over and over again I reviewed the x-rays that showed the fracture, then I set the bones, applied a cast, and then took another x-ray to make sure the fracture was in good position. I sent the patient home with a pair of crutches, a prescription for pain medicine, instructions to try and keep the limb elevated and a trauma clinic follow up appointment. If the post-cast x-ray showed the fracture was not in a good position, I removed the cast, set the fracture again, reapplied the cast and repeated the x-ray until a desirable result was achieved. The patients that had more serious fractures—like the femur (the long bone of the thigh), the hip, or any other bone that needed open surgical repair—were admitted to the hospital and prepared for an operation in a day or two.

That weekend I spent nearly all my time in the emergency room taking care of broken bones. That saved the ER Surgical Resident the burden of having to page me for every new patient with a broken bone that showed up. I just lined up the patients and took care of them one at time, like a Ford automobile assembly line. I slept in the trauma service office one hour on Saturday night and two hours on Sunday night. No, there was no bed in the office, not even a comfortable chair. I slept on the desk, the hardest "mattress" ever! The only thing that could wake me up, was hearing my name over the pager. I felt a lot of pain in both heel and hip areas, which made me understand how patients developed bedsores. On top of covering all trauma patients in the ER, I also had to address every problem of every patient that was on my trauma unit.

Patients with stab wounds were regular "clients" in the ER. Most of the stab wounds were in the abdominal area, chest and neck. Some of the patients with abdominal wounds had no pain at all, and no change in their vital signs that would indicate intra-abdominal organ injury, and/or bleeding. In that situation an abdominal tap and lavage was carried out, and if negative, the patient was admitted to the hospital for monitoring and observation. On the other hand, if there was severe pain, a drop in blood pressure or any other sign of serious organ injury or bleeding, the patient was rushed to the operating room for an "exploratory laparotomy." That procedure involved opening the abdomen and looking for the injury-causing problem and then repairing the issue. Injuries to the abdominal aorta—the main artery of the abdomen—or inferior vena cava—the main vein in the abdomen—cause an extensive rapid loss of blood, usually leading to death. The organs more likely to get injured by a stab wound, were the ones that were fixed in position, such as the liver, spleen, stomach, duodenum, aorta, vena cava, and portions of the colon.

The unit also saw frequent stab wounds to the chest, neck, head and extremities. I was called to treat one such injury, which presented in the ER in a spectacular fashion. A big, tall, man in his 50s arrived with a knife sticking out of his neck. The blade entered the skin at the left side of his neck, about two inches below the jaw. Most of the blade and the knife handle were outside the neck. The man was not very talkative and appeared to be mentally challenged, unable to explain what had happened. He was urgently taken to the operating room and given general anesthesia. In preparation for the knife removal, careful dissection and control of the carotid artery and jugular vein was secured. The knife was then pulled out by the anesthesiologist, allowing a careful, detailed, examination of the injuries. It appeared that the blade had passed flush with the left wall of the jugular vein, severing only small veins in the area. The left carotid artery was not injured. All the small vessels were ligated, and bleeding control secured. The wound was then cleaned, drained and closed. The next day when we made rounds, we asked him how he was feeling.

"I'm hungry man! Shit," he replied.

It was not the best way to relay that he had a good appetite, but we got his message loud and clear! We ordered a regular diet tray and took good care of him. He did well and was discharged home a few days later.

Patients with gunshot wounds were also regularly encountered at the ER, but their management was more complicated and challenging than the stab wound injuries. The bullet trajectory, and consequently, the specific organs in its path that might have been injured, was difficult to determine, especially when the wounded patient refused to cooperate. A case in point was a patient in his 20s with a gunshot wound in his left buttock and severe abdominal pain, indicating a catastrophic event in need of emergency surgery. I asked him what position he was in when he was shot, for example was he lying down, was he hit from the left or right. But he would not answer my question until we were outside the operating room and he was not any more helpful.

"Go f**k yourself," he told me.

That is one of the few times that I got pissed off by a patient.

"No, I will not go f**k myself, because if I do that, you are going to die," I responded.

On exploration, he was found to have an injury to the rectum and several holes in his small bowel. The bullet was found free in the abdomen and removed. The injuries were repaired, and a colostomy performed. The patient did well and was discharged home in 10 days, with a plan to bring him back in three months for colostomy closure.

The erratic course of a bullet was demonstrated in another patient, whom I saw for a gunshot wound in his right upper arm. That was the entrance wound and despite careful examination no exit wound could be found. To make things more puzzling and challenging, a chest x-ray, and x-ray of the right arm did not show the presence of a bullet! We saw a wound through which the bullet went in, but no wound of the bullet coming out, indicating that the bullet was still in his body, but it could not be seen on x-ray examination! Where did the bullet go? That was the million-dollar question!

I went back to examine the patient to find out where the bullet traveled by tracing his path of the pain. I started from the entrance wound and asked him to tell me if it hurt when I pressed around it. The pain path guided me to the right front upper chest, then to the left front upper chest, then to the left upper arm and midway between the shoulder and left elbow, I could feel the bullet. That was my "eureka" moment. The word "eureka" in Greek, means "I found," and that's exactly what happened: I found the bullet. Mystery solved! Evidently when the man was shot, he had his arms up, so the arms and upper anterior, front chest were on the same line. The bullet traveled under the skin along this line and wound up under the skin on the opposite arm.

I removed the bullet in the operating room, scratched my initials on its surface and surrendered it to the police to be used as evidence. There is a misconception about bullets that comes from watching too many western movies, which suggests that the bullet needs to be removed before the patient can recover. The truth is that the bullet itself resting in the body does not pose any significant danger. It's the travel of the bullet through the body that causes the damage, and poses danger to the patient's life.

At the trauma service we also had a lot of exposure and experience dealing with multiple injuries from car accidents. A particularly depressing incident I recall is when the ER surgical resident gave me a heads up about a couple on their way to the ER by ambulance. They had been traveling by car on the Brooklyn-Queens Expressway when another vehicle driving in the opposite direction, jumped the divider and landed on their car.

When the ambulance arrived on the accident scene, the couple ended up being taken to the morgue instead of the ER. They did not survive the crushing injuries from the accident. The ER surgical resident called me to cancel the alert.

Research with Dr. Harry LeVeen

On June 30, 1972 I finished the clinical PGY-2 year and on Monday, July 3, I started a year of research with Dr. Harry LeVeen, Director of Surgery, at the Brooklyn VA Hospital. My main project was to help him with the design of an operation for patients with intractable ascites (massive accumulation of fluid in the abdomen) caused by severe liver disease. He was working on a system of a valve between two silastic tubes, by which he tried to empty the abdominal fluid back to the vascular system. After he told me about the procedure he developed that kept failing, I recommended that we redesign the operation by positioning the drainage side of the tube through the jugular vein of the neck and into the superior vena cava (SVC), the big vein in the chest. The pressure in the vein is influenced by the breathing cycle, which creates a negative pressure inside the big vein in the chest, and will promote the flow of the fluid that is coming from the abdomen. He enthusiastically accepted my comments and recommendations for the new path of the tubing, and my job was to explore the results of the procedure that I designed.

I called Dr. LeVeen on Friday inquiring if he wanted me to go in on July 1, which was a Saturday. He was sort of surprised by my call and told me that I did not have to work on the weekends. That was a very welcome development because the only other time I was off on weekends was when I was on a vacation. The times I was off while working in clinical services did not start until Saturday afternoon, after morning rounds.

On Monday I showed up at the Brooklyn VA Hospital and had a meeting with Dr. LeVeen. We visited the dog lab we would use for our research and I met with Jerry, who was in charge of maintaining the premises. Then we got down to work and planned the course of action to explore my hypothesis and develop a physical treatment for intractable ascites.

The plan we developed consisted of two phases. In phase one, we would produce ascites in dogs. We would then proceed with the insertion of the LeVeen contraption with the one-way valve and the two tubes. We would place the collecting tube in the abdomen to collect the fluid and position the end of the drainage tube in the superior vena cava through the jugular vein.

The dog's weight, abdominal girth, water consumed, and urine output would be measured and monitored daily, starting from the time of the procedure that will cause ascites, through the development of ascites, the placement of the shunt and the resolution of the ascites. The ascites that is caused by the surgical procedure, normally resolves spontaneously over time, so we had to proceed expeditiously with the insertion of the shunt device once the ascites developed. The data collected would then be tabulated and examined. If the results revealed improvement or timely resolution of the ascites, then we would proceed to phase two.

Phase two would only take place if the operations on the dogs were successful, indicating a high probability of success of the second phase. The second phase of the project, consisted of inserting the devise in patients with intractable ascites, and studying the results of the procedure by monitoring the same parameters.

Dr. LeVeen instructed Jerry to give me a surgical instrument catalog so I could order what was necessary for the dog operations. I took my time and went through the pages and chose what I needed. Jerry placed the order, and we received the instruments in a few days. I operated on four dogs under general anesthesia. Within a few days the dogs developed ascites as expected. I then proceeded to insert the peritoneovenous shunt device, under general anesthesia.

After careful observation of the results and examination of the collected data, the new operation was clearly a success, and gave us the green light to proceed to phase two of the study. The results of the operation were clinically obvious, with the observation that the ascites had practically subsided, and quite quickly.

Having successfully attained the desired outcome of the peritone-ovenous shunt in the animal lab, we were in search of the right patient with intractable ascites for the new operation. The gastroenterologists at the Brooklyn VA Hospital who normally cared for the patients with ascites were skeptical about the effectiveness of the shunt based on past experience with Dr. LeVeen's procedure with the shunt. They were reluctant to refer any more patients for the experimental procedure.

Our first referral was transferred from the Orange VA Hospital in New Jersey. Frank P. was a man in his 50s with severe intractable ascites, which was so bad that the patient could not even turn on his side in bed, never mind get out of bed or walk around. He was very weak, had gener-alized muscle wasting and appeared malnourished. His abdomen was enormous, filled with ascites fluid, and tense due to the high intra-ab-dominal pressure. He had a history of alcohol abuse for decades, which caused liver cirrhosis (scarring and shrinkage of the liver), and conse-quently, collection of ascites, which became intractable over time. He had quit drinking by necessity, since the time he became unable to get out bed. We explained to him that this was a new procedure and though it was very promising we could not guarantee a desirable outcome.

He consented to the procedure and was taken to the OR. He had been transferred from the Orange VA Hospital to vascular service, and the operation was performed by the surgeons assigned to that service. I also scrubbed in to guide the team how to proceed. The collecting tube was inserted through an incision at the right abdomen close to the ribs, allowing the fluid to flow through the valve and out the drainage tube indicating patency and proper function of the system. The skin of the upper part of the incision was then lifted off the chest wall and bron-chial biopsy forceps with the end of the drainage tube tied to its end, pushed through a plane under the skin all the way to the right side of the neck over the jugular vein. A second incision over the end of the instrument, in the neck, was then made to free the drainage tube. The forceps were then withdrawn, and the tube pulled through the tunnel and trimmed so that once positioned through the jugular vein, its tip would be in the superior vena cava close to the heart.

The jugular vein was carefully exposed, and the collection tube inserted through the vein to the superior vena cava and secured in place. The wounds were then closed. Several 6-inch ace bandages were placed around the abdomen to maintain a higher abdominal pressure and facilitate the flow of the ascites fluid into the vascular system. A catheter was inserted in the bladder to allow free flow of the urine and accurate measurement of its volume. The patient was then taken to the recovery room. The operation went well, and everything developed as planned. As far as I was concerned, this was the time of truth, when the new procedure was going to be proven and take its place in the art of surgery or be a failure and bring our efforts to a disappointing end.

I stayed at the patient's bedside observing and monitoring the post-operative developments minute by minute. Diuretics (water meds) were given intravenously during the operation to help the kidneys get rid of the fluid that was diverted into the vascular system from the abdomen. The first signs were very encouraging. The bladder catheter started pouring out large amounts of urine and the patient felt reasonably well. His vital signs were stable, and the urine continued to pour out throughout the day and night. I left his bedside later in the evening feeling confident that he was going to do very well.

The next morning, I rushed back to the hospital early and I was glad to see his abdomen "deflated" and the ace bandages loose! The patient was able to breath much easier since the pressure on the diaphragm by the ascites had been substantially decreased with the diversion of the ascites fluid into the vascular system. The urine output from the time of the operation until the next morning was 11.5 liters, equivalent to 25 pounds of weight. That was a spectacular outcome. The patient was happy but not as happy as I was, though I imagined that Dr. LeVeen was even happier than me. He was extremely appreciative of my work and input, because with my design his dream operation was finally a reality.

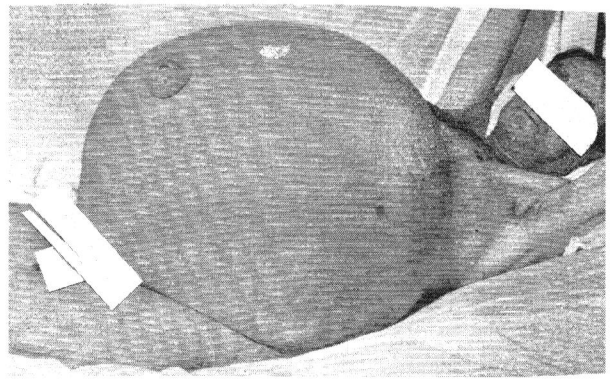

First Patient Before P–V Shunt

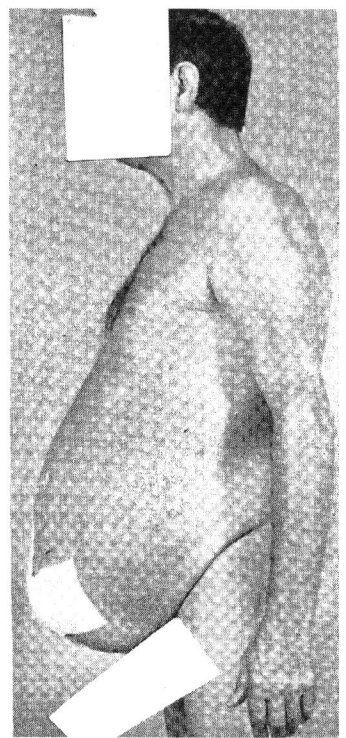

First Patient After P–V Shunt

The peritoneovenous (P-V) shunt, AKA LeVeen Shunt, received national recognition as a valuable contribution to the art of surgery. A scientific paper titled "Peritoneovenous Shunting for Ascites" with authors "Harry H. LeVeen M.D., George Christoudias M.D." was presented at the annual meeting of the American Surgical Association, Colorado Springs, Colorado, May 1-3, 1974, and was published in the prestigious surgical journal "Annals of Surgery" in October, 1974. Strangely enough the published paper had four more names as co-authors, giving Dr. LeVeen more recognition as the lead author. That did not bother me because I looked at it as an opportunity to show what I could accomplish. I was very appreciative for the opportunity and experience. Other research projects and scientific papers followed, but the "Peritoneovenous Shunting for Ascites" was head and shoulders above them all.

One of the advantages of working in research for a year was that I was working much less and that gave me more time to spend with Yih, Sheao-Ping, which translated form Chinese, means "Little Apple," and her name in America, Sharon. I saw my "Little Apple" often and I had the opportunity to learn mahjong and play at Lucy's place often enough. Lucy, Sharon's classmate in nursing school and best friend, lived in Jackson Heights, Queens with her husband Ming, and two toddlers, Howard and Jane. They were about 30 minutes from the Brooklyn VA Hospital, so we visited them often. My cousin Costas Kilaras had a diner in that neighborhood, on Hillside Avenue, and lived a few minutes away in Kew Gardens, so we frequently passed by to say hello. He was always happy to see us, as were Lucy and her family. We also visited my sister Anastasia, who was living in Teaneck with her husband Angelos and their sons Christos and Kyriacos. Of course, we also went to Manhattan regularly for dinner at the Greek restaurant "Paradeisos" on West 46th Street, and occasionally went to a movie.

One of those days was Sunday, June 3, 1973. I picked up Sharon at the Brooklyn VA Hospital Nurses Dorm and we went to New York

City in my brand-new Ford Maverick. I left my car in a parking lot and walked to the restaurant where we enjoyed a nice Greek meal. A walk around Times Square and a couple of hours at the movies capped the outing in the city. On the way home we took the West Side Highway to the Brooklyn Battery Tunnel. The traffic was relatively light because it was getting late. The weather was good and the roadway clear and dry as we went through the Battery Tunnel to the left lane of the Gowanus Expressway. Suddenly, something extraordinary happened—I saw a large car flying. It was traveling in the opposite direction and somehow, someway managed to lift off the ground and become completely airborne several feet above the highway divider. It was no more than 100 feet from my car, flying at a high speed but I did not think it would come in contact with my car. I was amazed by the spectacle.

"Jesus Christ! Look at that," I said to Sharon.

The next thing I remembered was that my car was not moving, the engine was off, my forehead was bleeding, and the windshield of the Ford Maverick shattered. Sharon was bent over on her seat and was completely quiet. A Rabbi was outside my door trying to pry it open.

"Sharon!" I called her.

"Yes," she replied.

"Are you All right?"

"Yes! Are You OK?"

"I am OK!"

The kind Rabbi managed to pry my door open and help me out of the car. Sharon's door was also opened by people from another car, who stopped to help. She was carried out and placed on the pavement behind our car. I ran to her. Her face was covered with blood as a result of multiple lacerations on her forehead. I asked her again if she was OK and if she had any pain. She said that her belly hurt. I had her lay down on the pavement of the highway and examined her abdomen. I did not find any signs of serious intra-abdominal injury, but I asked her to stay down until the ambulance arrived. I was in a daze and did not recall anything about the actual impact.

"Where are we? Where are we coming from and where are we going?" I asked Sharon.

She thought I was joking, but she answered my questions. I took a good look around. The traffic was a mess with two lanes of the express-way closed because of our accident. The people in the passing cars were screaming, looking at Sharon lying down on the highway pavement, thinking that she was dead. Several cars had stopped, and people came over to help. One man grabbed a diaper (a new one) from his car and placed it on Sharon's forehead. My car was mangled. The front end was totaled, and the passenger side roof crushed down to the seat. The damage extended to the trunk. A few feet behind my car I saw a Cadillac lying upside down. A man was carried out and placed on the pavement. I started putting things together with the different pieces of the puzzle falling into place. The image of the flying car flashed back in my mind and that made me realize what had happened.

The "flying Cadillac" must have been traveling over 60 miles per hour. I was going around 50 miles per hour, and since we were on the same path in opposite directions, we were approaching each other at a speed of over 110 miles per hour. It took only one second to collide. The front of the Cadillac landed on my car's engine, flipped over and hit the passenger's side and trunk of my car, and landed upside down several feet behind and to the right of my car. We were not wearing our seatbelts. At the time of impact, I was forcefully thrown onto the steer-ing wheel and the windshield, which I broke with my head, resulting in hundreds of tiny glass fragments penetrating the skin of my forehead and front scalp. The second I hit the windshield, I lost consciousness and the entire moment of impact was erased from my memory. Sharon saw the car coming and bent down in my direction so that at the time of impact, the rearview mirror got detached from the windshield and landed on Sharon's forehead, shuttering into pieces and causing multiple lacerations.

The ambulance arrived and we were placed on stretchers and transferred to the ER at Long Island College Hospital (LICH), which was the one closest to the accident site. I asked the paramedics if they could take us to Kings County Hospital instead, but they said they were obligated to take us to the nearest ER. The driver of the flying car that hit us was also taken to the same location. The surgical residents came and examined Sharon and me. Sharon's obvious injuries were the forehead lacerations. No other significant injuries were found. My injuries were also limited to my forehead lacerations and severe pain in my right wrist at the base of my thumb and my chest wall from hitting the steering wheel. I told the surgical resident that the findings indicated fracture of the scaphoid bone of my wrist, so he called the orthopedic resident to come and evaluate me. The orthopedic resident then examined my wrist, reviewed the x-ray, and found no evidence of fracture. I knew he was wrong, because I had all the clinical signs and findings of a fracture. The negative x-ray had no bearing on the diagnosis since it is common medical knowledge that a fracture of the scaphoid bone in particular, will not appear on x-ray for at least 2-3 weeks. But I was not about to get into an argument with the resident. By then, it was evident that we did not have any life-threatening injuries, so we declined any treatment and decided to take a taxi to KCHC-ER so I could pick the doctors who would repair Sharon's forehead lacerations and take care of my right wrist fracture.

Before we got in the taxi, Sharon went to the bathroom and came out very upset, crying profusely. She saw her beautiful face looking like minced meat and became inconsolable. Earlier when I was walking around, I saw an older man on a stretcher, crying for help. He was the driver of the Cadillac. His nose was swollen, evidently fractured, and there was significant swelling of his face, forcing his eyes shut closed. I went to him and asked him if he had any pain other than his nose.

He said no, just his nose, and was concerned that he could not open his eyes. I took his hand and reassured him that he was going to be all right, but I did not disclose that I was one of the victims of the accident he had caused.

We signed out of LICH Against Medical Advice (AMA) and headed for KCHC-ER. We arrived there in the wee hours of the morning. I got out of the cab and went inside the ER and asked a nurse to bring a wheelchair to the taxi where Sharon was waiting. Moments later Mitzie, the ER night supervisor, showed up with a wooden wheelchair and wheeled Sharon to the treatment room. As soon as I saw Mitzie I told her how I always said that if I had an accident, I wanted to be treated at KCHC, declaring my faith and trust to the great care administered there. She smiled as she rolled Sharon's wheelchair to the treatment room. I completed and signed the registration forms for both of us and waited for the plastic surgery resident to attend to Sharon's forehead messy lacerations. The surgical resident cleaned my forehead and removed multiple tiny fragments of broken glass. He placed a sterile dressing and held it together with a bandage around my head. That day was a soft tissue day, so the orthopedic service was going to take care of my wrist injury. The surgical resident also had a chest x-ray done to make sure I did not have any rib fractures since I had a lot of pain in my chest from the violent contact with the steering wheel.

The chest x-ray was normal and did not show any broken ribs. Dr. Moskowitz, the orthopedic resident, had completed a year of general surgery internship the same year as me and we knew each other. He examined my right wrist and pushed my thumb towards the wrist, which caused me pain, a pathognomonic (certain) sign of scaphoid bone fracture.

"George, you have a scaphoid bone fracture," he said. "I have to put a cast on."

That was no surprise to me. I had done the same maneuver myself when I was at the LICH-ER and reached the same conclusion. He proceeded to apply the cast, which was the first and last cast I ever had. I thanked him and went back to Sharon to see how she was doing. The plastic surgery resident was already there, taking care of her. It was Dr. Berman, the senior plastic surgery resident, on the last month of his training. I had worked with him before and I knew him to be a very competent plastic surgeon with excellent bedside manners. He cleaned the wound with antiseptic solution and irrigation with normal saline under local anesthesia. He worked tirelessly to explore the lacerations and traced and removed all fragments of the broken mirror he could find, which were embedded in the skin around the lacerations. He worked for over three hours meticulously debriding and approximating the tissues and closing the superficial layers of the skin in a plastic fashion, accomplishing the best possible result. By the time he finished the repair, the night departed and Monday daylight showed up.

We finished with the hospital treatments and we were ready to go home to my elevated basement apartment, but we had a problem. I had no car, and even worse than that I had no keys to get in, because they were left on the ignition of the Ford Maverick. I called the owner of the apartment, a Rabbi, who lived on the floor above and had access to my unit. He took a long time to answer the phone. He eventually picked up and I told him what happened and asked him to open my apartment door. I called a taxi to take us to my apartment at 295 East 48 St., just a couple of blocks from the hospital.

The owner was there with my door open, waiting for us. He was very sympathetic and offered to help if I needed anything. He gave me the extra key to my door until I could locate my car and retrieve my keys. I thanked him for his kindness, but the only thing Sharon and I needed was some sleep. We slept for hours and when we woke up, we were aching all over our bodies. Every muscle was tense and sore. My rib cage, which took the brunt of the deceleration force onto the steering wheel, was a bundle of aching bones and flesh, especially when taking a deep breath. My right wrist was also hurting from the scaphoid bone fracture, which was caused by the force of holding onto the steering wheel. We only took over the counter medication for our aches and pains, knowing that it was going to take over three weeks until the healing had progressed enough to soothe our symptoms.

We were still trying to come into terms with the fact that we were but a hairline's distance away from being crashed into a lifeless bundle of crushed flesh. A split-second difference was the determining factor between life and death. Had the flying car landed in front of my car, it would have been a head on collision and much greater force would have been transferred to the impact of my body to my car. The continuation of the Cadillac's path over my car, however, took away a large part of its kinetic energy. Simply put, the force that carried that huge car in the air several feet behind my car would have smashed my car like an accordion and killed us. On the other hand, if the car landed directly on us, we would have had the same fate as the couple that had their heads smashed in a similar accident on the Brooklyn-Queens Expressway, just a year earlier. We pondered how lucky we were to survive such a huge accident, in which we had the bad luck to be involved in through no fault of our own. One important thing that I concluded from this accident was the fact that when I regained consciousness after the head injury I had no recollection of any pain during the impact, so had I been killed in this accident it would have been a painless death, answering a question I used to wonder about for a long time. What is the last thing, people feel when dying from massive head injuries? How much do they suffer?

The next day, the first order of business was to rent a car so I could get around. I went through the Yellow Pages, a 3-4-inch-thick yellow telephone book listing all the business phones and addresses of an area. (The internet was still two decades away.) I found a local car rental place and then called the police to find out where my car was towed.

When I got to the shop where my car was to get my keys, I told them that I was the owner of the Ford Maverick that was crushed on Gowanus Expressway. Patrick, the owner of the towing service, looked at me, and came up with what I thought was a stupid question.

"You are still alive?"

I replied with an equally stupid answer. "No! But I was just raised from the dead to come and see you about my keys!"

He took me to the car, and I was stunned. No wonder he thought I was a goner! The maverick appeared to have gone through a wringer. I took some pictures and looked inside and saw my keys in the ignition. Patrick told me that I owed him $600 for towing and storing the car, but if I signed the car over to him, he would forgive the money I owed. The car was a complete wreck, so I did not hesitate to do it.

Crushed Car

Crushed Car

"Shall I write the amount of $600 as sale price?" I asked.

"No, no. Just leave everything blank," Patrick replied. "Just sign the title paper."

I signed the title, took my keys and left. Little did I know that signing the title and leaving everything blank was part of Patrick's insurance fraud scheme. I found out a few months later when I got a call from an insurance investigator. He asked me if I had sold my Ford Maverick, and for how much, because the new owner had reported it stolen. I informed him that the car was destroyed in a car accident that I had in June and that it was a total loss, and I signed the title to Patrick and received no compensation for it. I never heard back from him, but I guess they figured out the scam Patrick was running.

I drove over to the Brooklyn VA Hospital to finish up the loose ends of my research work. I talked to Dr. LeVeen about the accident.

"There is nothing wrong with cars flying, as long as they don't land on you," he remarked.

He then asked if I wanted to use his car since mine was destroyed. He said that he could do without it for a while since he was living on hospital grounds. That was a gesture that touched my soul, like finding someone that cared about me like my family. I thanked him very much for his offer to loan me his car, but respectfully declined since I had already leased a car.

We made an appointment for Sharon with Dr. Song, the Director of Plastic Surgery at SUNY-DMC, for a follow up. He took good care of her and gave her treatments that would result in minimal scarring. I was followed up by Dr. Shaftan, who was the chief of trauma surgery, for my scaphoid bone fracture, which healed well and gave me no trouble or impediment in carrying out my surgical duties.

With my research year coming to a close and the return to the hectic surgical schedule pending, I needed to purchase a new car. I went to the Yellow Pages again and found a Ford dealer in West New York, Brooklyn. I decided I wanted a Ford Mustang. I took a look at their inventory, picked the one I liked and paid for it. The salesman promised me that he was going to have it ready in two days, because I needed it to drive to Albany, New York, to take my FLEX (Federal Licensing Exam) test on June 12, 13 and 14, for Washington State. Why Washington State? Because I had an Exchange Visitor's Visa and the one of the few states that accepted doctors with that Visa was Washington. The exam was universal and was given and accepted by the majority of states, including New York, which did not take applicants with an Exchange Visitors Visa. I wrote to the Washington State Medical Board and applied for the exam, which I scheduled to take in Albany, since there was no opening for the New York City locations. I paid the fees and was all set to sit for the FLEX test. The rational was that once I pass the exam, I could get a medical license in New York State by reciprocity as soon as I changed my visa status to permanent.

I was planning to leave for Albany on Monday, June 11, but the Ford dealership did not have my new car ready, so I drove up to Albany in the rental car. I had been preparing for the Flex Exam for over a year, having taken advantage of the light 40-hour schedule during my research year to study. I arrived at a hotel in Albany on Monday afternoon. I did not take any reading material because I did not think that it was necessary. I believed that all the studying I had been doing was enough to help me take the exam successfully in all subjects: basic science, clinical knowledge and clinical competence. My only concern was the concussion I got from the big, forceful shaking of my head when it impacted and cracked the windshield just 11 days earlier. I wondered whether my memory would be affected by the injury. Despite the generalized muscle aches, I still felt pretty good and I was optimistic that I would score well and pass the exam. I relaxed for the afternoon and evening and had a good night's sleep. After a light breakfast I arrived at the exam location and was seated before the 8 a.m. test would begin. I felt healthy, rested and alert, my thinking was clear, and I was ready for the exam challenge. I had no problem whatsoever comprehending the questions, understanding the subject and easily picking the right answers. My memory was clear and sharp and my reactions accurate. After the long test, I left the exam hall content and confident that I did as well as I had hoped. I had the same feeling after the exams the following two days. I drove back to Brooklyn the next day and enjoyed another day of relaxation.

Back to Being a Surgical Resident at Kings County Hospital

I finished my research year with Dr. LeVeen at the end of June 1973 and went back to clinical duties. My year of light work was over. I had to get back to the regular schedule of being a surgical resident, working over 100 hours each week. In addition to that I did moonlighting in the ER from time to time for some extra cash. The payment of $25 per hour was generous compared with our resident's salary of approximately $3 per hour, with no overtime pay. I did not mind filling in when the Director of the KCHC-ER called me to work. I usually worked in the screening area where the first patient evaluation was carried out, so I evaluated a lot of people with a wide variety of problems and conditions. I either gave them the appropriate treatment and sent them home, or, If they had a more complicated problem, referred them to the proper ER department for further evaluation and treatment.

One of the patients I saw at the screening area was a heavy lady in her 50s, complaining of a "heavy feeling" in the lower abdomen. Two weeks earlier she had gone through an abdominal operation in the general surgical service for intestinal problems. I had her lie down and examined her abdomen. The scar up and down the middle of the abdomen was healing with unusual induration (hard inflammation and loss of pliability) on and around the scar. Something strange was going on but I could not be sure what it was, so I sent the patient for an x-ray of the abdomen. When I looked at the x-ray I was disturbed and amazed at what I saw. The largest, heavier, wider instrument that we used in the ER for abdominal surgery was sitting right in the middle of the abdomen behind the healing wound. I recognized the instrument right away. It was a malleable retractor, made of a malleable flat metal. It measured about 10 inches long by one-eighth of an inch thick and was 3 inches wide. The main function of this retractor is to hold the intestines and/or other organs away from the target organ or tissue we are operating on and provide exposure for a safe operation. At that time, it was also used to prevent injury to the bowel, when suturing close the abdominal wall, by placing it under the wound edges. This way the retractor shielded the intestines from the path of the suturing needle. It works pretty well as long as you remove the retractor before you complete the abdominal wall closure, something that her surgeon neglected to do.

This was the first and only time I saw a retractor of this size left behind inside the abdomen. I called the surgical resident at the department responsible for causing the problem and told him what happened. I then admitted the patient to that service for removal of the retractor. I did inform the patient that she had a very good reason to "have a heavy feeling" in the abdomen and explained to her what it was. The patient was taken to the OR within hours and the large retractor was removed.

When I applied for a residency at the SUNY-DMC, KCHC surgical program I had stated that had an interest in the thoracic surgery subspecialty and had several assignments to that service during my training. I had second thoughts about pursuing it, however, and decided that I was going to do a fellowship in cancer surgery instead, not because I did not love thoracic surgery, but because I loved general and cancer surgery more. At one point, Dr. Klotz, the surgical residency coordinator, asked me whether I was still interested in a thoracic surgery subspecialty. I informed him that I intended to pursue a fellowship in surgical oncology instead.

I had several rotations in thoracic surgery, the last of which was in 1974, a year before my chief residency. Other than the chief resident, there were three residents assigned to thoracic service, which at times was very slow. All three of us were in the later years of our training and very competent in carrying out the daily chores of the system. We were on call every third day (36-hour shift), and every third weekend (Saturday Noon to Monday evening). For some reason we decided that the resident on weekend duty should cover from Friday until Monday evening, so the other two could have a true weekend off from Friday night until Monday morning.

Dr. John Bivona was the resident on duty the first weekend. During his rotation there were not many patients on the unit and, surprisingly, there were no emergency admissions, something that was very unusual, taking into consideration the high incidence of chest injuries from stab and gunshot wounds, especially on weekends. Unbelievably, Dr. Bivona got bored, a very rare occurrence for any surgical resident on duty at KCHC! He caught up on his sleep deprivation and I was looking forward to doing the same the following weekend when it was my turn to be on duty. On Friday we all started at 7 a.m., finished our rounds, and then one of the residents went to the OR to assist in an open-heart surgery followed by another operation for removal of a lung lobe. The second resident went to do the bronchoscopies, which entailed placing a straight tube with a light at the end, through the mouth and down the windpipe, to look for any abnormalities, such as tumors or inflammation. I stayed on the unit doing the scut work—drawing bloods, changing wound dressings, obtaining lab, pathology and x-ray reports, addressing patients' needs etc.

The day finished at 6 p.m. with the afternoon rounds for everyone except me. My "day" was scheduled to finish 72 hours later, on Monday evening. It did not appear that it would be easy, like the prior weekend, because of the two post-operative patients, one with open heart surgery and the other with thoracotomy operation. They were both in the thoracic surgery ICU and the open-heart surgery patient was still on the respirator. I anticipated that she was going to need continuous monitoring by me. Just as everybody left, I received a call from the ER surgical resident that there was an older man with right-side rib fractures associated with a pneumothorax (air in the free chest cavity, outside the lung), who needed immediate attention. I rushed to the ER to evaluate the patient. This poor man had fallen at home and landed on the steps with the right side of his chest. He complained of severe pain and difficulty breathing. I reviewed the chest x-ray and saw that the right lung was completely collapsed and there were several ribs broken on the right side. A broken rib had punctured the right lung, which promptly collapsed, rendering breathing laborious and difficult. The only way to treat his condition was to insert a suction tube in the chest to create a negative pressure in the chest cavity, which would cause the lung to re-expand. I took the patient to the ER ICU and inserted a chest tube, secured it in place with a suture and connected it to suction. The patient felt better and an x-ray showed almost complete re-expansion of the right lung. There was a lot of air coming out through the chest tube, indicating there was a leak from the punctured lung. The wall suction was then increased, but no other measures needed to be taken. The lung puncture was expected to heal spontaneously as the healing of the lung tissue progressed. Eddy, that was his name, was transferred to the thoracic surgery ICU, in the "E" building, for continuous observation and monitoring. He was given narcotic analgesic injections for pain and the chest tube was connected to high wall suction. He was comfortable, but he had to be patient, waiting for "Dr. Time" to heal his lung. Like for every admission, I completed a detail history of the events causing his injury, his current relevant medical conditions, history of his past health problems and his family's medical history. I then recorded my findings of his complete physical examination from head to toes, documenting everything on my history and physical report, a process that takes a good hour or more.

As he settled down, I was asked to check the open-heart surgery patient. She appeared to be a little dusky, so I drew some arterial blood and took it to the lab for blood gas analysis. The results showed that her arterial oxygen was below the acceptable levels, so I adjusted the respirator settings to bring the gas levels back to normal and confirmed that by a repeat test.

Everything appeared to be under control but not for long. A few minutes later I was called to the ER to see a patient who was coughing up blood. I rushed over to the ER to evaluate the patient. He appeared comfortable, but he had an emesis basin on his side with bright red blood and some blood clots. I reviewed the chest x-ray and saw a cavity in the right lung, indicating that the underlying condition causing his hemoptysis (spitting up blood), was most likely tuberculosis. I proceeded to admit him to the thoracic surgery ICU and completed the history and physical with the associated report.

I notified the chief resident about the admission of this patient, knowing fully well that these patients were at high risk of massive bleeding leading to death and could need emergency surgery. The chief resident said he was on his way to see the patient. I had started an IV and gave the patient oxygen with a face mask. He appeared to be stable when, all of a sudden, he started coughing and spitting up large amounts of blood and clots. He was in agony. I tried to suction his windpipe and intubated him for better access to the breathing tube, but the amount of bleeding was overwhelming. The poor man was drowning in his own blood. He became cyanotic and unconscious and lost the battle of survival, as the chief resident was walking into the ICU! It was a very depressing scene indeed. A patient, who was fully alert just a few minutes earlier, was not breathing any more. His body was lifeless in bed, calm and serene. There was nothing more that could be done but that was no consolation for me.

It was already well past midnight, so I headed for the on-call room to get some sleep. Or so I thought. The ICU nurse called me that the heart surgery patient's blood pressure was dropping. I went back and made the necessary adjustments on the volume of the IV fluids until the BP reached acceptable levels. Then I checked on the other ICU patients too. The patient that had a lobectomy was fine, but the older man with the fractured ribs and the pneumothorax had a swollen chest wall around the chest tube area. On examination I could feel the crackling sound of the skin with subcutaneous emphysema, indicating the presence of free air under the skin. The presence of air under pressure in the chest cavity somehow found its way through the chest tube wound and into the space under the skin, causing it to swell. I increased the wall suction in the hope it would decrease the pressure of the chest cavity and stop the flow of air in the subcutaneous space.

It was about 5 a.m. when I thought I would try again to reach the on-call room and see if I could get some sleep. I slept for about 90 minutes when the next call came from the ICU. It was about the heart surgery patient, who was very restless. I washed up and went back. I repeated the arterial blood gases and drew more blood for routine tests, having increased the narcotic analgesics first. All the results were normal, so I decided to go for breakfast at the house staff building next to the "E" building where my patients were.

The dining room was actually like a first-class restaurant, with white tablecloths, all-you-can-eat eggs any style, fruit and cereal, all courtesy of the New York City Health and Hospital Corporation. I had a rich breakfast that more than made up for the dinner I missed the night before. I went back to the unit to do the scut work and made the morning rounds with the chief resident. Everybody was stable but Eddy had a big complaint: He could not see, and that made it impossible to have his breakfast since he could not see it! The subcutaneous emphysema got much worse and had extended all the way to his neck and face. The eyelids were blown up by a large amount of air under the skin and were completely shut closed. The poor man could not open his eyes at all. He had no pain, but he just could not see a thing. I went close to him and I gently squeezed the skin of the eyelids with my fingers, pushing the air out to the tissues close by, and like magic he could open his eyes wide and see again. He enjoyed his breakfast without the need for anybody's help. I showed him how to squeeze the air out of his eyelids because I suspected they would swell up again.

The admissions kept coming throughout the weekend. A young man with a gunshot wound to the chest had to go to the OR to control the bleeding. Two people in a car accident had chest injuries resulting in rib fractures and were admitted for treatment and monitoring. Then there was a patient whose x-rays showed a tumor on his left lung. He arrived at the ER complaining of a cough and spitting up blood. He was admitted for further work up and treatment.

The admission that topped them all was a man in his 30s who was caught cheating by his wife. She was not very forgiving and had stabbed him in the chest causing severe bleeding that needed an operation to stop it. By the time Monday's evening rounds came, I had only managed to get a total of five hours of sleep out of 82 hours of working straight. I went home, got in bed and woke up the next day. I had no desire to eat, watch TV or do anything but sleep. The next day my beeper went off. I called the operator who gave me a message to call the ER supervisor Mitzie. I wondered what she was calling me for, since I was not covering the ER that day.

"Yes Mitzie, you are looking for me?" I said.

"I want to ask you how Eddy is doing. He is my landlord," she said.

I was happy to hear her asking about the poor man. Nobody else asked about him, and no family showed up to visit him. I informed her of his condition and told her that he will probably be going home in a 7 to 10 days. His condition improved gradually and steadily and Mitzie drove him home after 10 days in stable, good condition. That rotation was my last in thoracic surgery, as I was going to my chief residency the next year.

My next assignment was at the tumor surgery service, a well-organized entity with joint conferences with specialists in medical oncology, radiology and pathology, which gave residents a solid foundation of this subspecialty. In addition to all the tumor admissions, we covered ER admissions for general surgical problems every other day. I always enjoyed the time I spent there, even the time that one of the residents got sick, leaving just me and the chief resident covering the unit for almost a month. I was on duty for 21 days and nights out of 30, with only nine nights off during the entire month. I worked very hard that month, but there was something good about it too. Other than the big cases, I did all the operations, which made me very happy. I slept in the hospital whenever things slowed down and, whenever I had the time, I went for breakfast, lunch or dinner, though I skipped many meals. There was always a high volume of operations, making the service a favorite rotation for the residents. We treated all types of benign and malignant tumors: stomach, pancreas and colon cancers; mouth cancers; benign and malignant thyroid tumors; benign breast tumors and breast cancers; skin lesions like melanoma and basal cell carcinoma; and fatty tumors, to name just the usual ones.

One of my assignments to the tumor service was on the year before my chief residency. The chief resident, Dr. McCauley, was a good and kind man as well as an excellent teacher and surgeon. He had performed almost all of the various kinds of cancer operations, except for one: abdominoperineal resection, which uses a double approach from the abdomen and the perineum, to remove the rectum and perform a permanent colostomy, a treatment for rectal cancer. The first day of the rotation before morning rounds, he gave the team a deal: Whoever finds him a patient with cancer of the rectum that can be treated surgically will get to do all the major operations for the month. Doing the very big operations is a privilege reserved for the chief resident, so getting to do those cases as a junior resident is a real treat, welcome by any and all junior residents. The chief resident usually guides all the junior residents performing surgery, and the attending surgeon guides and/or assists the chief resident when he is doing the surgery, unless it's something routine he can perform without supervision.

Rectal cancers are usually discovered with a rectal exam done with a gloved finger. For me it was conceivable that there could be a patient on the medical floors with a cancer of the rectum, so I set a plan to check that out. I went to the medical units, talked to the residents and found out that not all of them performed rectal exams as a part of their routine physical examinations. I reviewed the charts and made a list of the patients that did not have documentation of a rectal exam. Then I went around with a nurse to perform the exam and complete the physical examination. Just as I thought, I found one patient with a large fragile cancer of the rectum. Part of the tumor fell off the main mass during my examination. I promptly collected the detached part and submitted it to pathology for histologic examination. The patient was in his late 50s and without other major problems, making him a good surgical candidate. I had him transferred to our service, having secured a medical clearance for surgery by the medical resident, who was taking care of him. The results of the histologic exam confirmed the diagnosis of cancer, so Dr. McCauley was able to do the operation he was looking for! I got to do all the big operations of the service for the whole month and more importantly the patient god rid of his rectal cancer. Everybody was happy!

In 1972 there was a change at the top of the department of surgery at SUNY-DMC-KCHC. The department chairman Dr. Clarence Dennis who was there when I started my training, was stepping down. Dr. Dennis was a pioneer in the development of total parenteral nutrition (TPN) and made major contributions in the diagnosis and treatment of Crohn's disease. TPN is a method by which we "feed" the patient through a catheter positioned in the superior vena cava (SVC)— the big vein in the chest—providing all the necessary nutrients and calories that the body needs. It is useful in situations when a patient cannot eat, such as abdominal infections, small bowel fistulas and inflammatory bowel disease.

Dr. Dennis was replaced as chairman of the department of Surgery, by Dr. Samuel Koontz, a renowned pioneer in kidney transplantation surgery. An African American born in Louisiana, he came to SUNY-DMC from the University of California San Francisco (UCSF), where he had developed a successful kidney transplantation program and many major, enduring innovations and contributions to the field. I had the privilege to work with him in the fall of 1974, when I was assigned to the transplant service. Though I did not have a special interest in transplantation surgery, I really enjoyed my interaction with him, and I appreciated everything he taught me. I was on my fifth year of training and had advanced surgical skills, so he entrusted me with large parts of the operations, something that I totally appreciated. One thing he taught me was to learn to delegate tasks to the more junior residents since I was the most senior member of the surgical team assigned to his service.

"George! You cannot do everything yourself! You have to learn to delegate," he used to tell me over and over again. That made me adjust my actions and prepared me for the chief residency year, which was coming up shortly.

Three events happened during my work with Dr. Koontz that got stuck in my mind forever. The first was a patient who had been waiting a long time for a matching cadaver kidney transplant. We were so excited to notify him that a matching donor was found, and he should come to the hospital for the operation. Few people understand that the majority of doctors share the emotions of their patients, before, during and after treatment. Like the patient mentioned here, the transplant team really felt so happy that this unfortunate patient finally secured the opportunity to be treated effectively by an operation that could change his life.

The patient was prepared according to protocol and taken to the OR for the transplantation. The operation progressed smoothly and upon completion of the connection of the ureter to the bladder, and the artery and vein of the kidney to the iliac artery and vein in the patient, the clamps on the vessels were removed, expecting normal blood flow to the transplanted organ. Unfortunately, this did not happen. We saw the kidney become more and more dusky, with no flow of blood through its vessels. The operation failed right in front of our eyes by an immediate rejection of the kidney, caused by an attack of the body's immune system against the transplanted tissue. This terrible outcome is a rare but possible occurrence in the field of transplantation and has decreased significantly since the 1970s.

We knew that this kidney could not survive, so we went ahead and removed it. All that happiness of the transplant team had radically changed to shock and sadness, like riding a crazy roller coaster. That event was a traumatic experience for me and for that reason the specialty of transplantation was erased from my list of possibilities.

The second event that happened on that service was a patient in his 40s who did not gain any kidney function four weeks after receiving a kidney transplant. We discussed it with Dr. Koontz during a patient's visit to the clinic and a decision was made to bring the patient back for removal of the transplanted kidney. A date was set, and the patient was admitted at 6 a.m. on the date of surgery.

I saw him on admission, and he mentioned that he had some urine output in the past couple of days. Just to be sure, I ordered additional kidney function blood tests. I checked the results just before the patient was ready to get on the stretcher to be taken to the OR. I noticed that the creatinine and BUN—indicators of kidney function—had improved substantially, indicating that the kidney was finally working.

I talked to Dr. Koontz, who then cancelled the operation and sent the patient home, to be followed up and treated as an outpatient. The patient was elated to hear the good news, just as the transplant team was. The roller coaster had climbed up to the top. Everyone was happy, especially me, thinking that my due diligence in checking the parameters of the blood had made such a big difference in this patient's life for the better.

The third event that I encountered on the transplantation service had nothing to do with transplantation and a lot to do with the peritoneovenous (PV) shunt, the operation I had designed during my research year with Dr. LeVeen. Dr. Koontz was consulted for a patient who had malignant, intractable ascites that resulted from ovarian cancer. She was a lady in her 40s with such a tense collection of abdominal fluid that her ability to breath was severely compromised. The question was whether insertion of a P-V shunt could be helpful in relieving her ascites and improve her breathing. Dr. Koontz asked for my opinion, since I was very familiar with the PV shunt. After careful consideration, I reached the conclusion that it would be helpful as a temporary measure to relieve the breathing problem, but the end result would be the implantation of the malignant cells from the ascites to the lungs, where the cancer cells would grow into new tumors. In the case of malignant ascites, there are billions of cancer cells inside the fluid, so if we diverted the ascites fluid to the large vein in the chest, the fluid would go to the heart first and from there to the lungs, where the cancer cells or clumps of cancer cells would "stick" and eventually grow into bigger tumors resulting in the patient's demise.

To my knowledge the PV shunt had not, as yet, been used in the treatment of malignant ascites. We talked to the patient and explained everything to her, including the likelihood that the cancer would be transferred to the lungs if we went ahead with the operation. The poor lady was so desperate that she accepted the complications as long as she had the chance of being able to breath better, even for a brief period of time. We proceeded with the operation, which fortunately relieved the intra-abdominal pressure and breathing problems for a few weeks, providing a desirable improved quality of life to the unfortunate patient. The end result, as we anticipated, was the growth of cancerous tumors in the lungs and along the course of the tubing in the chest wall. The patient was not cured but at least she was relieved of the acute breathing problems, even if just for a few weeks. That gave me a feeling of accomplishment for being instrumental in helping a fellow human being. Dr. Koontz appeared to be impressed by the result.

"George, you come up with another innovation like that, and I will make you a full professor," he remarked.

The year 1974 was a good year professionally, but it was a catastrophic time for my birthplace, the Island of Cyprus. I took my one month vacation in May and went back to Cyprus to spend some time with my family and visit Karavas, the village where I was born, and where my family had lived for many generations. It was heaven on earth!

Karavas extended from the Mediterranean Sea along the valley and up the foothills of the Pentadaktylos Mountains. It covered an area of about three miles and was the eastward extension of the Village of Lapithos, which was founded 3000 years ago by the king of Sparta and hero of the Trojan War, Praxandros. The main crop of the entire area was lemons, which accounted for the main income of the population, though the fertile land and availability of water allowed farmers to grow practically almost anything: apples, plums, grapes, onions, potatoes, wheat, beans, carobs, olives, almonds, walnuts, even tobacco. Every February the abundance of blooming almond trees all over the village washed the town in white. But the most amazing time was when the lemon trees were blooming. The thousands upon thousands of lemon trees extending throughout the village and surrounding areas, bloomed with innumerable white blossoms and filled the air with a pleasing, beautiful, calming and mesmerizing aroma that spread harmonically throughout the region.

There were several churches, at least one in every neighborhood, and a historical monastery of Virgin Mary by the Mediterranean Sea. According to legend a piece of the Holy Shroud was brought to the monastery in early Christian times. Next to the monastery there were the ruins of "Lampousa," meaning "Shining City," that flourished during the Byzantine times. Lampousa was destroyed by a catastrophic earthquake a long time ago and became a location attractive to treasure hunters. Two silver trays were retrieved from the ruins by one treasure hunter and somehow found their way to the Metropolitan Museum of Art in New York City, where they are still on permanent display. The ruins were also the source of a lot of stone blocks used for building the homes of many villagers. The centuries old church in my neighborhood on the west side up the hill was dedicated to Saint Irene. That is the church that my family regularly attended and where my Great Grandfather Stavros Spanoudis was baptized and got married, as were my grandparents and parents, and many more of my ancestors before them. It was where I was baptized too and where I planned to get married whenever the time came. The other church in the uptown area up the hill, on the east side, was Saint George's Church, where my family sponsored the liturgy on Palm Sunday every year. Being the sponsor on Palm Sunday meant that a member of our family would carry the icon around the church during the St. George's Icon Procession, and after the liturgy was over, hosted lunch for the priest and the cantors of Saint George's Church. It was a blissful occasion that everybody enjoyed.

The people of Karavas were generally happy, witty, and liked to joke around. They were also adventurous, curious, intelligent and restless and immigrated to all the continents of the world. Everybody had a nickname and, most of the times, that was the only name by which they were known. The nicknames were attached to them and were based on their looks, behavior, place of origin, actions, or for no specific reason at all. For example, my father was known as "Yemenis," meaning the man from Yemen, just because he used to sing a song titled "Yemenis." My maternal grandfather,Costas, was known as "Yennadios," meaning "fertile brain" because he had a sharp brain with a lot of ideas. My Yiayia, his wife Eleni, was known as Yennadiena. Other nicknames were: Catsinioros (scorpion), Sifounas (tornado), Kaouros (crab), Aniftos (unwashed face), Aloupos (fox), Pittas (flat bread), Kotchinos (red), Tsacrocolos (crack ass), Thkiolloitis (two colored eyes) etc., with each one having its own story.

Many people from Karavas immigrated to the U.S. during the late nineteenth century and most of them settled in the metropolitan area of New York, New Jersey and in the Washington, D.C. area. A society named "Lampousa" was founded by immigrants in 1937 in the New York-New Jersey area, and is still active in 2020.

When I went to Cyprus in 1974, I spent some time in the capital, Nicosia, and visited friends and relatives. I also spent more time in my village where my mother still owned the family home, which was built in 1869, as well as other properties. In Cyprus, the day temperatures in

May go as high as 90 degrees Fahrenheit, so it was perfect weather for the picturesque sandy beaches of Karavas. The sea was generally calm and the waters crystal clear and soothing. The village was about 20 miles from our house in Nicosia, so sometimes we made it a day trip, and sometimes we stayed over at the family house. I usually took my mother with me when I traveled to our birthplace, for which she was very thankful, just as I was. I walked around the village taking pictures of every place I spent time in my childhood and teenage years. I visited the monastery by the sea, Saint Irene's Church, Saint George's Church, and my neighborhood, taking hundreds of pictures.

In Nicosia I had an outing with my high school classmates and "forever friends" George Drakos, Nicos Polemidiotis and Stelios Papantoniou. We had a rich, delicious Cyprus meal, and they sang some Greek songs popular from our university years. I pretended that I was singing but I actually was just listening because I did not want to destroy the beautiful melody with my terrible voice, to put it mildly. While I was in Cyprus, the U.S. Secretary of State Henry Kissinger came to Cyprus and had a meeting with the President of the Island Archbishop Makarios. He had requested the establishment of an American Military Base on the island, which Makarios unwisely denied. That denial had catastrophic consequences.

The Cyprus vacation went by very fast and it was time to get back to work in Brooklyn. As the plane took off from Nicosia Airport for Greece, where I could change planes to New York, I had a very strange sad feeling. Along the route as we passed over Karavas, I broke into uncontrollable sobbing, tears pouring out profusely, having a terrible premonition that I will not see my village again. I could not explain it at the time, as I never felt anything like that in my life.

I returned to Brooklyn with a few days to spare before returning to work. This gave me enough time to take care of things and spend some time with my Little Apple. I called Sharon the first day I arrived in New York and picked her up from work. We talked about my trip to Cyprus and all the pictures I took of the places I had spent my childhood. I gave her all the film to have it developed at the VA Hospital, where she worked. It was nice to be able to go out and relax without being tired from 36-hour shifts and without having to worry about getting up at 6 a.m. the next morning. The days went by fast and it was time to get back to work. Unfortunately, the film was lost, and I never saw the pictures of Karavas I had taken during my last trip.

I was assigned to pediatric surgery in June, which was the last rotation through that service for the rest of my residency. The director, Dr. Peter Kottmeier, ran a tight ship, but I was much more comfortable with the high demands of the service as a well-trained resident, but I still had to do 36-hour shifts. We were busy with a plethora of routine operations like hernia repairs, circumcisions, and appendectomies. The pediatric surgery ER was as busy as ever. Hot weather and summer recess allowed children more time to run and play outside and get hurt in the process, winning a ticket to the ER.

On Sunday, July 14 I had the day off, so I relaxed during the day and spent the evening reviewing and studying surgical procedures and subjects of surgical interest in different surgical textbooks and scientific papers. I went to bed by 11 p.m. that night, preparing for an early rise the next morning for 7 a.m. morning rounds. Then, something very strange happened. I woke up at about 2:30 a.m. feeling completely awake, alert, and agitated. I could not figure out what was going on. I never woke up during the night, not without an external stimulus, such as the phone ringing, the noise of the beeper or hearing my name being paged by the operator when I was dozing off in the hospital. I turned on the radio to listen to music in an attempt to calm down, and then there it was, the reason for my agitation. The music was interrupted by an announcer:

"We interrupt our program for breaking news." There was a "coup d'état" in Cyprus. "Makarios, the president of Cyprus is dead."

This was catastrophic, terrible, heartbreaking news and explained my premonition when I was on the airplane from Nicosia to Athens, and the tears I shed that day looking down at Karavas from my window seat in the plane. During my vacation in Cyprus, I had noticed a severe, deep division of the population among supporters of President Makarios, who stood for an independent state, and the supporters of General George Grivas, who led the recent uprising against the British and who supported unification of the island with mainland Greece. The people were fanatic, irrational, and arrogant, with complete polarization of the two sides, creating a fertile ground for civil war.

President Nixon was also under fire for the Watergate break in and had practically relinquished the foreign policy decisions totally to Henry Kissinger, a move that meant bad news for Cyprus. Greece was under dictatorship by the military junta, led at that time by Ioannides, a military man under the control of Kissinger, who strongly disliked Archbishop Makarios, the president of Cyprus. Following the instructions of Kissinger, the military junta, (Ioannides, Patakos and Makarezos) organized and executed the coup d'état against President Makarios, using the Greek Military contingent assigned to the island at the time. Makarios escaped capture and certain death finding refuge at the British Sovereign Bases, and from there, fleeing Cyprus and eventually arriving in the United States.

In Cyprus, the coup d'état evolved into civil war between the two divided sides of the Greek Cypriots and even worse than that, Kissinger gave Turkey the green light to invade the island, as was then reported by the New York Times. The pretext was the protection of the Turkish community, which comprised 18 percent of the Cyprus population. As the two factions of the Greek Cypriot population fought each other, I was watching the news showing the Turks amassing a military force at Mersin, a port at the south coast of Turkey across the sea from Cyprus.

I saw the "writing on the wall"; the Turks were going to invade Cyprus. On July 19, Makarios addressed the United Nations and condemned the coup d'état perpetrated by the Greek junta. On July 20, Turkey's troops landed on the beach where I had been vacationing just two short months earlier. They attacked Cyprus with their air force, navy, 300 American tanks and 40,000 troops. They attacked Cyprus, whose air force consisted of a helicopter, a navy made up of a speed boat, and an army equipped with arms from the Second World War. The Turkish Army forcefully expelled 200,000 Greek Cypriots one third of the population, from their homes and occupied 38 percent of the Island, which corresponded to 60 percent of the country's Gross Domestic Prodct (GDP). They raped and killed innocent civilians and looted establishments. Thousands of Greek Cypriots, civilians and over 150 American citizens could not be accounted for. The 3,000 people from my village of Karavas, as all the people from the occupied area, fled to the south of the island. Dozens of my civilian relatives were executed in cold blood by the Turkish invaders.

I was devastated by the catastrophic events in Cyprus, as Sharon stood by my side, accompanying me to all the demonstrations at the United Nations. She helped me type letters to Congress asking members to impose an arms embargo on Turkey for using arms and equipment provided by the United States for defensive purposes in a savage attack on Cyprus.

My pediatric surgery colleagues were supportive and did everything to comfort me. Everyone asked if my family was safe and I did not know the answer to that, as the Turks were bombing civilian targets with Napalm bombs. Dr. Kottmeier mentioned that wars are associated with unfortunate atrocities, but eventually it comes to an end. Dr. Francesca Velcek, who was doing her fellowship, gave me flexible hours, as I went to New York City to enlist with the Greek Volunteers of America, willing to offer my services to the country where I first saw the light of day. As the invasion was happening, a point of interest was a call I received from the KCHC telephone operator. She informed me that the KCHC anesthesiology resident from Turkey called her screaming his lungs out.

"Where are the Greeks? Find me a Greek! I want to KILL a Greek!"

To which I responded: "Thanks for letting me know. He knows where I am."

What went through my mind was, "a barbarian remains a barbarian even if he became a doctor."

The Turks slaughterd 1.5 million Armenians, during the 1915 genocide. They killed another 1 million Greeks and Armenians in 1920-22, and expelled hundreds of thousands Greeks, Jews and Armenians from Constantinople in 1955. When I mentioned the incident of the Turkish resident's bullying to Dr. Kottmeier, his answer was much sharper.

"He doesn't have to kill a Greek. He has already killed too many Americans with his anesthesia!"

I did not see that Turkish anesthesiology resident anymore, nor did I hear what happened to him, but I have a feeling that the only thing he accomplished with his "outstanding bravery" was to kill his future. The events had caused a huge wound on my heart and soul, which, with time, evolved into a permanent, ugly scar.

I tried to help collect clothing for the refugees in Cyprus, and Sharon and I sponsored some children through the "Cyprus Children Fund" entity. Despite everything happening though, I had to carry out the duties of my residency too.

The last year of residency before reaching the chief resident level was easier than the earlier years, since reaching that milestone practically guaranteed a spot in the senior year and completion of the surgical training. Before that, at the end of each year every resident had to be evaluated to advance to the next level. The Surgical Residency at SUNY-DMC, KCHC followed a pyramidal system, by which there were more residents at the lower levels, and before they climbed up to the next year, they had to be evaluated at a special meeting, where some were advanced and the rest were rejected. The residents that were not advanced usually moved to a different specialty.

The residents that were going to advance to the chief residency level had to provide their preferences for rotation, three months ahead of their chief year. There were a total of eight services available between KCHC and Brooklyn VA Hospital. I thought that the best services were general surgery at the VA, vascular surgery at the VA, tumor surgery at KCHC and trauma surgery at KCHC, which I requested in that order. I was thrilled when I found that my requests were approved, by the directors of each service.

Chief Residency at the Brooklyn VA Hospital

On Sunday, June 1, 1975 I started my chief residency year with the general surgical service at the Brooklyn VA Hospital as I requested. All the chief residents graduating that year went on vacation for the month of June, so all the incoming chief residents took command of the surgical services. Because it was a Sunday, I made rounds with the junior resident on call to familiarize myself with the patients. The actual chief residency started the next morning with the new team and it turned out not to be such a good beginning.

Before I even started morning rounds at 7 a.m., Dr. S., an attending surgeon from South Africa who was hired by Dr. LeVeen, came to the unit and wanted to talk to me. Dr. S. was not well respected by the surgical residents because he had no surgical skills to speak of, no surgical critical judgment and absolutely no manners. The residents had raised numerous complaints to the Chairman of Surgery Dr. Samuel Koontz during their regular meetings with him, about the poor quality and lackluster skills of Dr. S. Evidently, the chairman brought the subject up with Dr. Leveen who got enraged. He threatened the residents who complained that he would see to it that they never passed their boards. Dr. S. was so inept, that when he performed a peritoneovenous shunt operation with a resident, he placed the drainage tubing in the vein without trimming it, so the end of it wound up in the femoral vein in the thigh instead of the superior vena cava (SVC) in the chest. As expected, the shunt never worked, so he had to take the patient back to the OR, pull the tubing out of the vein, trim it and reinsert it in the SVC to achieve a functioning shunt. He then had the audacity to write and publish a paper about the incident, presenting it as somebody else's mistake.

So, Dr. S. wanted to talk to me before I started my morning rounds, on my first day of my final year of surgical training. Though I had no high regard for him, I obliged out of respect to Dr. LeVeen. We went in the corridor of the unit a few feet away from my assembled team.

"I am listening," I said.

He looked at me with a stern face. "George. You are a smart guy, with a good reputation and a very bright future."

I was wondering where he was taking the conversation. "You have to listen to me and do everything I want you to do, otherwise I will destroy you and your future!"

This clueless moron was completely out of order to come and threaten my career at the very beginning of my chief residency. I did not take this abuse from anybody, and he was not going to be the first one to threaten me without getting a proper response. He was not even the attending assigned to the service where I was the chief resident. I did not know exactly how to react, but I considered several options. Option one, punch him in the nose and chase him off the unit. No that was too radical and risky, an action that could help him ruin my career. Option two, say nothing, turn my back and go back to my team. No, that would make him more abusive and abrasive. Option three, have a shouting match and see who has the louder voice. No, that was too embarrassing with all the staff and patients listening.

I finally went with option four. Looking at him with a piercing eye, I addressed him in a calm, stern but low volume voice. "Dr. S, let me inform you that the person who will destroy my career was never, and will never, be born! I will do what is right irrespective of your threats and desires. Don't challenge me, because you are going to be the loser if you do."

He was stunned. He turned around and went away. This idiot was already in hot water with the department of surgery for his incompetence so he thought that by intimidating me, he could prevent me from exposing his shortcomings during the routine meetings of the chief residents with the chairman of the department of surgery. He could not be more wrong and the only thing he accomplished was to erase any good will I had towards him.

I went back to my team and we made our rounds, visiting and evaluating every single patient on our unit, taking more time than usual to get acquainted with each person and the problem that brought them to the hospital. The patient population consisted of WWII and Korean War Veterans, with an increasing number of younger Vietnam War Veterans. The Vietnam War ended just a few months earlier on April 30, 1975, but the number of veterans coming for treatment was continuously growing. A good number of them were addicted to drugs and were admitted to the hospital for detoxification. But we did have some surgical patients, usually needing a hernia repair. It was depressing to see so many young men, were impacted so negatively by an unwanted, unpopular and catastrophic war. To make matters worse, the American population not only neglected to consider them heroes for answering the call to serve, but instead treated them with distaste, despise, disapproval and disrespect, as if they were the ones that started the war and continued the hostilities on the other side of the globe. It was heartbreaking to see these young men appear lost and struggling to find their way back to society. I always made sure on my service that they were treated with the proper respect because I had the firm belief that they had earned it.

The general surgery service was very busy. We admitted everybody with a hernia, a fatty tumor, a gastric and/or duodenal ulcer gallbladder stones and colon tumors. I was fortunate enough to have the Great Maestro of Surgical Technique, Dr. George Stergiopoulos, show me all his tricks that made an operation proceed smoothly with practically no complications. There was one patient in particular who stuck out forever in my mind. He was a polite African American man who complained of severe, continuous pain in the upper abdomen that didn't respond to antacids or other remedies. An upper Gastrointestinal (GI) series (x-rays of the stomach and small intestine, after ingestion of radio-opaque solution) showed an ulcer of the distal stomach. I explained the findings to him and recommended an operation to remove the affected part of the stomach and reconnect it with the intestines. I explained to him that, though I could not guarantee anything, I expected everything to go well and the pain to go away when the wound healed. He accepted my recommendation and we proceeded with the operation the next day.

The operation advanced smoothly until local exploration revealed a big surprise. We discovered a large tumor on the head of the pancreas that had all the findings to suggest it was cancerous. The stomach ulcer appeared to be in the area of the pancreatic tumor, suggesting that it was a result of the tumor growth into the stomach wall. The tumor appeared to infiltrate the other surrounding tissues and large veins, and this was most probably the cause of the poor man's severe, relentless pain. There was no cure for this patient and no surgical excision was indicated, because the tumor had gone too far. But there was something that might, at least, take care of his intractable pain and alleviate his suffering for whatever time he still had left to live.

I had recently read in a scientific paper that the pain could be treated by injecting 70 percent alcohol in the celiac plexus or ganglion area, around the aorta, where the artery to the stomach originated. The celiac plexus, or ganglion, is a net of nerves, which carry the pain signals from the area of the pancreas to the brain. This pain path from the pancreas to the brain can be interrupted and the pain alleviated if the celiac ganglion is destroyed, by injecting it with phenol or 70 percent alcohol. Though I had never seen or done this procedure before—called Chemical Celiac Ganglionectomy—I felt obligated to at least give it a try for this patient's sake.

A "frozen section" immediate biopsy of the tumor was done during the operation and was reported as carcinoma, confirming our clinical impression. The pharmacy sent a container with the 30 cc of 70 percent alcohol I had requested, which I injected to the area of the celiac ganglion, with a prayer that I get the same results that were documented in the scientific report. Save for the surprise cancer of the pancreas, the operation did go well, without other complications. Post operatively the patient progressed normally and smoothly. The day after surgery there is usually a lot of pain because of the large surgical wound, so when I asked him how the pain was, he said that it was quite a lot, but it was different than the pain he had before surgery. That was encouraging, indicating that the chemical celiac ganglionectomy might have been successful, though it was still difficult to tell because the patient was on narcotic analgesics for pain control. By the third day after the operation, the incisional pain and the amount of pain medication needed had decreased. It became clear that there was a definite improvement, if not complete relief of the pre-operative pain that brought the patient to the hospital. On the fifth day after the operation the patient had minimal incisional and no other pain, proving that the desirable effect of the injection was definitely achieved.

The patient was grateful that I cured his pain but despite the ganglionectomy success, I was weary. I was trying to decide how and when I was going to tell this poor gentle soul, who was thanking me profusely for curing his pain, that he did not have much time to live. How was I going to tell him that he had cancer of the pancreas, which was going to kill him within a few months? My feelings notwithstanding, I had to find the courage to deal with this daunting task. I invited him in a private room on the unit and sat down with him. By then, I had prepared the line I was going to follow in letting him know about his condition, as he was again expressing his gratitude for taking his pain away.

I started the conversation. "Sam, I am very glad that your pain has gone away, but I am sorry to say, that I have bad news for you. The ulcer you have is a result of a tumor of the pancreas. The tumor is what irritated the nerves around it and caused your pain. I destroyed those pain nerves and that is why you have no pain anymore, but the tumor could not be removed."

Sam was stunned by the news. He managed to utter a few words. "What does that mean?"

"Sam, you have a bad tumor, which cannot be cured."

He looked at me as tears blanketed his eyes. "Doc! How long do I have to live?"

"Only God knows for sure, Sam, but based on past experience with patients with your condition, not very long. You have to take it a day at a time. Learn to live and enjoy yourself every single day that you feel OK until the time comes."

As I spoke, tears streamed down my cheeks. Cancer of the head of the Pancreas is a terrible disease, with no effective treatment when it extends into the surrounding tissues or organs. The only time we could offer a surgical treatment is when the cancer is discovered at the very early stages, especially if the cancer originates in the bile duct that goes through the pancreas. The surgical treatment, called Whipple Procedure, is a very big operation, involving removal of the head of the pancreas, the distal common bile duct, the distal stomach and the duodenum (proximal portion of the small intestine), and then putting everything back together. The operation takes several hours to perform and can be associated with high incidence of complications.

In Sam's case the tumor was growing into the surrounding tissues, so he was not a candidate for a Whipple operation. He was discharged home in a few days, totally relieved from his pain, with the expectation of the certain demise in the few months that followed. Since that time, I had the opportunity to use the chemical celiac ganglionectomy numerous times, with excellent relief of patients' pain. And I faced the daunting task of being the first person to tell a cancer patient of his diagnosis, a task that was never easy, but I was obligated to do it, nonetheless.

In the three months of my chief residency at the general surgery, we performed quite a lot of major and minor operations. I was lucky to have a good, hard working team comprised of knowledgeable residents who made me look good with their diligent work. The only operations that I did as a surgeon, with the guidance and assistance of Dr. Stergiopoulos, were the stomach, colon and pancreas procedures. The junior residents got to do all the other procedures with my assistance and guidance.

My next assignment was the vascular service at the Brooklyn VA Hospital. The attendings of that service were Dr. LeVeen and Dr. Carlos Diaz. Dr. LeVeen rarely scrubbed in, while Dr. Diaz was a standard fixture in the OR. He was a master technician with excellent surgical skills and teaching abilities. The service did all the vascular operations and a lot of general surgery operations on the patients admitted to the hospital. At that time, Dr. LeVeen came up with a special rule that every colon operation had to be done with Dr. S. as the attending. I thought that was a terrible decision, only intended to help S. get some experience with colectomies and improve his non-existent surgical skills. The intent of the surgical program was to provide residents with the experience needed to become competent surgeons under the guidance and assistance of a competent attending surgeon. Instead of that, Dr. LeVeen appointed a totally incompetent and dangerous person as attending, so that he could learn how to operate at the expense of the residents. Even worse than that, he put patients' lives at risk. I tried to talk to Dr. LeVeen, but he was adamant about his decision, so I had no choice but to accept it.

The vascular service was busy with restoring arterial blood flow to the legs and the carotid arteries that supplied blood to the brain. The biggest vascular operation was the resection of an abdominal aortic aneurysm, which involved the removal of a portion of the body's main artery that carried blood to the abdomen and the lower extremities. The section removed was replaced with a portion of synthetic tube. We also worked a lot on the venous system, removing varicose veins of the lower extremities and taking care of venous ulcers. These procedures alone kept the service busy. My most experienced junior resident and also my favorite was Dr. Steven Hornyak, a very talented hardworking doctor with whom I had worked many times. I had a competent, hard-working team that kept my service running like a well-oiled machine.

Dr. LeVeen had a standing challenge to all the residents to find a patient with erectile dysfunction who was willing to accept an experimental treatment for his condition — an arterial bypass between the femoral artery and the penis. As a reward he promised $50 to the resident who found such a patient. It is common knowledge that impotence is not a rare condition. Many men had it and had to live with it, since we are talking about a period before the era of Viagra and sialis. I asked every patient I interviewed, whether he had any trouble getting an erection. If the answer was "yes," I would ask whether he was willing to try a new procedure that could help him with that problem. Within a week I found a candidate and a $50 bill.

The candidate's name was Robert and I sat down with him and explained that we were going to take one piece of his thigh vein and use it to connect the artery in his groin to the base of his penis. I told him that the expected result will be an erection, though a potential complication may arise — inability of the erection to deflate. If that turned out to be the case, we would possibly have to remove the bypass. Robert understood the risks and expectations of the procedure and consented to the operation. Dr. LeVeen was happy he had someone who agreed to undergo the operation that he designed. I actually discussed with Dr. LeVeen the real possibility that the procedure could result in Priapism, a condition consisting of a continuous erection, which was associated with pain and inability to urinate. But he wanted to see the results of the femoral-penis bypass.

After careful preparation the patient was taken to the operating room where I harvested a segment of the saphenous vein of the right thigh, placed it in a tunnel I created between the right femoral artery and the base of the penis. I then connected the one end of the vein to the artery and the other end to the penis. The results were immediate and impressive. The wounds were sutured closed, a sterile dressing applied over the wounds, and the anesthesia terminated. The patient was then taken to the recovery room, fully awake. He looked down towards his genitals and amazingly he saw a tent formation, indicating a success! He was very happy, but not for long. The next day on morning rounds I asked him how he felt.

"Doc, I cannot pee, I cannot shit, and I cannot get out of bed to walk around, because my dick is flying out the (pajama) window!"

I inserted a bladder catheter that alleviated the urine problem, but the priapism needed to be addressed. Me and my team had a meeting with Dr. LeVeen and Dr. Diaz, trying to find a solution. Dr. LeVeen was convinced that a spinal anesthesia would resolve the erection, so we tried it, but after it was administered, there was still no improvement.

In the meantime, other patients heard about the "magnificent" transformation of Robert's penis and asked to have "the same operation Bob had," a request that could not be honored. The next step with Robert was to decrease the amount of blood flow to the penis by placing a synthetic material circumferentially around the vein graft to decrease its diameter. Back to the OR we went. But that did not work either and the priapism persisted. We eventually had to do the right thing. We took Robert back to the OR and tied closed the vein graft, eliminating the flow of arterial blood into his penis. Robert was disappointed as were so many other wannabes, though Robert's famous words were, "I've never seen it so good"!

The time finally came when a patient on my unit was diagnosed with left colon cancer and lymphoma and was scheduled for removal of the left colon and spleen. As per the director's rules and orders, Dr. S. had to scrub in for the operation as the attending. I was not ready or willing to allow him to do anything that could harm my patient. I knew that at this stage of my training I had done enough operations to be able to perform the colectomy and splenectomy without an attending's assistance and/or guidance. I opened the abdomen and had Dr. Steve HornyaK give me exposure with a large Deaver Retractor. Everything was exposed beautifully, and I was ready to start freeing the left colon to prepare it for resection.

All of a sudden Dr. S. says, "Let me show you how to get the spleen out" as he inserted his "five thumbs" right hand inside the abdomen and grabbed the spleen that I had just exposed. He pulled it so forcefully, the spleen ruptured, causing profuse bleeding.

The first thing I did was to scream at him, "Get your f**ing hand out of the belly" and I grabbed and pulled his hand out. The second thing I did was clamp the spleen's artery and vein to control the bleeding, as the anesthesiologist called the blood bank for 2 units of blood. With the bleeding under control, I did the third thing. I grabbed the Deaver Retractor from Dr. Hornyak's hand and raised it up towards S. and screamed "Get the f** out of my operating room before I hit your stupid head with the Deaver!" He ran out stunned. The maneuver he tried to do to bring the spleen out before identifying, dissecting, clamping and transecting the splenic artery and vein, required a transection of all the ligaments that hold the spleen in place. Instead, being clueless, he tried to pull it out with the ligaments still attached, causing the spleen to rupture, causing profuse bleeding. I was livid and infuriated by S.'s actions and the rule Dr. LeVeen had initiated that almost killed my patient right in front of my eyes.

I knew I had to calm down for my patient's sake. I took a big breath, apologized to the doctors and nurses for my outburst and my language, and proceeded to complete the operation in a flawless fashion. The patient, whose blood pressure had dropped after the bleeding caused by S., recovered fully, with normal vital signs within minutes after blood transfusions. With the operation completed, the abdomen closed and the patient safe, I asked Dr. Hornyak to take care of the post op orders and stay with the patient in the recovery room until I returned.

I headed for Dr. LeVeen's office, determined to solve this S. problem once and for all. Dr. LeVeen was in his office and the door was open. I knocked and asked if I could come in. He invited me in and asked me to have a sit, but I remained standing, and started the conversation.

"Dr. LeVeen. I just finished the operation on Mr. Jennings and S. scrubbed in. He put his hand in the abdomen and almost killed the patient. I know about your rule to have him scrub in for all colon operations and I fully respect your decision, but I have one problem and one request. My problem is that I cannot stand witness to patient abuse by this clueless person, who presents himself as a surgeon. So, my request is to transfer all my colon patients, in the future, to one of the other Surgical Services. This way I will not have to scrub with him, and he can continue to scrub on all the colon operations."

He listened to me without interruption, responding only after I finished. "George, I spoke with Dr. Vincent P., who helped you with an emergency gastrectomy in the middle of the night two weeks ago, and he told me that you are not such a good surgeon either."

I scrubbed with Dr. Vincent only once and I was not impressed with his skills either. He did not show the finesse, skills and abilities that Dr. Stergiopoulos and Dr. Diaz demonstrated every single time I scrubbed with them. But I was not about to debate Vincents's opinion of my surgical skills. To the contrary, I thought that Dr. LeVeen's comment gave substantial support to my position.

So, I responded:

"I want to thank Dr. Vincent for making my point. It is true that I still have a lot to learn, but I think it is appropriate that I scrub with people who are seasoned, experienced surgeons, and have something to teach me, and not somebody who has no idea what he is doing."

I asked him if he was agreeable to divert all the colon cases to the other services. He said he was going to think about it, and we left it at that. I went back to the recovery room to see the patient. He was doing fine, which helped my nerves and calmed me down. The next day there was a new communication from the director of surgery stating that the rule requiring that Dr. S. be the attending for all colon operations was discontinued. Dr. LeVeen did not even talk to me about that, but the whole thing about Dr. S. made me feel betrayed. I could not figure out what it was that compelled Dr. LeVeen to act irrationally by allowing an incompetent person to risk the lives of the VA patients. All my life I was taught to do the right thing and stayed true to those lessons and that conviction. I expected all my friends and the people I respected to hold the same values and treat me with the same respect, I treated them. It was my impression that despite all the respect I showed to Dr. LeVeen, he failed to reciprocate, and that turned me off. I was not going to work with him after the completion of my training, as he had asked me to in the past. Instead, I was going to seek other opportunities.

My assignment at the Brooklyn VA Vascular Service came to an end, bringing me to the mid mark of my chief residency and the end of my service at the VA hospital. I left the hospital with mixed feelings. First, I was glad I was given the opportunity to contribute in the development of a new operation, the Peritoneo-Venous Shunt, and other less significant research, with Dr. Harry LeVeen. I was also grateful to work with Masters of Surgery Dr. George Stergiopoulos and Dr. Carlos Diaz and "steal" from them every detail I could about their surgical techniques that placed them head and shoulders above the rest of the faculty. I was glad I ran two busy services during my chief residency, with over 300 operations between them two, with excellent results, making me, and the residents of my team, proud. On the other hand, I was upset with Dr. LeVeen's dreadful rule regarding Dr. S. that placed patients in harm's way. I was further upset that Dr. LeVeen refused to lend me an ear when I protested his ridiculous rule. I resented the fact that S.'s moronic threat was my "welcome ceremony" to a place I loved so much. My feelings notwithstanding, it was time to move on to my next rotation. Of interest is the fact that dr. S.'s Medical License was revoked, at a later time.

Tumor surgery was the next service I was assigned to and it was one I had requested for my chief residency. I had a special interest in the specialty and the way it was run with organization, great conferences, and competent faculty, making the service a hub of knowledge. The vast majority of the operations were for the treatment of all kinds of cancers and other benign and malignant tumors located anywhere in the body. In addition to tumor operations, on allocated days the service also admitted general surgery patients through the ER.

I was happy to have Dr. Steven Hornyak on my team again. I was demanding and expected every member of my team to know all the results of a patient's lab tests, pathology reports and x-ray reports. I believed that only then could the best care be provided to the patient. Steven was a hard worker who always had everything under control, and we both functioned on the same wavelength. The other two members of my team were at the PGY-1 level (first year after medical school graduation) and it was the first time I ever met them. The team also included four medical students assigned to the service who were involved with taking a patient's history and completing a physical, as well as reading relevant material about a patient's diagnosis. They also scrubbed in the OR, where they were given minor roles during the operation.

I again ran an extremely busy service with a high volume of operations. The service ran the breast clinic, which by itself brought in about six to eight breast tumor operations per week, mostly noncancerous, on a younger patient population. A fair number of breast cancer patients were in need of radical surgery, and some patients had advanced tumors that were beyond surgical treatment. We also had a lot of colon cancer patients, and a number of rare types of cancer that presented challenging management decisions, like desmoid tumors, originating in the connective tissue. My first Whipple operation was for cancer of the duodenum, the first part of the small bowel, located around the head of the pancreas. There were also a number of stomach operations for cancer, as well as a lot of thyroid operations for both benign and malignant tumors. We also handled some procedures for cancer of the mouth, tongue and larynx. Operations for fatty tumors under the skin were the bread and butter for the PGY-1 residents, who enjoyed the opportunity to get plenty of experience in minor surgical procedures.

During my time on tumor service, we had visiting professors from all over the United States, and one of them, Dr. Seymour Schwartz, author of one of the top textbooks of Surgery, gave us a lecture about liver resection. He told us a story about how difficult and bloody his liver resections were until he visited Dr. Lee in Taiwan, who was doing liver resections quickly, with little blood loss. What Dr. Schwartz observed was Dr. Lee was using the "finger rapture technique," which consisted of incising the liver capsule and then fracturing the liver tissue by compressing it between his fingers. The pressing caused the tissue to break down while leaving the arteries, veins and bile ducts intact, at which point they could be obliterated with a tie or a clip and cut without significant amount of bleeding. From that time on he adopted Dr. Lee's technique and was able to achieve the same good results. That was an interesting revelation and I was looking forward to finding the opportunity to use the new technique while on tumor service. That chance never happened. This gave me the same feeling of disappointment I had on vascular service when I was hoping to operate on a raptured aortic aneurysm, but I never had that opportunity.

My team was competent and hardworking except for one PGY-1 resident who did not seem to be with it. He was not a good worker, most of the times he did not know the lab and pathology results and/

or x-ray reports and did not show up for work three times in the first six weeks. The funny, or rather tragic, thing was that his excuse, each and every time was that his father died. The third time I could not hold back. "How many fathers do you have!" He did not answer. I called Dr. Klotz, who was in charge of the residency program, and informed him that the resident in question was not fit for the challenges of a KCHC surgical residency. I then called the resident, told him I did not want him on my team anymore, and sent him to go see Dr. Klotz, who in turn gave him his "walking papers."

Being a surgical resident anywhere is an extremely hard job, but it is a much harder job when you are a surgical resident at SUNY-DMC, KCHC. It takes commitment, dedication, endurance, extreme stamina and above all, an unconditional love for the profession. We worked endless hours, too many to count at times. What kept me going was my dream of reaching that stage when I would make a positive, significant difference in people's lives. Many doctors who start a surgical residency quit after the first year and chose a different specialty. Some of them last a year or two more before deciding they had enough. At the time of my residency, there was no limit to the hours a resident had to work. I remember one time I finished work at 6 p.m. after a 36-hour shift and started my vacation only to be called back at 7 p.m. because "I was needed in the OR", where I worked for another three hours. Many years later a patient died in a New York City Hospital and the death was attributed to the resident's fatigue after having worked for over 20 hours straight. That event precipitated the passage of new legislation restricting residents' working hours to a maximum of 80 hours per week, which is much less than what my fellow surgical residents and I worked during our training at KCHC-DMC.

One day that I will always remember is the day I was in the operating room doing a gastrectomy, a stomach operation for cancer. That day our service was taking all the emergency admissions coming through the ER. I received a message from Dr. Hornyak stating that he was

admitting a patient with severe abdominal pain due to acute perforated diverticulitis of the colon and wanted to know whether I wanted
him to schedule the patient for emergency surgery. That condition
consists of an infection of the colon with perforation and acute peritonitis, which needs an emergency operation. I asked Dr. Hornyak to go
ahead and schedule him for surgery and prepare him for the OR right
away because we would operate on him as soon as I finished the stomach operation. The gastrectomy went well and as soon as the operating
room was cleaned, we brought in the perforated diverticulitis patient.
The routine preparations were completed before starting the operation.
I was the surgeon of record, Dr. Hornyak was assisting me, and Dr.
Orces, a general surgeon, was the attending surgeon present. A medical student was also scrubbed in the case to assist with retraction and
observe the operation up close.

When I made the midline (up and down) incision and entered
the abdomen I saw that all the tissues were infiltrated with blood and
pushed forward, indicating severe bleeding at the back portion of the
abdomen. There was also a pulsatile motion associated with these
tissues, while the colon was perfectly normal. Right away, I realized
that the diagnosis was not perforated diverticulitis but a ruptured aortic
aneurysm. That was what I was waiting for when I was at the vascular
service, but never saw one. The blood bank was notified to send up the
units of blood prepared as part of the pre-op routine process. The surgical field was prepared with retractors placed appropriately, to give me
the proper exposure for the removal of the aneurysm. Dr. Orces was
not a vascular surgeon, but stayed with me until Dr. Powers, a vascular
surgeon arrived. The truth is that I had enough experience with elective
aortic aneurysm operations from the time I was at the vascular service
that I could finish the operation without an attending. The steps of both
operations were the same. The only difference with a ruptured aneurysm is that it is already open and bleeding and could quickly kill the
patient. There was no time to waste.

The first thing I did, was to secure the best exposure, as I had learned from the Masters of Surgery at the VA hospital. Then I chose the clamps I was going to use to shut the blood flow to the aorta. Next, I open the peritoneum to enter the compartment where the aorta is located and where the bleeding was happening. I felt the pulsating aorta and slipped the aortic clamp around it and closed the clamp to occlude it. The iliac vessels where then identified, dissected and closed with special vascular clamps. As Dr. Powers arrived in the OR to relieve Dr. Orces, he complimented the progress we made. I proceeded to open the aneurysm wide, remove all the clots from inside, and replace the damaged portion of the aorta with a synthetic graft extended to the femoral arteries. The patient did very well postoperatively, had no complications, and was discharged home 10 days after the operation. I was quite happy about my management and outcome, taking into consideration that the survival rate at that time, of patients operated on for ruptured aortic aneurysm, was only 50 percent.

With the completion of the tumor service rotation, my general surgery training was coming down to the wire. I only needed to go through my final rotation as a chief resident to be recognized as a fully trained general surgeon. I already felt I could face any situation, of any problem, any time and take care of it competently, effectively and efficiently, achieving the best possible outcome every time.

The next and final assignment I had, was at the trauma service. The unique characteristic of the service was that it did not focus on the treatment of any specific body part, but instead dealt with any injured organ or tissue. We treated practically any condition that happened as a result of physical force, from broken bones to lacerations, abdominal injuries from blunt trauma, stab wounds and gunshot wounds, and, oh boy, did we have a lot of those! My team was again very good, with my friend Dr. John Xanthopoulos serving as the surgical resident who was on top of things. He also had a great work ethic and kept everything under control when I was busy in the operating room. I had already seen a lot of strange and unusual things during my previous assignments on the service over the past five years of my training. This time I came across even stranger things than before.

A prisoner was brought in, complaining of abdominal pain after he swallowed a TV antenna. He was transferred from the regular jail to the KCHC jail unit, which was located on the second floor. I went to the jail unit to examine him, and sure enough, I could feel a hard object under the skin at the upper abdomen where the stomach was located. The x-ray showed a metal, straight object extending from the chest to the anterior abdominal wall. The patient was taken to the operating room under police escort.

The anesthesiologist gave him IV sedation and I injected a local anesthetic over and around the hard object I could feel. I made a small incision over the TV antenna and under the skin I found the end of the antenna, which had perforated through the stomach's front wall to the abdominal wall. I used more iodine solution to wash out the infected area under the skin and gently and slowly pulled out the over one-foot long antenna. I then trimmed the stomach edges at the perforation and repaired the opening. I left a drain around the repair, which I brought out through a small skin incision nearby and closed the wound. After the recovery room the patient was returned to the hospital jail and a few days later he was returned to his regular cell. Prisoners that swallowed all sorts of things, like coins, spoons and other objects, was a usual occurrence because it was used as a ticket to the hospital and out of jail for a few days.

One evening after finishing rounds I started walking home, which was about three blocks from the Hospital. As soon as I arrived, before I even sat down, I got a call from Dr. Louis, one of my residents, informing me about a patient in his 50s he had just seen in the ER who had a foreign body in his rectum. An x-ray showed a sizable vibrator in his rectum. This man's story was very strange.

"I was walking in the street and all of a sudden, two men grubbed me, pulled my pants down, and shoved something up my rear end," he said.

Yes, sure. I don't know if he expected anybody to believe his fairy-tale, but that was irrelevant anyway. What really mattered was that the man had a foreign body in his rectum that had to be removed, irrespective of the way it landed there. I told Dr. Louis to prepare him and book him for surgery and let me know when the OR was ready so I could walk back to the hospital. The patient had eaten lunch between 12 and 1 p.m., so he was booked for surgery 9 p.m. because we had to wait at least eight hours after a meal before surgery. In the OR, the patient was given general anesthesia, which relaxed the abdominal wall completely, and on palpation of the abdomen the vibrator could clearly be felt. A rectal retractor was inserted in the anus and the vibrator manipulated by Dr. Louis from the top through the abdominal wall and pushed it gently down to the anal canal, from where it was carefully removed, solving the patient's problem.

Every Saturday morning, we had the Mortality and Morbidity (M&M) conference in the hospital's amphitheater. The chief resident of every service had to present every complication and every death that happened on their service, as well as the total number and type of operations performed during the preceding week. The presentation was made with the help of slides and a projector, which showed pictures, x-rays and text on a big screen for everybody to see. The conference was well attended by the faculty and residents and moderated by the chairman of the department of surgery himself. The floor was open to everybody for questions, comments, critique and discussion. There was plenty of criticism especially by some members of the faculty who would find something to say, no matter how ridiculous their comments were at times. One such doctor was Dr. Garzon, a thoracic surgeon and member of the faculty who had at one time criticized me about a patient who was still on a respirator 10 days after an operation for a perforated ulcer, peritonitis, and pneumonia. The patient also had fallen before coming to the hospital, resulting in rib fractures and pneumonia, in addition to the perforated ulcer with peritonitis. It was taking a long time to resolve his pneumonia and he needed the respirator to help him breathe in the meantime.

Dr. Garzon's question was, "The patient was not on the respirator when he was brought to the hospital, so why is he on the respirator now?"

Another member of the faculty who was the tumor surgery service attending, Dr. Horace Herbsman responded: "Do you really mean that the only patients who can be placed on the respirator are the ones that come to the hospital already hooked to one?" The whole room burst into a loud laughter, forcing Dr. Garzon into absolute silence.

The week that I was planning to present case of the foreign body removal from the rectum, I was following the thoracic surgery presentation. The Thoracic presentation had a slide with 12 consecutive operations for pacemaker battery change, followed by a description of each operation. After he was done, he took his slides and stepped down from the podium, and I walked up, ready to address the audience. I placed the slide of the patient's x-ray with the vibrator on the projector's receptacle. A huge image showed up on the screen and I explained on the microphone, "J. P. 55 years old came for a battery change." Most people thought it was funny, but some people did not get the joke. An older, visiting doctor stood up and asked for clarification. "Can you explain what that thing is?" to which I replied not so kindly, "Sorry sir, but we don't provide sex education at this conference."

Another interesting event concerned a young man who was brought to the ER with a stab wound in the mid-upper abdomen. I evaluated the injured man, who was complaining of severe abdominal pain. On examination, I discovered he had signs of severe peritoneal irritation, indicating an injury that caused spillage of gastric or intestinal juices in the free peritoneal cavity. The liver dullness was replaced with a tympanic sound indicating the presence of free air in the abdomen, confirming an injury to a hollow organ, such as the stomach or intestine. I explained to the patient that he needed an emergency operation to repair the damaged organ.

He was prepped and taken to the OR. On exploration, he was found to have a lot of bile-tinged free fluid in the abdomen, suggesting injury to the small intestine. Adequate exposure was secured. After conducting a careful exploration, multiple issues were discovered. There was a laceration of the left lobe of the liver, with transection and partial separation of the injured portion from the main lobe. There was also active oozing from the row surface of the liver. I packed the area with a lap-pad (a multilayer absorbent gauze), and applied pressure over it to temporarily control the bleeding.

Further exploration revealed a small laceration of the first part of the small intestine—the duodenum, with a lot of spillage of bile-tinged juices into the free peritoneal cavity. The knife blade touched the side of the wall of the inferior vena cava (IVC) without causing injury to it. Injury to the IVC can kill somebody in minutes from severe bleeding, so this patient was lucky that the blade did not hit him a couple of millimeters to the left, or he might not have made it to the emergency room. I repaired the duodenum and turned my attention to the liver. This was my opportunity to perform a liver resection! I exposed the injured liver and fractured the lacerated edges exposing the vessels, which I grasped with a clamp and obliterated with a hemoclip to control the bleeding. The portion of the liver that was still attached, I removed using the finger fracture technique, which I found amazingly effective and helpful.

The patient was kept on IV fluids only, for several days before he was given a liquid diet to avoid distension of the repaired area, as a precaution. The patient was discharged home in good condition eight days after the surgery.

About three weeks later, we were called to the ER to evaluate a car accident patient who had sustained multiple injuries. She was a middle-aged lady complaining of severe abdominal pain, having received a direct blow to the right, upper portion of her abdomen. She was hypotensive and had a rapid heartbeat, indicating loss of a significant amount of blood from internal bleeding.

We prepared her promptly for surgery, making sure the blood bank prepared six units of blood ASAP. An IV with normal saline was started in the meantime and we rushed her to the OR. Under general anesthesia I made a midline incision and entered the abdomen. Exploration revealed a large amount of blood in the free peritoneal cavity. The blood was aspirated, exposing a severely injured right lobe of the liver. A large part of the right lobe by the right side of the rib cage was smashed to a paste, associated with active bleeding. This injury was much more serious than the liver stub wound I had treated before. I packed the area of the injury and applied pressure to decrease the blood loss and extended the incision transversely to get the best possible exposure. I used a vascular clamp to temporarily occlude the vessels to the liver and control the bleeding while I resected the badly smashed portion of the liver. As a matter of courtesy, I asked the nurse in the OR to notify the surgical attending on call that I was planning to do a liver resection. She said he told her that he was coming in because he wanted to see it. I clamped the liver vessels and using the finger fracture technique, transected the destroyed part of the liver. The clamp that was occluding the vessels was then removed. I applied some more pressure on the row surface for a few minutes, and then checked the resection margins. The bleeding was fully controlled, and the vital signs of the patient started returning to normal values.

As I was getting ready to close the abdomen, the attending surgeon on call entered the room. He had driven from Long Island where he lived, more than an hour's drive, and he was disappointed that he missed the whole operation. I showed him the damaged part of the liver I had removed and the resection margin of the liver. I explained to him what I did, including the finger fracture technique I used. The operation was very gratifying for me because I demonstrated that I could perform a major liver resection successfully. The patient spent some time in the intensive care unit, but she eventually went home in good condition, returning to normal activity. I knew then that I could do anything that was doable and that I received the best possible training at the best available program.

Part 4: Real Life Begins

Graduation to a Fully Trained Surgeon

Pondering What Is Next

June 1976 was vacation time for me and Sharon, after having gone through the final stretch in my quest. My surgical training was complete, and I was now a fully trained surgeon. My beeper was a victim of my graduation and it died after being forcefully hit against the wall. Now wherever we chose to go on vacation, nobody could bother us! We decided to travel through New York and Canada and explore our surroundings. We started from Brooklyn and headed to the Adirondacks where we stayed in a Lake George Hotel overnight. We toured the beautiful area that was surrounded by tranquil waters and guarded by magnificent trees at their borders. It was an environment that radiated a calm feeling to visitors, something greatly welcome by both of us. We stopped for dinner at a restaurant by the lake and appreciated that we could talk and discuss things without the noise of the beeper or the ring of the phone. We slept well enjoying the sounds in the heart of nature.

The next day we drove north to Canada and reached Montreal where preparations for the 1976 Olympics were in full throttle. At that time, people could order sets of the Olympic commemorative medals, which would be shipped after being circulated during the games. We placed an order for a couple of sets as a future reminder of our trip to Canada.

We continued our travels across Canada to Toronto and crossed over to Buffalo, New York, where we visited my high school and medical school classmate Dr. John Christodoulides and his wife Nancy. John was practicing urology in the Buffalo area. Many years had passed since we had seen each other, so it was nice to get together and shake up old memories. While in the area, we made sure we visited the impressive and majestic Niagara Falls, which proved to be an unforgettable experience. Never before had I seen such a huge amount of fresh water, diving from such a height, coupled with a thundering sound while triggering a vast cloud of raindrops in the process. It was breathtaking. We left Buffalo in the afternoon and drove to Brooklyn in a marathon trip, arriving home at 282 East 45th Street, very late at night. As we entered my apartment, at the ground floor, we heard the TV blasting from the basement where the landlord Aaron Alperowitz lived. He had a serious hearing problem and always had his TV blasting. I just couldn't figure out whether he developed the hearing problem because of the blasting TV, or whether he had the TV blasting because he had the hearing problem first.

I opened the door to the basement, went down and turned off the TV, as I did so many times before when Aaron fell asleep watching it. Aaron was an interesting man. He worked at his brother's butcher shop and used to supply me with all the meats I needed. He would offer me a cut of meat or a pound of ground meat at a certain price and then I would bargain with him, just for the fun of it. I always paid him the asking price, which made him proud, convinced that he won the bargaining match. He was a kind man and told me all the perceived problems he had with his daughter who lived on the apartment above me, on the top floor, of the two-story dwelling. She was pressuring him to transfer the ownership of the property to her, something he was not willing to do, hence the friction between them. I did not know the family dynamics, but I quietly listened and offered no opinion. The only thing I kept bugging him about was to see an ENT doctor and get a hearing aid. One day, while walking back from the KCHC after a long day, I found Aaron outside my back door waiting for me.

"Doctor I got a hearing aid as you told me. Talk to me!"

I was about 10 feet away from him. I stopped and I moved my lips as if I was talking but made no sound.

"I cannot hear you. Darn thing is not working!" he said disappointed. But he heard my laughter that followed.

"Aaron, relax. I am just joking. Your hearing aid is working," I reassured him, bringing a wide smile to his face.

The last day of my chief residency we had a farewell party at the trauma unit with plenty of food. We went down memory lane of the past years and contemplated the future. I had actually secured another year at the SUNY-DMC, KCHC Program, as a fellow of surgical oncology, at the tumor service. After the party, I went home being free to spend some time with Sharon. I took my beeper off my belt and propelled it against the wall! My beeper had been a symbol of slavery for more than 5 years; destroying it was an act of deliverance and a declaration of independence. During the year I was chief resident, I did not have a single day off. I was responsible for the patients on my unit 24/7. Now, all of a sudden, I found myself at a point where I could rest, sleep, or do anything I pleased, without having to be available for urgent or emergent matters. I generally don't like alcohol but to cap the day off, I drank a lot of brandy and got wasted for the first time in my life. It was no surprise I threw up all night, but thank God, Sharon took good care of me!

Graduation day was approaching, and the ceremony was planned for mid-June 1976. It was always a well-organized event, with all residents and most faculty in attendance. There was a formal dinner followed by speeches from the chairman of the department of surgery, the director of the residency program and by every single member of the graduating class of general surgery, thoracic surgery and pediatric surgery. I pondered whether I should bring up Dr. S's threats I was showered with, on the first day of my chief residency, or whether I should let the subject go and forget about it. After all, it was a joyous occasion, which could be adversely affected by the mention of some ridiculous threats by an even more ridiculous man.

On the day of the graduation ceremony, we had a full house. The graduating class consisted of nine general surgeons, two thoracic surgeons and one pediatric surgeon. The general surgeons, in alphabetical order were:

John C. Bivona, MD

George C. Christoudias, MD

Charles R. Dennis, MD

M. Arisan Ergin, MD

Moon Wai Ip, MD

David L Friedman, MD

Condapurum E. Pasupathy, MD

Walter S. Ramsey, MD

Gregory E. Rauscher, MD

The thoracic surgeons were:

Satish C. Khaneja, MD

Chukuma J. Okadigue, MD

The pediatric surgeon was:

Anthony C. Petrillo, MD

Dr. Samuel Koontz, chairman of the department of surgery, was seated on the dais with all the graduates and almost every faculty member was in attendance. The ceremony started with a speech by Dr.

Koontz, along with the traditional congratulations to the new surgeons, followed by each graduate's address that thanked the faculty for guidance in teaching them the art of surgery. Two attending surgeons—Dr. George Stergiopoulos and Dr. Carlos Diaz—received gratitude from every general surgeon "for teaching me how to operate."

When my turn came to take the microphone, I was a little nervous, but at the same time I was glad I had the opportunity to thank everyone who had contributed to my transformation and development from a neophyte into a competent, secure, self-confident surgeon. I started by thanking Dr. Koontz for teaching me how to delegate responsibility and apologized to him for not "meeting his expectations" when I was on his service. He looked at me with amazement, like he was asking me: "What gave you that idea?"

"The first day I started on your service you told me that the way you judged if a resident was good, was by whether the resident contracted hepatitis or not. A resident that got hepatitis is a good resident! I did not get hepatitis therefore, I did not meet your expectations," I explained.

He laughed, as did many in attendance. (The hepatitis virus is transmitted by a transfusion or contact with infected blood and/or needles. The kidney transplant patients had a very high incidence of hepatitis, which could be transmitted to the members of the health professionals treating them.)

I then thanked Dr. Harry LeVeen for the opportunity he gave me to participate in the development of the peritoneovenous shunt, and for generally being good to me and offering his car after my accident. After considerable analysis and thought, I decided to bring out the fiasco of the unqualified attending surgeon at the Brooklyn VA Hospital.

"I am very sorry that our relationship soured because of Dr. S.'s actions. I generally don't like to talk bad about people that are not present, but I consider it my obligation to reveal my unpleasant experience with Dr. S., so as to make everybody aware of his character," I said. "The welcome I received at the Brooklyn VA during the first hour of my first day as a chief resident, was a bunch of threats by Dr. S., who promised to 'destroy my bright future' if I did not abide by his instructions and decisions or if I fought him in any way."

This incident was common knowledge among the residents and many faculty members, but I thought that by bringing the issue out in the open it could force a resolution and protect the VA patients from harm.

The rest of my comments were to thank Dr. George Stergiopoulos and Dr. Carlos Diaz for teaching me the technical intricacies of general and vascular surgery. I also thanked Dr. Kottmeier, Dr. Klotz, and Dr.Francesca Velcek from pediatric surgery; Dr. Antonio Alfonso and Dr. Bernard Gardner from tumor surgery; Dr. Shaftan and Dr. McCauley from trauma surgery; and every faculty member and resident that contributed to my experience and education. I also thanked all the junior residents that were members of my team during my chief residency, for their invaluable help.

Fellowship in Surgical Oncology

During the academic year of July 1, 1976 to June 30, 1977, I did a fellowship in surgical oncology at SUNY-DMC, KCHC. Since I had spent the previous five and a half years at the same institution, I was familiar with the people and the hospital's inner workings. I was given a lot of responsibility scrubbing in the OR and assisting the chief residents and residents during operations.

I also did a lot of research and studied the clinical and pathological parameters of patients treated at KCHC. One of my goals during my fellowship year was to get a scientific paper published. I decided to review the cases of all 273 patients with benign thyroid tumors who had been operated on at KCHC over a seven-year period. Some had presented with symptoms of non-cancerous thyroid tumors associated with the compression of the trachea (windpipe) and esophagus (food-pipe). Others had come to the hospital with serious problems due to delayed medical treatment. When neglected, thyroid masses kept growing and eventually caused compression of the trachea and/or esophagus, which presented with difficulty breathing and/or swallowing. Out of the 273 patients, 91 had symptoms of tracheal or esophageal compression and they comprised the subject of my study. I submitted the study for publication to the American Journal of Surgery and it was published in September 1981.

While my professional life progressed, my personal life was in turmoil. The coup d'état by the Greek junta against President Makarios, led to a Turkish invasion and the illegal occupation of 38 percent of the island of Cyprus. During the coup d'état, my younger brother John got stuck in London since all flights to Cyprus were canceled. He had gone there to see his girlfriend and her father, who was having an operation. When John called to fill me in, I told him he was welcome to come and stay with me in New York.

I picked him up at JFK Airport and we drove together to my Flatbush apartment in Brooklyn. John was two and a half years younger than me. Not only were we close in age, we were close socially and belonged to the mutual admiration society. It was a treat to have him with me despite the terrible circumstances. John had a doctorate degree in structural engineering from Milan Polytechnic and owned a land development company with our eldest brother Stavros. The savage Turkish invasion and illegal occupation was a major blow to their holdings and company plans since a big portion of their land fell under Turkish control. There were 200,000 Greek Cypriot refugees, one third of the population, who fled the advancing Turkish forces, seeking refuge in the free portion of the island. There was a strange sight of families living in tent cities with their Mercedes cars parked outside their tents! Cars were the only possession people managed to take with them as they quickly fled away from the Turkish hordes. As far as John was concerned, there was no rational reason to return to Cyprus at that point.

The Turkish invasion hung over us like a dark cloud, but we were happy to be together again as we discussed the catastrophic events that transpired. Since John was forced by circumstances to stay in the United States, he prepared for and passed the qualifying competency tests so he could practice his profession in America. His girlfriend Aphrodite—an American citizen born in Santa Barbara, California—left London with her mother and joined us in Brooklyn. John and Aphrodite got married in a civil wedding ceremony at the Brooklyn Court House, deciding they would have a church ceremony after everything settled down. He found a job at an engineering company in New Jersey that had a contract for the construction and maintenance of nuclear plants. He, Aphrodite and his new mother-in-law then moved to an apartment in Lodi, New Jersey, about an hour away from my Brooklyn residence. We made it a point to see each other often.

Wedding Bells in Cyprus

Once again, I had time alone with Sharon, who had become my soul mate and partner and was very supportive about all my worries about the Cyprus tragedy. Things were getting serious with us and although we spent a lot of time together, it never felt like it was enough. It was frustrating that we could never plan anything because we could never predict when my beeper would go off, but we endured. Things got a little better when I finished my chief residency and started my fellowship year in 1976. We were able to spend more time with each other and considered making the commitment of spending the rest of our lives together. I had always insisted that I was going to be the last of the seven siblings to get married, so when John got married, I thought that my time had come too.

We discussed our options and decided to go to Cyprus to get married. We were both filled with happiness and joy! John was sad because he had the impression that I was not going to be there for his wedding, and I did not tell him otherwise.

I called my eldest sister Irene and asked her to make the arrangements with the church. She told me what certificates were required, which I gathered and sent to her. Sharon was christened Greek Orthodox, at Three Hierarchs Greek Orthodox Church in Brooklyn. She took the name Eleni, the name of Helen of Troy and my grandmother. Her godfather was our friend Dr. Stratigakis, an Orthopedic Surgeon, finishing his training in Brooklyn.

John went to Cyprus in August ahead of his wedding, which was scheduled for Aug. 28. I was planning to arrive on the Island on Aug. 24 and our marriage was set for Saturday, Sept. 4, at Kykkos Church in Nicosia where the bishop's seat was located. When the bishop heard that I was coming from the United States with a Chinese girl to get married, he volunteered to perform the wedding ceremony. Papa Yiakoumis, the priest who christened me 33 years earlier, was also going to participate in the ceremony, something that touched my heart and soul. Papa Yiakoumis was now a refugee after the Turkish invasion and illegal occupation of our village, but Irene made sure she located him and informed him of my desire to have him participate in the wedding ceremony and he was happy to oblige.

We flew on Olympic Airways by way of Athens and arrived in Cyprus on Aug. 24 expecting to surprise John by showing up for his wedding. Irene and my mother were supposedly the only ones who knew we were coming and planning to get married, but my mother's composure and behavior convinced John that she was hiding something. After serious pressure she relented and admitted that there was "something" she was trying to keep secret. She then spilled the beans that I was going to Cyprus with Sharon for his wedding and was also planning to get married a week after him. John was excited to hear the whole family was getting together to celebrate two weddings.

Irene came to the airport with our mother to pick us up. I gave them a big hug and introduced Sharon to them. They were both happy to meet her and welcome her to the family. Irene then took us to her house, where we would be staying. We had a really big problem, however. Our luggage with Sharon's wedding gown was lost. We had no clothes to wear and more importantly, we did not have a wedding gown! We expressed our frustration to Olympic Airways, and they promised that they would find our luggage and get it to Cyprus the next day. Sharon had invested a lot of time getting measurements and adjustments at the wedding gown store in New York City's Bowery neighborhood. We could buy clothes and anything else we needed in Nicosia, but it would be impossible to find and tailor a wedding gown in just a few days.

We settled down in my sister's house, took showers and then played a trick to my sister Anastasia, who was just as close to me as John. Sharon called Anastasia and told her that she was the operator from the United States and her brother wanted to talk to her. At the time, the only way I knew how to call anybody in Cyprus was through the operator, so Anastasia believed the story. I took the phone and talked to her about John's upcoming wedding. She told me how disappointed she was that I would not be able to be with them. She said Aphrodite's family was staying with her, and as John's wedding was going to be at her house, she was busy with the preparations. We said our goodbyes and hung up. I then got in the car with Sharon, my mother and Irene and headed for Anastasia's house about 5 minutes away. When we arrived, Irene and my mother got out of the car first and started walking towards Anastasia's house, which was about 10 yards away. It was dark so that when Sharon and I got out of the car, Anastasia could not see us yet. She shouted over to Irene and our mother.

"Irene, you just missed George! He called from America!"

She was then shocked to hear my voice ask, "What did he have to say?"

She was stunned and speechless for a couple of seconds but as I got closer, she leaped on me and gave me a big protracted hug. She was so shocked that she was trembling, and her children, Christos and Kyriakos, stared in amazement. She thought I was thousands of miles away and that she had just hung up with me, and all of a sudden, I appeared right in front of her!

Anastasia welcomed Sharon, whom she had already met when she was living in the United States. She was happy to see Sharon again. She treated us with some cold drinks and talked about the wedding dinner and party she was planning for John and Aphrodite. She volunteered to do the same for me one week later.

The next day and every day after that, I kept going to the offices of Olympic Airways to keep the pressure on and ensure they delivered our suitcases. But they couldn't care less about our predicament and their responsibilities. After the disappointment of not having our clothes delivered and with John's wedding coming up, we went to the heart of the shopping area in the old city within the walls. I found a ready-made suit and asked if they could finish the alterations by the next day, explaining the fiasco with our suitcases and the pending wedding. The tailor of the store said he would do it for me, so I took my pants off to try on the suit. The guy was shocked and turned away because I had no underwear on.

"Don't be surprised," I told him. "All my clothes are in the lost suit-case, somewhere. That's the next thing I'm going to buy after I'm done here!"

We continued our shopping spree to replenish our lost items. Sharon found a nice dress for John's wedding, so we were both set for the time being and would be dressed appropriately for John's big event.

The wedding took place in a church up the hill in Strovolos, Nicosia on Saturday, Aug. 28. It was a typical Greek Orthodox ceremony, in the presence of many aunts, uncles, and cousins, whom I had not seen for ages, as well as many friends. Before the invasion, whenever I went to our village of Karavas, I always saw hundreds of relatives. But after being forcefully chased out of their homes, everyone was spread all over the Island, and indeed, all over the world from Europe to America and from Africa to Australia. This happy occasion was an opportunity for so many in the family to get together.

Anastasia and Angelos hosted an evening dinner party at their house. There were a lot of guests and I had the opportunity to introduce my bride-to-be and invite them to our wedding too. At the time, there were no formal wedding invitations because no one knew the where-abouts and addresses of many friends and relatives from the occupied part of Cyprus. The invitations were instead published in newspapers, potentially reaching everyone.

On Monday, I again went to the Olympic Airways office to check the status of our missing suitcases and again they were anything but helpful. The situation was finally saved a day before the wedding by my eldest brother Stavros. He had some business in Athens and while at the airport, he walked through the suitcase storage area to look around. The first thing he saw were our suitcases, with our nametags and Cyprus address in plain sight. Stavros called us with the good news when he arrived at Nicosia Airport just 15minutes away from Irene's house. Sharon, and everybody else for that matter, breathed a deep sigh of relief that everything was sorted out just in the nick of time for a smooth walk down the aisle. We took that as a sign from God that no matter what difficulties we encounter, things would always work out in the end.

The preparations for our big day were well under way and under control. The only missing piece, the wedding gown, fell into place and brought everything smoothly together. The photographer and videographer were reserved, the announcements and invitations were published in the main newspapers, the meats for the barbecue were ordered and plenty of traditional Cyprus dishes were in the process of being prepared. As per the Cyprus tradition, the bride and groom leave from different locations and meet at the church for the ceremony.

Saturday, Sept. 4, 1976, was a clear, sunny, dry and hot day like all September days are supposed to be in Nicosia, Cyprus. It was also the special day Sharon and I would officially join our lives together, forever. We were not just going to walk side to side down the aisle. We were going to walk together through the rest of our lives, share everything, be there for and support each other, laugh together and cry together.

Sharon was getting ready at Irene's house and a hairdresser was there to set Sharon's hair and apply her makeup, which was followed by the fitting of the gorgeous wedding gown. My cousin Eftychios Lefkaritis, who used to have a flower shop in New York City, designed and created an extraordinarily beautiful bride's bouquet with red roses that perfectly complemented Sharon's elegance and beauty. Irene's husband Socrates was going to escort Sharon to the Kykkos Church of Virgin Mary and walk her down the aisle.

In the meantime, I got ready at Angelo's and Anastasia's house. As per tradition, I was shaved while a violinist played traditional wedding music. I then put on my black suit and was ready for the big leap in life. The ceremony was scheduled for 3 p.m. so we left Anastasia's house to arrive at the Kykkos Church 10 minutes ahead of the scheduled ceremony. The church was located in the heart of Nicosia and under the control of the Kykkos Monastery. The monastery is dedicated to the Virgin Mary and is the wealthiest and most famous monastery in Cyprus. It was founded in 1100 AD by the Byzantine Emperor Alexios I Komnenos and was located high up on the Troodos Mountains. Among many precious religious treasures, it houses the Icon of the Virgin Mary, which was painted by the Apostle Luke and transferred from Constantinople when the monastery was founded. The monastery was almost 900 years old and had full control of Kykkos satellite

Church in Nicosia. Parenthetically the oldest Monastery in Cyprus was Stavrovouni, Greek for "the hill of the cross." It was founded in 327 AD and houses a piece of the holy cross, brought there by its founder Saint Helen, mother of the Byzantine Emperor Constantine the Great.

My godfather Charitos Aspris walked me to the church from the street parking and through the church yard, a duty usually carried out by the father of the groom but not possible in my case, since my father had the misfortune to depart from this life long before my ceremony. We stood outside the church and waited for Sharon to come. The guests were already gathering and included many relatives that traveled from all parts of the island. As I looked at them while waiting for Sharon, I was pondered how nice it would have been if our land and homes had not been grabbed by the Turkish hordes, and our churches had not been desecrated, and our families were not pushed out of their homes and scattered all over the world. How nice it would have been if I could walk the same street from home to the Saint Irene Church where my father and mother, and her parents and grandparents walked to for their own marriages. I thought about how much I would have wanted that, but then the bishop's voice brought me back to reality.

"Where is she? I have another engagement later and I don't like to wait," the bishop said.

It was just five minutes after the scheduled starting time of 3 p.m. and he was getting impatient. But just as he finished his words, Sharon came shining through the great arch to the church gate, escorted by my brother-in-law Socrates. We walked into the church and down the aisle to the altar. The church's art and decorations were impressive, as were the centuries-old icons, adorned with gold and silver. We faced the altar with our witnesses, which included 20 maids of honor on Sharon's side and 20 ushers on my side. My best man was Nicos Polemidiotis, one of my three best friends that I had always kept in touch with. There is no required set number for witnesses of a Cyprus wedding. They can be as few as one or as many as 30 or more. This way no one who wants to be a part of the wedding party is left out and everyone is happy. Two big rolls of two-inch wide white silk ribbon were given to the witnesses, one each for the ladies and men. The ribbon was unrolled and each of the witnesses wrote their name. The ribbon was eventually given to the new couple as a testament to the witnesses present at the ceremony. The church was filled with family and friends as the ceremony started, led by the bishop and assisted by Father Papa Yiakoumis and two cantors stationed to the left and right of the altar.

The ceremony started with the exchange of the rings. The bishop placed the rings on our right ring fingers and chanted three times, "The servant of God, Georgios, is betrothed to the servant of God, Eleni" and then "The servant of God, Eleni, is betrothed to the servant of God, Georgios." After he exchanged the rings between our ring fingers, he then chanted our declaration that we went freely and without prior commitment to be joined by God as husband and wife. We were then crowned with two wreaths adorned with white pearls and joined by a white silk ribbon, a symbol of our participation in the Kingdom of Christ.

The epistle (epistoli means letter in Greek) of St. Paul to the Ephesians was then chanted, representing the cornerstone of the Greek Orthodox vision of marriage. "As Christ gives Himself totally to and for his Church, the husband will give himself totally to and for his wife." There is also a verse in the ceremony "and the woman shall be afraid of the man." During this part of the ceremony the groom at times, will step on the bride's foot to claim his dominance over her, a move that the church—and more specifically the Bishop—did not approve. I was told before the wedding that when that verse was read during another ceremony officiated by the same Bishop, the groom did step on the bride's foot. The Bishop expressed his displeasure by smacking the groom's face. For the record I did not step on Sharon's foot because I was not interested in provoking the bishop's discontent, and more importantly, I did not believe that fear should be a part of my married life. I was looking forward to a marriage with mutual love and respect.

The ceremony continued with the common cup, where Sharon and I shared a sip of blessed sweet wine, symbolizing our common life together. The dance of Isaiah followed, which consisted of a triple procession around the center table, led by the bishop, who held our joined hands. We walked around the center table three times with the bishop chanting three hymns on the theme of martyrdom and union with Christ. The best man followed us in the procession holding the crowns over our head.

The ceremony ended with us facing the altar and removing the crowns. We prayed that God would receive the crowns into his kingdom. We then turned around and faced the assembled relatives and friends, who in turn, came to congratulate us. There were a lot of people at the service that I had not seen for many years. They saw the announcement and invitation in the newspaper and decided to honor us with their presence. I was happy to see so many friends and relatives and receive their congratulations and best wishes for Sharon and myself.

A married couple now in the eyes of God and the minds of mortals, we got into my brother Stavros' white, antique Jaguar and headed to Anastasia's house. We took pictures in front of the house, close to the huge jasmine plant that was full of white, fragrant flowers. Many relatives who traveled far and long to come to the wedding formed a joyous procession as they followed us to Anastasia's house. We talked and traveled through time and relived the memories of life in our paradise, the beautiful village of Karavas. Anastasia, Irene, Angelos and other family members prepared traditional Cyprus dishes, including the classic Souvla, which is made by slowly rotating big chunks of lamb over charcoal. The dinner tables were set in the yard around the house, where everybody enjoyed the rich dishes on a perfect day with dry weather and balmy temperatures.

Wedding Picture

Everybody seemed happy but my mother was the happiest of all. Her main goal in life was to see all her children get married and be successful and happy. The married part of her goal was fulfilled for five of her children, but for John and me. Now, suddenly and unexpectedly, her goal was reached with two weddings in eight days. My mother had a tough life after my father's death in 1961. She became a widow at the age of 49 and her time was consumed by the grocery store, where she continued to help out my brother Costas who inherited the business. She also helped by taking care of her grandchildren. Irene had two daughters, Mary and Cleo; Costas had a son and a daughter, Christos and Evgenia; Stavros had two daughters, Maria and Charis; Anastasia had two sons, Christos and Kyriacos; and Theodora had two daughters, Christina and Ioanna. My mother took great pleasure providing toys and candy to all her grandchildren, like most grandparents do. Most of all she showered them with the most precious ingredient of life: unconditional love. Some of the newcomers to the family were not very kind to her, but she took it in stride, not letting anything interfere with her strong love for her family. Any shred of disrespectful behavior towards my mother by some of the in-laws bothered me immensely and tainted my opinion of them. I believed that my mother had earned the highest level of respect from all of her children and their spouses. From day one of every child's life, she made countless sacrifices. Respect was the very least every one of us owed her.

An example of my mother's selflessness was the time I gave her money to spend as she pleased. My first cousin Helen Stillman, who lived in Queens, New York, sold a piece of property in Karavas, and she asked me if she could give that money to me in Cyprus and I could pay her back in dollars so she would not have to go through the trouble of money transfers through the bank. I asked her to have her representative give the money to my mother—about $1,800—and I would pay her back in dollars. I wrote to my mother about it and asked her to deposit it in the bank under her name and use it any way she pleased. I was disappointed to find out that she did not spend a single penny.

"Mamma, why didn't you use any money?" I asked.

"You work so hard for your money, my son. I don't want to spend it," she said.

Her response left me totally flabbergasted. "Mamma, you worked so hard for me and the whole family all your life and it's about time that you start spending some money on yourself without any concerns about how hard I work. Money is made to be spent and as time goes by a point will come that I will make much more than I can spend, so please promise me that you will use the money for anything you please," I said.

She promised me she would try though she said that she really did not need much money. But she kept her promise and spent small amounts to buy toys and candy for her grandchildren. My parents lived to support, serve and help their children in an unselfish, altruistic way.

The party ended and the guests dispersed. We were finally able to get some rest and relax away from the noise and the handshakes. The next day we headed for the Troodos Mountains for our honeymoon. My brother-in-law Socrates graciously loaned us his car and Sharon and I made the one hour drive to Mount Olympus, which has an altitude of 6,400 feet. We stayed in the nearby tourist village of Troodos. The village had several hotels that were always packed in July and August with visitors wanting to escape the scorching heat of Nicosia. The village became a ghost town in September until the ski season started, usually sometime in January.

In early September the high temperatures in Nicosia are in the mid to upper 80s. Troodos was a much nicer, cooler climate, with pine and cedar forests creating a beautiful green scene. Centuries-old villages on the side of the mountains capped the panorama of the valley below. We arrived at the Troodos Hotel and checked into a room with a panoramic view of the mountainside below. We walked around the plaza of the village enjoying the cool and comfortable air that was tinged with the scent of pine. We rested on a bench and talked about our journey through the future. We walked to the vendors lined in the center of the square, selling everything from pears and plums, to dehydrated crunchy country bread called "baximadi," to a sweet soft stick made from grape juice called "shooshookos." We noticed that several government-owned bungalows in the area were already closed for the summer as people returned to their jobs in Nicosia.

The next day we drove along the narrow road on the southwest side of the mountains and stopped along the way to look at the many villages we came across. We enjoyed the centuries-old scenery, houses, buildings and churches that time had forgotten. We stopped at a village and sat down at a coffee shop. We had Greek coffee and some sweets and we were pleasantly surprised when the shopkeeper said another patron paid our bill. He raised his hand to salute us and we thanked him for his courtesy and hospitality.

We continued on our way and headed to Paphos, a city founded 3,000 years ago. In ancient times it was the seat of one of Cyprus's ancient kingdoms. The famous Temple of Aphrodite, the Goddess of Love, Beauty and Fertility, was also located there. According to Greek mythology, the Goddess Aphrodite was born by the surf of the sea on the shores of Paphos. The shoreline was exceptionally beautiful and could be seen from the road traveling from the city of Limassol to Paphos.

When we arrived at Paphos that night, we didn't think we would have any trouble finding a hotel room since the tourist season was practically over. But we were so wrong, and not making reservations proved to be a big mistake. We stopped at every hotel and got the same answer, "Sorry, we have no vacancy!" I finally asked the last hotel keeper I talked to, whether he knew if there was any hotel in the region that had any vacancy.

"You can try Polis," he said. "Hotel Marion may have some room." I asked him if he could call them for me and their answer was a beautiful "yes." The kind man made our reservations and gave us directions. I thanked him from the bottom of my heart, and we got on our way. I knew where Polis was, but I had never been there despite having spent the first 20 years of my life in Cyprus. Even when my high school had an excursion to Paphos during my senior year, I could not go because I had an appendectomy operation the day before.

It was easy to get to the road leading to Polis since there was only one road going northwest. Polis means "city" in Greek and is 23 miles northwest of Paphos. It is also a town with a rich history spanning 3,000 years. It is separated from Paphos by the tail of the Troodos Mountains, easing down to the Mediterranean Sea. The road was narrow and winding, leading up and down the hills and valleys, going through villages whose names I recognized from my high school geography lessons but had never visited before. I remembered a British teacher's statement I had heard as a student at the English School in Nicosia. "The roads in Cyprus were designed by the donkeys, not the engineers! Wherever the donkeys formed a path, that is where the road was built!" It appeared to be so true! It took us close to an hour to go the 23 miles and arrive at the Marion hotel, which was on the main road. "Marion" was the name of Polis in the ancient times. The hotel Marion was family owned and run. They were kind, welcoming and hospitable. We checked in and went to our room, relieved that we could lie down and relax. The trip turned out to be too long and too rough, especially for Sharon.

We had a good night's sleep and woke up fresh and full of energy, ready to explore a gorgeous part of Cyprus. The hotel offered an appetizing breakfast with eggs, famous Cyprus halloumi cheese, various fruits, cereal, coffee and tea. Halloumi cheese is a unique white cheese that is made usually from goat and sheep milk. It is served fresh, fried, grilled or cooked without melting. We enjoyed our rich breakfast and headed for the baths of Aphrodite, a picturesque area where legend says the Goddess of Love, Beauty and Fertility used to bathe. We parked the car and walked slowly up the hill, which passed a large rock with a spring cascading into a pond. The area was completely encircled by greenery, with several fig trees coming out of the pond's edge. The water found its way to the sea, a couple of hundred yards downhill, to the top of a cliff, which towered from the water's edge. On top of the cliff and near the parking area, there was a restaurant/coffee shop with a breathtaking, majestic view of the crystal-clear turquoise waters that made up the shoreline. Rocks of various sizes lined the coastline, like soldiers guarding the land of the Goddess. The waters were so clear, that we could see the bottom of the sea and everything that was in it, even though it was 100 feet below us.

The climbing up and down the hill stimulated our appetite. We sat down for lunch at a table overlooking the water. We ordered grilled fish that was freshly caught just hours earlier from the surrounding sea. The whole fish, head and tail included, was grilled to perfection and served to us with oil and lemon sauce on the side. We also had a Cyprus salad, French fries and village bread, and then topped it off with a demitasse of Greek coffee.

I don't know whether it was because we were very hungry, or because of the serene surroundings, but Sharon still insists that it was the best fish she ever had.

We stayed in the area for a couple of days and then headed back to Nicosia. On the way back we toured the city of Paphos, where Saint Paul was whipped with 39 lashes at a synagogue. Paphos is a picturesque city with an old medieval castle on the coastline. There was a lot to see, from ancient sites to restaurants, hotels and tourist attractions. The city had a history of attracting visitors since the ancient times when the Temple of Aphrodite was a sought-out destination.

Outside of Paphos we also stopped at a farmer's roadside kiosk and bought a locally grown watermelon. After that, we started heading towards Limassol, which was the main seaport of Cyprus. About half-way there, the car overheated and stalled. We were stuck on the side of a narrow road in the middle of nowhere. It was a hot, sunny day, and we were thirsty, but there was no water around. Every problem has a solution, however. I picked a sizable rock and cracked the watermelon into pieces. The fully ripe watermelon was a fiery red color and had a rich aroma. It was the best tasting, thirst quenching, invigorating and refreshing watermelon we ever had. When the car cooled down, we managed to get back to Nicosia without further ado.

We spent the rest of our vacation time in Nicosia with the family. My mother was impressed and pleased by the attention and care Sharon gave her and so was I. Sharon was a great daughter in law that cared for her and treated her with kindness and respect. Sharon even helped my mother bathe since the Parkinson's disease made it difficult for her to do on her own. Sharon repeatedly invited her to come and stay with us in America, but she declined, stating that she did not want to become a burden.

When it was time to give hugs and kisses before heading to the airport for our trip home, Sharon again invited her to come and visit us. My mother's answer was solemn and grave.

"Have a safe trip my children and take good care of yourselves, because I don't think I am going to see you again. I was blessed to see all of you get married and I feel that I have fulfilled my purpose on this earth. I feel I will be traveling to go meet with your father again!"

I was stunned and urged her to think positively, because she had a lot to live for. Her grave statement, however, remained etched in my memory throughout my life. Sharon then addressed her and told her "Sagapo", meaning 'I love you" in Greek. That was the best gift she ever received, putting a big smile on her face!

Back to Work as a Fellow

Being a fellow in surgical oncology on the tumor service was much less stressful than being a surgical resident. The 36-hour and 60-hour shifts were now a thing of the past. I had the opportunity to do a lot of studying and research, as well as assist often in the operating room by guiding the chief residents and their teams through the procedures. I was also called in to help, by the chief residents of other services, whenever they came across a difficult situation, which they could not handle. The chiefs were my interns and residents in the previous years, so they felt comfortable asking for my help and advice whenever they faced a difficult problem in the operating room, even at odd hours. I never let them down since I lived only three blocks away from the hospital. We saw a lot of thyroid tumors that were big enough to interfere with the patients' breathing and/or swallowing. I decided to review the experience of this specific problem in our department. That study resulted in a publication of a scientific paper in the American Journal of Surgery in September of 1981 with the title, "Tracheal or esophageal compression due to benign thyroid disease."

In the Autumn of 1976, my Uncle Christ Loucas had an accident and was found to have an irregular heartbeat. I had him admitted to the University Hospital at Downstate for a work-up and treatment. His christened name was Christodoulos, which means servant of Christ, but he shortened it when he came to America in the 1920s. From servant (doulos) he became Christ, the boss. He had spent the better part of his life working as a shoemaker in the Bronx and finally retired in 1974. He took a suitcase full of his savings and returned to his birthplace of Karavas to live out the rest of his life. The Turks had other ideas, however.

Just a couple of months after he arrived in Cyprus, the Turkish forces attacked and invaded the island about two miles from Karavas. My uncle and his wife found refuge at an American radio station in the village and managed to escape the advancing invasion. From there they were airlifted by an American helicopter to an American Navy ship in the waters nearby. They returned to America with only the clothes on their back.

Uncle Christ then moved to Asbury Park and opened a new shoe repair store to make ends meet. He had always been kind to me since I came to the States and I felt that I needed to take care of him. He had a son Constantine who lived in Ronkonkoma, New York, with his wife Joan and two children, Nicholas and Nancy. He also had a daughter Helen who lived with her husband James Rotsettis and their son Christopher in Toms River, New Jersey. Uncle Christ's wife, Fero, came to stay with us while uncle Christ was in the Hospital, as we were trying to find out what was going on with his health.

A couple of days later I received a phone call from my cousin Constantine, asking about his father's condition. I told him that we were still doing tests and did not have a clear picture of what was going on. He surprised me with an angry argument. He said he had talked to a doctor on Long Island who told him that we should have figured out the problem by now. Constantine was anything but appreciative. I was doing so much for his father so I could not take his attack passively.

"Listen cousin!" I responded. "Since you have better doctors where you are, just take your father to them, and take your stepmother too so I can enjoy my honeymoon with my wife! After all, taking care of him is more your responsibility than mine!"

"Oh no," he complained. "I just went through hell taking care of my terminally ill father in law. I cannot deal with this anymore!"

I could not believe my ears. He was so rude and ungrateful, it made me even more angry. I could not help but reciprocate in kind.

"Cousin! If you don't know how to say thank you for everything I am doing for your father, then shut up and don't call me anymore". I was angry but did not lose sight that whatever I was doing for my uncle, I was doing it because of my uncle and not his son.

It turned out that my uncle had cancer of the transverse colon. Dr. Gardner, the chief of surgical oncology, removed the tumor but unfortunately the cancer had spread beyond the colon, making his condition incurable. He was taken home to Asbury Park by his daughter Helen, a week after his surgery. As his condition deteriorated, his wife could no longer take care of him. He found comfort and care in a nursing home in New Jersey, where I visited him frequently.

In the meantime, married life was good for Sharon and me. Sharon quit her job and became a house wife. Her appetite increased a she started baking some delicious treats, which served her pregnancy well. I don't know how, but she learned to create the best tasting New York cheesecake I have ever encountered. And she kept baking them much too often. She also baked the most flavorful Cyprus blackolive bread, which is a meal by itself. It is so good, that every time it came out of the oven, I quickly devoured an entire loaf.

As Sharon's pregnancy progressed, she started gaining weight. Out of sympathy I gained even more weight than she did. Of course, the fact that I was no longer working never-ending shifts, coupled with Sharon's fabulous cooking, had a lot to do with my weight gain. I was thoroughly enjoying married life.

I was notified by the American Board of Surgery, that my written exam for the boards, was scheduled for Dec. 13, 1976 in New York City. I was determined to pass the exam, so I devoted a lot of time studying and paying attention to the most rare and complex conditions and surgical techniques. On exam day I felt completely alert and fully prepared for the test. At the end of the allocated time for the test, I still had some questions left to do. Although I didn't get a chance to answer all the questions, I was confident about my performance. All of the questions I answered were in the scope of my knowledge.

I had taken the day off for the exam, so afterwards I went back home to spend more time with Sharon. I called Cyprus to talk to my mother and let her know that I had finished the exam. I was shocked to learn that she fell and fractured her hip. She had been in the hospital for three days and her surgery was still not scheduled. I asked the my sister why she did not let me know when it happened, but she said that my mother did not want her to, so that it would not have an adverse effect on my exam.

I was feeling indecisive as to whether I should stay home with my pregnant wife or rush to Cyprus to see my mother. Sharon encouraged me to go, but I had doubts whether my presence in Cyprus would change the situation, so I decided to stay home. I talked to my brother and asked him to have her transferred to a private clinic for better care and a timely performance of the operation.

The operation was done the next day and the surgeon told my sister Irene that everything had gone well. The next day I went to work and scrubbed in several operations. By the time I finished, I felt engulfed by a dark cloud. I walked home feeling depressed, upset and unhappy. My mood was obvious; when Sharon saw me, her first question was, "What's wrong? Did something bad happen? Why do you look so upset, so depressed?"

"I don't know. I just feel terrible, and I have no idea why," I said.

It did not take long to discover the root cause of my sudden depression. The phone rang and it was Irene calling from Cyprus.

"George, I have bad news. Mother had a pulmonary embolus and died," Irene said.

My mother was only 65 years old. She died on December 16, 1976. I recalled the last words, she uttered to me and Sharon at the airport, before we left Cyprus. She had said she did not think she was going to see us again and that her purpose in life had been fulfilled. She said that, as if her only purpose in life was to serve her children. She must have had a premonition.

I broke down and cried because my mamma, whom I loved with all my heart, had an acute medical problem and there was nothing I could do to help her. Just like that, in the blink of an eye, she was gone, and I was not there to say goodbye.

Although she was gone, she remained alive in my heart, soul and existence, just like my father. Her words, prayers and good wishes still resonate with me: "To act with honesty and integrity and with love for the world. To become a productive member of society, treat people well and fight for what is yours. Take care of yourself and your family and treat everybody with respect."

When I was just a little kid, she told me a story that greatly shaped my understanding of how to treat our parents in need. Every time I think of the story, my eyes tear up.

An old lady's house collapsed after a storm. She was not hurt, but her house was uninhabitable. She went to her daughter, who lived nearby with her husband and children and knocked on her door. When her daughter opened the door, she told her she had nowhere to stay because her house was ruined by the storm and asked if she could stay there. The daughter told her there wasn't enough room, but she could stay in the stable with the donkey and the goats.

The woman thanked her daughter and walked slowly with her cane to the stable on the side of the house. Her daughter thought for a while and then picked up a blanket and summoned her own daughter. "Bring this blanket to your grandmother in the stable because it is very cold." The granddaughter unfolded the blanket and tore it in two pieces. She then folded both halves and left one behind. She took the other half and she started heading to the stable.

"Why did you tear the blanket in two and why are you only taking half a blanket to your grandmother?" the woman's daughter asked.

"Oh mamma! I am saving the other half for you, when your time comes to move into the stable," she said.

The girl's mother was taken aback by that answer. She opened the door and walked to the stable. She asked her mother for forgiveness, telling her that she found room for her in the house.

Sharon tried to console me. I looked at her and came up with a big statement, "You are my mother from now on."

New Beginnings

The year of 1976 was a time of blessings and heartbreak. That was the year I had finished my general surgery training, got married and found out I was going to be a father. And then it was the year I lost my mother.

The year 1977 came with the promise of an addition to the family. My first son was born on March 22, 1977. Sharon was in labor for 24 hours before the little boy decided to come out. We named him Christos, after my father. My brother John was the godfather and we christened him at the age of eight months at the Church of Saint John the Theologian in Tenafly, New Jersey.

Christos was a bundle of joy. He gave our life a more specific purpose, which was to nurture him and bring him up to be a productive member of society, just as my mother had always wished for me. Christos was very responsive to me and was always laughing, playing and full of joy. He spread delight and happiness and was a great pleasure to the family.

I continued the routine of my fellowship on the surgical oncology service and was offered a faculty position at SUNY-DMC, KCHC as assistant professor of surgery. The director of the service, Dr. Bernard Gardner, offered me the position and the department's chairman Dr. Koontz was happy to approve it.

"George, you make another contribution like the P-V shunt and I will make you a full professor," he reassured me.

Dr. Koontz had always expressed his appreciation for my surgical skills, knowledge and potential for innovations, so I considered it a privilege to be a member of the surgical faculty under his leadership.

An offer by Dr. Leonard Lieberson, a general surgeon at Christ Hospital in Jersey City, did not pan out. During my internship there, he had suggested that I come to see him when I finished my training so we could work together. When I went to see him, he Initially said he was interested in hiring me, but he then reneged on his offer. In the meantime, Sharon and I had purchased a home in Paramus and moved there in June of 1977, from where I commuted to Brooklyn every day.

While my life progressed, Uncle Christ's condition deteriorated. He ended up being transferred to a nursing home in New Jersey where I visited him frequently. During one of those visits, we started talking about our ancestors. He told me about his grandfathers and their siblings, going back to the mid-1800s. I recorded those conversations and the information allowed me to trace my family tree to the 19th century. He died on May 3, 1977, at the age of 73 years old.

His last words were, "They are all here. They came to take me." And then he aske a question: " Maritsa died too?"

He was referring to my mother Maritsa, who was his youngest sister and had died five months earlier. No one told him that she was gone. But he found out on his death bed. He saw her among the others who came to take him. That incident had always made me wonder what lies beyond our death.

On July 1, 1977, I was appointed assistant professor of surgery at SUNY-DMC, KCHC, Division of Surgical Oncology. It was a salaried position associated with private practice privileges. I was given an office and a secretary and a payment of half of my liability insurance premium. It was a descent deal and I was quite satisfied. But then another event changed everything again.

In 1977, Dr. Koontz had traveled to Africa for a visit. Shortly after his return, he got a bad headache and knew that something bad was happening to him. From what I heard at the time, Dr. Koontz called his right hand man, Dr. Khalid Butt, and told him that he was headed to the hospital. He asked Dr. Butt to meet him there and take care of him. By the time Dr. Butt arrived, Dr. Koontz was in a coma and never regained full consciousness. He died four years later in 1981.

Christos was growing fast and was a source of joy to me, and Sharon. I left home every day before 6:30 a.m. to make the commute from

Paramus to Brooklyn before the onset of heavy traffic. Sharon was home alone with the baby and there was not much I could do to help her. My niece, Mary Socratous, Irene's daughter, was also staying with us while she attended Fairleigh Dickinson University. She was too busy with her studies to be of any help to Sharon, who started getting home sick.

On Jan. 19, 1978, she left for Taiwan to visit her mother and the rest of her family. It was a beautiful sunny day without a cloud in the sky, when her plane took off but that did not last long. By the evening, the clouds moved in and completely covered the skies. Soon after, it began to snow hard. The snow came down until the next morning and dropped 15-plus inches across the metropolitan area. I tried to open the back door to go to the garage, but the screen door would not open; it was completely blocked by the snow. That morning I was forced to do my morning exercise and shoveled a whole lot of snow before I managed to clear a path to my car and driveway, which I also had to clear before heading to work. Sharon's stay in Taiwan gave her a breather, with her family helping out and having fun with little Christos. She returned home six weeks later, and I was disappointed that Christos did not recognize or even respond to me. He had already forgotten who I was, but he gradually got used to me again.

Part 5: Career and Life Plans

Staking my Path

Decisions, decisions

After Dr. Koontz's disability, it became obvious to me that SUNY-DMC and KCHC had nothing exciting to offer me. The stabbing of a doctor on hospital grounds convinced me that I had to start looking elsewhere to build my practice and career. I looked at advertisements for available positions in every surgical journal. I went for an interview in West Virginia, driving up the mountains with the radio playing, "Country road, West Virginia," a perfect song for the occasion. The area was isolated from civilization as we knew it and Sharon had no interest in spending her life in the mountains there. I also traveled to California with Sharon and little Christos for an interview in Corcoran and Visalia. That hospital liked the fact that I had extensive trauma experience because they treated a lot of patients with stab wounds and other such injuries. That indicated to me it was a high crime area and was not exactly what I had in mind. I liked the climate and landscape because it reminded me of Cyprus. But I was not looking to go from one high crime area to another, 3,000 miles away. I made it known that I was not interested in that "opportunity."

While in the area, we traveled up the mountains to the redwood forest. The sky-high redwood trees with their massive, gargantuan size and their towering heights seemed to touch the sky. I had never seen or imagined trees with such massive dimensions. I was in awe of the unusual and overpowering surroundings. We descended towards the valley and Visalia, where we noticed a brook with a lot of people having a picnic. We stopped to rest and enjoyed the countryside and its beautiful landscape. We walked around next to the brook and stopped to feel the water. It was ice cold, which prompted me to say, "I will not get in this water for a million dollars!"

Somehow, Christos slipped into the water before I could grab him. He was carried downstream to a deep huge water mass a few feet away and disappeared. Alarmed and desperate, I jumped into the deep water and tried to find him, but I just could not locate him. I finally swam under a huge rock and with my right foot I felt him underneath it. I grabbed him by the diaper, but it came off. I tried again and grabbed him by the thigh. One thing was certain; I was not going back to the surface unless I had him in my hands.

I managed to grab him firmly by the thigh and dislodged him from the rocks. I came up to the surface with him only to find that Sharon was in the water too. She saw me going down and disappearing, so she jumped in too, but she did not know how to swim. Now, not only did I have to help Christos out of the deep waters, I had to do the same for Sharon too. Fortunately, some people saw us struggling and came over to help us out of the water. We waited to dry out and then went back to the car and drove to our hotel. Before we left we noticed a sign close to the brook: "WARNING! Waters are treacherous. Do not get in the water!" I seconded that, though my family's entrance into the treacherous waters was not exactly intentional. We took that as a bad omen; California was not for us.

We returned to New Jersey, disillusioned about my prospects of finding the perfect location to start my practice. At SUNY-DMC they taught me how to operate and how to manage any and every difficult medical emergency, but nobody taught me how to start a surgical practice. During one of our discussions, Sharon asked me a simple, but important question.

"Where do you really want to practice?" she asked.

I did not hesitate. "Bergen County, New Jersey," I said.

"So, let's do it," she said.

Home, Practice, Hospital Privileges

I still had my academic appointment and private practice at Downstate Medical Center, so there was no urgency to move. We went through the steps involved to proceed forward with the goal of establishing a practice in the area we lived. But first I had to find a new house that was suitable for both my home and my office. Then I had to apply for privileges at the area hospitals.

I was busy working in Brooklyn between my academic duties and my private practice, so Sharon took on the burden of house hunting for something that would also be suitable for my practice. She finally found a house in New Milford, which was designed as a home-office combination and used to belong to Dr. York, a long-gone general practitioner. The house was centrally located on a county road across the street from New Milford High School. The building included an office with a separate entrance, which perfectly suited my needs. The owner at the time had moved out of the house, but the office was still rented to a dentist. It was a huge house and I thought I could construct a temporary office on the ground floor to use until the dentist's lease expired.

Our $100,000 offer was accepted, and the closing was set for Dec. 21, 1978, which was also Sharon's birthday. We then proceeded to put our house in Paramus on the market and quickly found a buyer. We also set that closing for Dec. 21. When the day came, we emptied out our Paramus house and loaded everything into a truck. The closing of our Paramus house sale was then completed, followed by the closing for our new home. After closing on the New Milford house, we emptied the truck into our new home on River Road. Thanks to Sharon's perseverance, the first step of setting up my new practice was done.

The next steps included applying for privileges at local hospitals and getting approval from the Borough of New Milford to construct a temporary office until the dentist's lease expired six months later. When I initially moved to New Jersey I applied for a Medical License by reciprocity. My application for medical license was approved by the New Jersey Board of Medical Examiners, so I was licensed to practice Medicine and Surgery in the state.

I had some problems with New Milford's building inspector Mr. Coleman. He told me in no uncertain terms, "I will never allow you to practice because every time I go to my doctor there is no place to park."

He got me angry, so I responded accordingly. "Mr. Coleman, I earned the right and license to practice with my blood, sweat and tears. You have absolutely no power to stop me from practicing my profession," I said and walked out. His attitude reminded me of Dr. S's shenanigans; that is why I was so rough with my words.

I knocked on the doors of all my neighbors and asked them to sign a petition supporting my application for variance, to establish a temporary office in my house, which I had already submitted to the town's planning board. At the planning board hearing, the building inspector did not show up to oppose my request. The variance was unanimously approved, and I was allowed to proceed with my plans. I asked my brother John, who is a structural engineer, to design the office. He then helped me build dividers to convert the living room into a waiting room, the dining room into my consultation room, and the sunroom into two examining rooms. It cost me less than $1,000 and allowed me to hang my shingle "George C. Christoudias, MD, General and Tumor Surgery", on the front loan and start seeing patients.

The applications I had submitted for hospital privileges were still dormant. Englewood Hospital in Englewood, New Jersey was the first to reply. I went for an interview in a room that looked more like a tribunal than a professional interview. Several surgeons and administrators asked me questions, and, in the end, they offered to grant me admitting privileges only if I quit my academic appointment as assistant professor of surgery at the SUNY-DMC. I was concerned about severing my income by giving up my academic position, but I accepted their terms with the caveat that I would be allowed to give SUNY-DMC three months' notice before terminating my employment with them. They accepted and another hurdle was out of the way. In retrospect, that was the best thing that could have happened because it allowed me to focus on my New Jersey practice and devote 100 percent of my time to its success.

The first application for hospital privileges I had submitted was actually to Holy Name Hospital in Teaneck, New Jersey. Several months had passed without hearing from them. I called to find out the reason they did not respond to my application and I was informed that they completely changed the application form and process, so I had to reapply. I thought it was their way of saying, "stay away, we do not want any competition." Regardless, I went there and picked up the new application and resubmitted it for consideration. It had a lot of ridiculous requests, like submitting a letter from my "spiritual advisor," which had nothing to do with my qualifications or competence. I thought it was requested as a way to complicate and/or delay the process and discourage new applicants, thus protecting their turf from new competition.

I finally received a response from Holy Name Hospital and was scheduled for an interview with the director of surgery, Dr. Richard Mazzara, in June of 1978 on a hot and dry day. He asked if I was Greek, and when I said that I was, he started reciting Homer's Iliad in the original text. He stopped after the first two verses, at which time I continued delivering the verses that followed. I had spent endless hours in high school studying Odyssey and the Iliad in the original text and had memorized several verses from both of Homer's epic poems. I was taken aback when Dr. Mazzara started reciting the Iliad in its original text. There are few Greeks that have the knowledge and ability to do that, let alone people who were non-Greeks. I was pleasantly surprised with his knowledge of Homer's 3,000-year-old epic poem.

After that, he asked me routine questions about my training, office location, and plans for the future. The interview went well, and I was granted admitting privileges to Holy Name Hospital. I also was quickly accepted to Bergen Pines Hospital without much ado since most of the operations done there, were charity work for uninsured and indigent patients.

All of the pieces to the puzzle came together and presented a rosy picture for mine and my family's future. I had been trained at one of the most prestigious institutions in the world and had experienced every surgical condition that could be found in any surgical textbook and then some. In addition, I had already performed every operation that I could possibly face in private practice. I had worked like a dog for countless hours and I was prepared to continue working just as hard. I firmly believed that all of these accomplishments put me on the road to success; eventually, that proved to be the case.

Two of the busiest surgeons at Englewood Hospital, Dr. Berlin and Dr. Halsted, asked me to assist them in their big operations, which gave me a steady source of income. When I started, I also treated patients for non-surgical problems, since I had extensive experience from my previous rotating internship and the many hours I worked in the relevant specialties while moonlighting in the KCHC ER. An important contributor to my success was having the support of the Greek community who looked to me to treat their relatives who did not speak English. I was also on the emergency room roster for both hospitals and handled all the surgical emergencies on scheduled days.

My practice grew at a relatively fast pace. By the time I resigned from my academic position at SUNY-DMC, I had enough income to meet our basic needs and cover essential expenses. During my training I was taught how to diagnose patients, care for them and operate. But no one taught me how to run a practice or file insurance claims. Sharon had to start from scratch to find out how to handle all of the bureaucratic intricacies of running a surgical practice. There were strict Medicare rules and procedures to file claims. She went to the social security office for guidance and found out where she had to call for the Medicare information. She took similar steps to get the other health insurance companies' information. Within 30 days she had everything figured out and the office was fully functional.

As these changes were taking place, we were blessed with a new addition to the family, Stavros George Christoudias, born on Aug. 27, 1979. We named him after my great-grandfather and my brother. Sharon's mother came from Taiwan to help with the newborn as well as our toddler Christos, who was now two and a half years old. Sharon's sister Joy and brother Teddy also came from Taiwan and were a great help, taking care of the kids.

Sharon recovered fast after the second delivery and handled the office phone and set appointments. She also supervised the reception area during office hours and took on nursing duties. In addition to all that, she was also in charge of billing, insurance filing, collections and bookkeeping. The practice was growing quickly and steadily, and my patients were my most important referral source. My concerns about having the patient load necessary to maintain a practice while also earning enough money to provide for my family had completely dissipated. All the work, which I used to do for free at KCHC, was now a source of steady income in my private practice. Most importantly, I continued to enjoy every minute of my profession. The ability to make a difference in people's lives was an important ingredient of my happiness and complemented my family life. I felt blessed!

Hospital, Surgical and Family Life

Over the course of my 45-year career, I performed well over 15,000 operations, some small some big, and some unique. Each operation had an impact on the patient's life, as well as my own.

I remember rushing to treat a patient on a Saturday night in the Summer of 1979 at Holy Name Hospital. He was in his early 50s and was brought to the ER with a kitchen knife sticking out of his neck after a failed suicide attempt. He had pushed the knife into the left, upper side of his neck near the carotid artery and internal jugular vein. He used his left arm to stab himself because his right arm was amputated following an injury from an earlier failed attempt to kill himself. There was no significant bleeding, but the knife was pulsating, indicating its proximity to the carotid artery. I was amazed to see this patient after having treated someone with an identical situation at KCHC.

I had to remove the knife and repair any damage it might have caused. I asked the nursing supervisor to call in the OR team and the anesthesiologist. About 90 minutes later, the patient was prepared, taken to the OR and placed under general anesthesia by Dr. Subbarrao. As I proceeded to prep and drape the neck the anesthesiologist questioned me about my experience with this kind of operation. He feared the procedure could end in disaster. I assured him that I was fully trained in this type of surgery and there was no need to worry.

I made an incision at the area of the injury and carefully exposed the right carotid artery and internal jugular vein. I gained control of both vessels, with the knife still in place, its blade covering a portion of the artery and vein. I asked Dr. Subbarrao to pull the knife out.

"I cannot," he said. "It's against my religion."

The truth was, he was afraid that if he pulled the knife out, the patient would bleed to death, and he would get in trouble for causing the patient's death. The circulating nurse, Linda, took care of it after I reassured her that I had full control of the situation and nothing bad was going to happen. The only damage the knife caused was a laceration of the internal jugular vein, which I promptly repaired without incident. Post-operatively the patient did well, and recovered fully. The patient was discharged home, under psychiatric care I had requested. His name was Willie and he lived with his mother. He was on disability. His bill totaled $500 and he sent a $5 check every month to pay it off. After about a year I felt bad that I was taking his $5; I thought he needed it more than I did. I discussed the situation with Sharon, and she agreed. She sent him a letter telling him that we appreciated his payments, but his balance was now written off and he did not need to send any more money. His response surprised me more than my letter surprised him. He replied that he knew his responsibilities and would continue making payments until my fee was paid in full. Sharon and I concluded that it was best to let him continue sending the $5 monthly installments, because maybe it gave him a purpose in life.

At that time there were no hospitals designated as trauma centers to handle seriously injured patients. Every community hospital received patients with severe and multiple injuries and we had our fair share at Holy Name Hospital. In 1980, an Irish family was involved in a car accident and three people sustained multiple injuries. One was brought to HNH and the other two were taken to Hackensack Hospital. The patient at HNH had just arrived from Ireland to visit his family in New Jersey. He had a ruptured spleen, multiple soft tissue injuries and a fractured collarbone on his right side. I took him to the OR for removal of his spleen and an orthopedic surgeon, Dr. Morrissey, repaired his collarbone. The patient was doing well until the fifth post-operative day, when he developed a fever. The wound appeared infected, and when I drained it, I could smell the characteristic odor of a dangerous bug called pseudomonas. I sent a culture and sensitivity specimen to the lab and started him on the proper antibiotic for pseudomonas. He responded well to the treatment and two days later the culture results confirmed my clinical diagnosis.

Complicated Cases

My successful completion of complex situations boosted my reputation resulting in many referrals by patients, nurses and physicians. Although this irked some of the older, more established surgeons, it did not bother me. I maintained that my results were an open book for everybody to see, and nobody could harm me. I continued to make myself available at all times and the opportunities to demonstrate my expertise, competence and effective management of difficult situations continued to grow.

On March 24, 1981, I was called to the ER to manage a car accident victim who had suffered catastrophic injuries. Zoe was a 19-year-old young lady who drove into a main thoroughfare from a side street before she realized that there was another car coming her way. She froze as the other car careened into her vehicle on the driver's side. She sustained multiple injuries from the direct impact and had to be extricated from the wreck.

On first evaluation the patient was in critical condition. Her blood pressure didn't register, and her pulse was rapid and barely palpable. She was also dusky, agitated and confused. At one point while I was examining her abdomen, she grabbed my arm and pushed her nails into my skin. After I reviewed her chest x-ray I saw that she had multiple rib fractures on both sides, which made her breathing problematic and caused low levels of her blood oxygen. These issues resulted in her agitation and confusion, exacerbated by the blood loss from her injuries. The patient was very close to death and there was no time to waste.

I called the OR, and Linda answered the phone.

"Linda do you have a room available?" I asked.

"Yes," she replied.

"Great, I am bringing this patient in with multiple life-threatening injuries for a laparotomy (operation of the abdomen)."

"No," Linda said. "We are not ready."

"There is no time to get ready. I am coming up with the patient now or she will die."

I ordered four units of blood talked to her parents and obtained consent for surgery and rushed to the OR with the patient. The OR team was still preparing for the operation as we quickly moved the patient to the operating table. An additional nurse was assigned to the room to facilitate and accelerate the preparations. The first thing we did was to have the anesthesiologist intubate the patient (place a tube into her windpipe) and connect her to a respirator. In rapid sequence, I placed a CVP (central venous pressure) catheter in position and started transfusing O-negative blood while she was given general anesthesia. I then inserted two chest tubes, one on the right and one on the left side of the chest, which were connected to an antiquated system of two bottles, where the blood will drain and be collected. Upon connection of the chest tube to the collection bottles, a half-liter of blood drained immediately in them. Despite the transfusions the patient was still in shock and the anesthesiologist said he could not record a blood pressure.

As we opened the abdomen, we noticed that the abdominal cavity was full of blood. We aspirated the blood and did a full exploration, examining every organ and every structure that could be visualized or palpated. The findings were discouraging. There was a retroperitoneal hematoma, a collection of blood outside the posterior border of the abdominal cavity, indicating bleeding. I knew that this bleeding was a result of the pelvic fracture, which had showed up on the x-rays when she arrived at the ER. There was nothing to do about the bleeding, which was self-limiting and controlled by the pressure created by the accumulating blood.

The other findings were a smashed spleen with active bleeding and a crushed upper half of the left kidney. I asked the nurse to place a call to a urologist as I proceeded to control the bleeding from the injured spleen. I clamped the artery and vein connected to the organ, and then removed the mushy splenic remnants. A urologist responded to my call and joined me to take care of the injured kidney.

We removed half of the left kidney and left the other half in place. That was enough to sustain life if for whatever reason the other kidney was lost in the future, due to disease or cancer. Once again we see the wisdom of nature, providing the body with a pair of some important organs like eyes, ears, kidneys, ovaries and testicles, so if one is lost, the remaining organ can still sustain life.

Once we finished with everything we had to do in the abdomen, and despite transfusions of numerous pints of blood, Dr. Dermit O'Herlihy, the anesthesiologist, said he could not record a blood pressure and the pulse rate was too high. This indicated that there was likely another source of blood loss. I closed the abdomen, applied the wound dressing, and directed my attention to the chest. First, I checked the drainage bottles connected from the chest tubes to the wall suction. I noticed that one of the "corks" was loose and failed to completely seal the bottle, rendering the suction ineffective. I reapplied the "cork" correctly and established a seal, which resulted in several liters of blood draining from the right chest tube. That was the reason there was no detectable blood pressure.

There was a serious injury to the right lung, which prompted the need for a thoracotomy (opening of the chest cavity) in order to identify and control the source of bleeding. I asked the nurse to call in a chest surgeon.

I went to talk to the patient's parents waiting near the ER; Zoe was their only child. I informed them of the findings and the type of operation I performed. I also told them that there were additional injuries to the right chest that had to be addressed by a chest surgeon. In the meantime, the chest surgeon, Dr. Roe, responded to the call and I told him the situation. He said he was on his way to the hospital. I had the parents sign the consent for the operation and went back to the OR. I prepared and positioned the patient for a right thoracotomy (opening the right side of her chest)..

The scrub technician got the thoracotomy instruments and the thoracic surgeon, Dr. Roe, arrived in the OR but he was not feeling well. When it was time to make the incision, he handed me the scalpel. I did not hesitate to proceed. This was not the first time I did a thoracotomy. I had spent substantial time during my training in the thoracic surgery service.

The chest cavity was fully exposed and exploration revealed a laceration of the lung's upper lobe with active bleeding. I controlled the bleeding and then proceeded to do a wedge resection of the upper lobe portion that was injured. The anesthesiologist kept transfusing more blood and finally was able to record a blood pressure. I washed out the chest cavity and closed the chest wall. Completing the operation.

The patient now had a blood pressure, albeit low, as we prepared to transfer her to the ICU. I thanked everyone for their help, especially Linda S., the nurse that stayed with us through the operation. She had really worked hard.

"Do you really think she is going to make it? Do you think all of this was worth it?" Linda asked me. She had just finished her shift and was going on vacation.

"She has two things going for her", I said. "The first is her young age and the second is her good health before the accident." I could have added a third, "she had me taking care of her," but I did not want to sound bombastic. I thought I will let my results speak for themselves.

The post-operative course was expected to be stormy, with a strong likelihood of serious complications. When someone sustained numerous life-threatening injuries to so many areas of the body and had also lost a lot of blood that required multiple transfusions, a person's ability to fight infection would be severely compromised and predisposed to major complications.

Zoe had suffered multiple rib fractures, contusion and laceration of the right lung with bleeding. Then there was crushing injury to the spleen and upper part of her left kidney, and fracture of he pelvis with bleeding in the surrounding area. That is quite a combination of life threatening injuries, pushing her very close to death.

I talked to her parents and explained that she was in critical condition and breathing with life support. It was expected that she would have to stay on a respirator for about three weeks because the multiple broken ribs are interfering with her ability to breath. I told them I could not guarantee anything, but I was very optimistic that she was going to pull through. The trick with Zoe's care was doing a detailed and comprehensive evaluation of her condition daily or even more often, like two, three, or more times a day. Frequent evaluation would allow me to identify and address any problem as it arose, and before it became unmanageable.

I ordered a TPN, (total parenteral nutrition), which was a method of feeding a person through a vein. I also requested a pulmonary consult to manage the respirator settings. I stayed with the patient in the ICU until late at night and adjusted the fluid intake and evaluated her blood level. The patient became stable with normal vital signs (blood pressure and pulse) as well as good blood oxygen levels. I headed for home after I left strict orders to be called for any changes in the patient's condition.

The next morning when I arrived at the ICU, I was told that the patient's chest and face were swollen, but she was otherwise stable. I was not alarmed and when I examined the patient, I found the characteristic crackling sound caused by subcutaneous emphysema—the escape of air from the chest cavity to the space under the skin through the chest wound. This caused her chest, neck and face to swell and even forced her eyes closed shut. It looked bad even though it was an innocuous condition that would subside as healing progressed. I had seen this before with an older man named Eddie who was brought to Kings County Hospital with fractured ribs.

Zoe was given narcotic analgesics and was in an induced coma to allow the respirator to function without patient interference. The blood results indicated that there was no evidence of active bleeding and the kidney function was good. Her vital signs were stable, and the oxygen blood levels and carbon dioxide were within the normal parameters.

Her mother had literally camped in the ICU waiting room, agonizing over her only child's life. She was alarmed when she saw her daughter's face and neck blown up like a balloon, but I reassured her that the swelling will subside on its own and will not influence her daughter's chance for survival.

I continued to update Zoe's parents about their daughter's condition every time I visited. Thankfully, I generally had good news for them every day. Zoe continued to improve slowly and steadily. I made numerous adjustments to her treatment every single day according to what the blood or culture results demanded. In general, her youth and good health before the accident worked on her side. She did not present any major complications or unexpected problems.

A week after her operation I removed the breathing tube through her larynx (voice box) and replaced it with a special tube, inserted directly into the windpipe through a cut in her neck. The procedure — a tracheostomy—was done to prevent permanent damage to the voice box caused when a breathing tube stays through the voice box for an extended period of time.

It took a week for the chest, neck and face swelling to go away and for Zoe to look like herself again. After three weeks, she regained the ability to breathe on her own, as the ribs healed enough to provide stabilization of the chest wall. She was disconnected from the respirator and allowed to breath on her own, through the windpipe tube, which was left in place. A day later, the blood oxygen and carbon dioxide levels were normal and confirmed her ability to breath on her own. Once I removed the tracheostomy tube, Zoe could speak again, which made her mother and everyone, including Zoe of course, very happy. Her nutrition, with the support of the TPN, was good, her hemoglobin normal and her breathing restored. All her body functions had returned to normal. She was started on a liquid diet and subsequently given solid food, but her recovery was far from over. She still had a mountain of intensive physical therapy to climb before she returned to normal. The relative immobility for over three weeks, the extensive damage to the tissues from the accident, the operations of her abdomen, chest and neck, the fractured pelvis, all took their toll on her ability to even stand up straight, let alone walk without help. She started physical therapy right after she was taken off the respirator and would continue as an out patent after she was discharged.

When she was transferred out of the ICU, I sat down with her and explained her injuries and the treatment she received. I then told her what treatments she still needed before she returned to normal. She was amazed at the description of her injuries and told me she did not remember anything about her stay in the ICU, which was a blessing in my estimation.

The OR nurse, Linda S., had returned from her vacation and the first thing she wanted to know was how Zoe was doing. "What happened with that patient with the multiple injuries that you operated on before I went on vacation?" she asked.

I responded that the patient was alive and well and she was expected to fully recover from her injuries. Many people were interested to know how Zoe was doing because of the extent and severity of her injuries and her relatively smooth recovery, especially Mary R., the new OR technician who was Zoe's classmate in high school.

Zoe went on to achieve a full recovery and live a normal life. She called me one time from Florida for an emergency. Her mother had sustained a bad laceration of her right leg and they were boarding a plane to New Jersey. She wanted me to take care of her mother's injury. I am sure that there were plenty of surgeons who could have effectively treated her mother in Florida. Because of her love for her mother, or her trust for me, or maybe both, they decided to get on a plane and come to me for her mother's care. From the airport, they went directly to the HNH-ER and called me upon their arrival. I repaired the extensive laceration of her mother's leg in the operating room under general anesthesia and kept her in the hospital overnight. I was really touched by their trust in me, though I felt confident that I had earned it. I am still in touch with Zoe. I talked to her recently, in 2019, 38 years after her accident, and I am happy to say that she is in good health and doing well.

Another interesting situation evolved on Greek Easter, April 26, 1981, one week after Catholic Easter. Sharon, myself, and our children were dressed up and ready to leave the house for midnight mass. As we were going out the door, I heard the phone ringing. I went back into the house and answered it. It was HNH's ER doctor informing me that he had a patient with "acute abdomen" and free air in the abdominal x-ray. The patient needed an emergency operation and I was the surgeon on call. It was a dire situation that needed my immediate attention. I apologized to Sharon, who had to attend midnight mass alone with two small children—four-year-old Christos and 20 month-old Stavros. She headed for the church as I rushed to the ER.

When I arrived at the ER, I interviewed and examined the patient, who was a 61-year-old man in excruciating pain. His name was Wayne. The first thing I did was put my hand on his belly to assess the situation. His abdomen was rigid, hard like a board, which indicated acute peritonitis and the need for emergency surgical intervention ASAP. The patient told me that he hadn't been feeling well recently and was plagued by abdominal cramps, abdominal distention and constipation, since his

Easter a week earlier. His doctor had referred him to a specialist, but he hadn't yet gone. A couple of hours before he came to the ER, he said he felt an "explosion" inside his belly that caused instantly excruciating pain which persisted since.

After I reviewed all the tests and x-rays, I diagnosed that he had a blown intestine caused by a blockage. I explained to him that he needed an emergency operation and probably the removal of part of his intestine.

"Anything Doctor! Do anything to take this pain away," he said. "And do it right now!"

It was past midnight by the time all of the necessary OR preparations were done. With the patient under general anesthesia the abdomen had become completely soft. When I opened the abdomen, a strong putrid fecal smell filled the room. The abdomen was filled with the patient's Easter meal from the week before, along with feces, which fully explained the patient's excruciating pain. Pieces of lamb chops, peas and corn could be seen in every crevice and corner of the abdomen, together with liquid stool. All these belonged inside the intestine not in the free peritoneal cavity. I had seen many contaminated, dirty abdomens, but that one was the worst and the most complicated, covering the entire surface of the abdominal cavity.

I did a fast exploration and discovered the source of the contamination. The right colon had ruptured and ended up in the center of the abdomen. There was a cancer at the colon, which closed up the lumen. All the bowel content was backed up, and the colon was blown up, inflated by the stool and the gas, until it exploded inside the belly like an over inflated balloon. The content of the bowel was scattered allover the abdominal cavity. I used a large clamp to close off the hole of the ruptured right colon to stop the continued soiling of the abdomen, and then proceeded to irrigate the belly with over 20 liters of normal saline. I poured the saline in, one liter at a time, manipulating the structures inside the belly, and using suction canula to aspirate the dirty saline out. I spent over an hour picking chunks of lamb, peas and corn from all over the abdomen until the cavity was clear of any visible contaminant.

I then proceeded to perform the definitive operation. I connected the small intestine to the colon after resecting the right colon (large intestine) and distal end of the small intestine. I removed a hard tumor, which had caused the blockage of the bowel and the backup of the stool, the distention, and the explosion of the colon. Clinically, I thought the tumor appeared to be cancerous. I again checked the liver and the entire abdomen looking for possible spread of the cancer, but thankfully there was no visible sign of cancer metastasis (spread of the tumor, beyond its point of origin). I was sure that this poor man was going to have a stormy post-operative course, with probable formation of intra-abdominal abscesses (pockets of pus inside the belly) and a wound infection due to the large volume of germ-ridden contaminants that came into contact with the patient's tissues.

After the connection of the small intestine to the colon I placed some drains inside the abdomen and closed the main long incision. Because of the patient's critical condition, I transferred him to the ICU. The most serious complication would have been a breakdown of the anastomosis—the connection between the small intestine and the colon. To avoid that I kept the patient NPO (nothing by mouth) and placed him on total parenteral nutrition (TPN), giving him all the necessary nutrients and vitamins through a central venous catheter to the superior vena cava, the big vein in the chest.

The post-operative course was stormy as expected. The patient, after all, came to the hospital with the worst possible peritonitis. He was in critical condition and it was my duty to try my best to help him recover. He developed a bad wound infection, which I cleaned and washed out every single day. I put him on wide spectrum antibiotics from the time I first saw him and continued to adjust the type and dose of the antibiotics based on the culture results of the specimens I sent to the lab during the operation, and the wound cultures obtained every three days thereafter.

Wayne had now become my friend after seeing him at least two times a day. I was the only doctor taking care of him. Nowadays, a patient in his condition would require an intensivist (specialist in intensive care), to follow him in the ICU, a cardiologist, an infectious disease specialist to write the antibiotic orders, in addition to myself taking care of the wound and the nutrition. The problem with multiple specialties attending the patients is that there could be lack of coordination of the patient's care. Sometimes having too many subspecialists weighing in could have an adverse effect on the patient's health. After all everybody knows that "too many cooks, spoil the soup".

Wayne was in bad shape, but he was improving slowly and steadily. My experience had taught me that no matter how bad the patient's condition was, as long as he/she was improving, there was an excellent chance of recovery. After 10 days in the ICU, he was well enough to be transferred to a regular bed, where he continued to recover at a steady pace. Twenty days after the operation, he was already walking around, feeling strong, and the wound drainage had decreased substantially. When I listened to the abdomen, I heard good bowel sounds, indicating normal function of the intestines. The albumin of the blood was trending towards normal levels, a positive development that indicated he was at a stage where he could be started on clear liquids by mouth and on his way to full recovery. The danger to his life had decreased substantially and he would be ready for discharge in a few days.

I went to make my morning visit and prepared to tell him the good news.

"Good morning Wayne, how are you today?"

"Good morning Doc," he said. "Do you know what I was dreaming about last night?"

"No. What was it?" I replied.

"I was dreaming of an ice cold 7-Up!"

I smiled.

"Wayne, I am happy to inform you that your dream will come true this morning!"

I turned to the nurse and asked her to "please get the patient an ice cold 7-Up."

I explained to Wayne, that his life did not appear to be in danger anymore and everything was going as well as anybody could hope. I explained to him that the pathology report showed that he had cancer, but all the lymph nodes were negative, an indication that the cancer was most likely localized in the colon that was removed. I also informed him that while in the operating room, I checked for signs cancer spread but found no sign of cancer anywhere else.

I changed his wound dressing and then went to visit and care for my other patients. When I finished rounds, I went back to Wayne. As soon as he saw me, he was happy to tell me that he had his 7-Up.

"Doc, I could never imagine, that 7-Up could taste so good!"

That made me happy. I smiled, wished him well and left the floor. The next day I advanced his diet to full liquids, and the day after to a regular diet. Wayne was a landscaper who worked alone and had no insurance. I wanted to get him home as soon as possible. I found out that he was my neighbor, living diametrically opposite my house on the same block in New Milford. His house was adorned by a beautiful rose garden with hundreds of roses blooming at the same time of different varieties and colors. I always admired his rose garden whenever I happened to pass by his house, which was actually very often. After he tolerated the regular diet, I told him that he could be discharged, and I would pass by his house every day to change his dressing.

I did see him every day and changed his dressing until his wound had healed completely, about six weeks after his discharge from the hospital. At that point, he was walking outside and started doing some work too. I sent him a bill for my services, which read: "Exploratory laparotomy, abdominal lavage and right hemicolectomy, charge $3,000, minus rose rights, $1,500. Balance due, $1,500. I wanted to give him a break since he had no insurance and would not be able to work for another month or so.

On his next visit to the office, he paid his bill and also handed me a clipper. "Doc, this is for you, to cut as many roses as you want, whenever you want!"

A couple of weeks later, I heard loud banging noises in my backyard, very early in the morning. I looked out the window and saw Wayne creating a rose garden for my house. His gesture really touched my heart, seeing the special way he had chosen to show me his appreciation for saving his life. I went out to the back yard and thanked him for his thoughtfulness.

I kept in touch with him and his wife, who later developed a tumor of the colon. I did her operation and she did fine. Both Wayne and his wife consulted me for every health-related matter, and I referred them to the right doctor for treatment. Wayne was cured of his cancer and so was his wife and they lived a long happy life. They reached the milestone of their 50th wedding anniversary, which they celebrated in a grand fashion, an event I had the honor to attend. The lamb, corn and the peas picked from Wayne's belly during surgery was discussed plenty of times among the OR staff, who were repeatedly asking about the patient's condition and showed their concern about his health. Wayne died in his 80s of causes unrelated to cancer.

I was busy at both Holy Name and Englewood hospitals, but I very rarely received any calls from Bergen Pines Hospital in Paramus, which is now called Bergen Regional Hospital. I did a big operation for free on an indigent patient who had cancer of the gums. I removed part of the floor of the mouth and part of the patient's right jaw. I also removed the musculature and lymph nodes from her neck, starting from the jaw to the collar bone. The patient did fine and recovered well.

The other operation I was called to do at Bergen Pines Hospital was for a ruptured spleen that was caused by a car accident. I took the patient to the operating room for removal of the ruptured spleen that was bleeding. When the patient was put to sleep, I asked the nurse to insert a catheter into the bladder to monitor urine output during the operation. She placed the catheter, but no urine was coming out.

"Are you sure you put the catheter in the bladder?" I asked and she assured me that she had. I was scrubbed and ready to start the operation but did not feel comfortable going ahead without the certainty that the patient had a catheter in place. I scrubbed out and went to check the catheter myself. Sure enough, the catheter was in the rectum! I asked for a new catheter placed it at the right place in the bladder, and 400 cc of urine drained out.

"What is your name?" I asked the nurse. She refused to tell me. "Never mind. The important thing is that if you cannot tell the difference between the rectum and the urethra you don't belong in the operating room."

The operation went well, and the patient recovered. She was discharged home in five days. The day after she was discharged, I handed in my resignation from the medical staff at Bergen Pines Hospital.

I was at the end of my second year of my practice in New Jersey and I was getting too busy in both Holy Name and Englewood Hospital. Covering both hospitals was getting problematic. One time, the situation came to a crisis. I had to attend to a patient with severe, active bleeding from the gastrointestinal tract at Holy Name Hospital, and at the same time I had a patient with acute gallbladder infection scheduled for surgery at Englewood Hospital. The gallbladder patient was in the pre-op holding area, and the bleeding patient was in nuclear medicine department having a test to determine the source of his bleeding. There was no way I was going to leave the bleeding patient alone, so I called the OR at Englewood Hospital and told them to take the gallbladder patient back to her room, and I would let them know when I was ready to proceed with the operation. I had scheduled that patient early in the day, but they waited to finish everybody's operations before they gave me a spot to operate since I was "the new kid on the block".

The test of the bleeding patient revealed that the bleeding was coming from the mid small intestine. He was already scheduled and prepared for the operation, so I rushed him to the operating room for an exploratory laparotomy and small bowel resection. By the time I started the operation, it was already 10 p.m.. I finished at 11:30 p.m. I was able to identify that the bleeding originated from a small bowel polyp. After resecting that portion of the intestine, I reconnected the remaining intestine.

The patient was stable, and his problem was solved, so I turned my attention to the other patient with the gallbladder problem. I called the Englewood OR and told them I would be there in 10 minutes. I saw the patient in the pre-op holding area and apologized for the delay. I started her operation at 30 minutes past midnight and finished by 1:15 a.m. By the time I finished writing the post-operative orders and note, and dictated the operation, it was already 2 a.m.

This situation made me uncomfortable, so I decided to resign from the active staff at Englewood Hospital since most of my work was done at Holy Name Hospital (HNH). I also liked the HNH better because they had a superb nursing staff and better relationships among the surgical staff. I decided to focus my practice on HNH only, which made life much easier.

Not only was I busy with my patients at HNH, I also assisted the busiest surgeon at HNH, Dr. Abad, with all of his operations. The big operations associated with difficult and challenging problems kept coming my way.

I had not seen any patients with gunshot wounds at HNH until one Friday night when I was called in for a patient in the ER who was shot in the belly and was complaining of severe pain. I rushed to the hospital, interviewed and examined the patient and reviewed the x-ray and blood work results. The patient was a 27-year-old man from Teaneck with an entrance wound in the left upper abdomen and an exit wound in the left flank back area. He was in severe pain, which indicated an injury to vital organs. I called the anesthesiologist and the operating room team, prepared the paperwork and had the patient sign the consent for the operation.

At exploration he was found to have injuries to four vital organs. He had an injury to the stomach, with spillage of gastric juices into the abdominal cavity. His spleen was injured and actively bleeding, and the tail of the pancreas was shuttered. In addition to all of that, the upper half of the left kidney was injured. The bullet had caused a lot of damage, but I had seen such cases before many times at KCHC. I removed the spleen, resected the tail of the pancreas and half the kidney, and sutured closed the holes in the stomach. He did not develop any complications and was discharged home a week later.

My office was getting too busy, and Sharon's workload was getting too much to bear. We went on and hired our first employee in 1983, a resident of New Milford. Pat Stagno had worked at another surgeon's office before, so she was familiar with the task in hand in assisting Sharon. A good and loyal worker, she remained with us until she retired 30 years later.

In 1983 Debbie called the office very upset. She was a family friend, who had lost her mother from breast cancer, and she just noticed a breast lump. She was in her 40s, and that was the age of her mother, when she was diagnosed with the breast cancer that killed her. I told her to come right to the office so I could examine her and decide what to do. She was there in 10 minutes, terrified with the thought that she could meet the same fate that her mother had. She had three children in their teens and wanted to see them grow up.

I found the tumor she had described. It was a hard lump, measuring about one half of an inch in diameter, a small mass relatively speaking. Clinically it had the characteristics of a malignant tumor, taking her family history into consideration.

I discussed my findings with her and did stress that despite the fact that it did appear to be a cancerous mass, we could not be sure until I took it out and examined it under the microscope. The tumor could be examined at the time of the operation and if it were positive for cancer, the breast would be removed together with the lymph nodes of the armpit. I also tried to calm her down, stressing that even if it were a cancerous tumor it would still be in the early stages and it was possible she could be cured, but she was inconsolable.

Three days later I removed the tumor, which turned out to be cancerous. I proceeded to remove the breast and lymph nodes, as we had discussed. She recovered well and before she was discharged home, we received the final pathology report of the removed breast and lymph nodes. The tumor was 1.5 cm in diameter and no other tumor was identified in the breast or in the lymph nodes. The fact that all the lymph nodes removed were negative was a very good indication that the cancer was localized in the breast, which indicated that, it was in stage 1, with a relatively good prognosis. I explained the findings to her and asked her to see a medical oncologist for possible chemotherapy. She declined, stating that she did not want to go through chemotherapy. I followed her with annual exams until I retired in 2016. She is now 80 years old. Debbie was cured from the breast cancer. She lived long enough to see not just her children, but also her grand children grow up!

Another patient I will never forget, is Tom, a 59-year-old Irish man referred to me for abdominal pain and weight loss of several weeks' duration. He also complained of feeling tired and had lost his appetite.

On physical examination he had a palpable mass in the right upper abdomen associated with moderate to severe pain. He was admitted to the Hospital and work up with a barium enema revealed a tumor of the right flexure of the colon, next to the liver, and an abscess next to it. His white blood count was over 20,000, which confirmed the abscess diagnosis. I explained to him that he had a tumor of the colon, which had probably perforated, causing a collection of puss and that he needed an operation to remove a portion of the colon and evacuation and cleaning of the abscess. He consented, so we proceeded with the operation.

During the operation I found that the tumor had extended beyond the colon directly into the right lobe of the liver, with contamination and an abscess formation. There was no sign of distant spread, so I proceeded to remove the right lobe of the liver together with the cancerous portion of the colon. I then connected the small intestine with the remaining colon. The abscess was a part of the specimen removed. This was a very big operation, but it gave the patient the possibility of cure. If no distant spread of the cancer had occurred, something that would be determined from the pathology report, as well as the passage of time.

Post operatively the patient recovered well. The pathology report was received before he was discharged home. It showed that the margins of the liver and the colon were free and clear from cancer, indicating that the tumor was removed completely locally. It also showed that all the lymph nodes removed with the specimen were free of tumor. This was a very encouraging sign, because that would be the first area that the colon cancer would spread, reinforcing the possibility that the patient had a good chance of being cured! I explained everything to Tom before he went home and asked him to make an appointment in one month with my office for follow up. During his visit in my office he told me he felt terrific. His appetite had returned, he started gaining weight and he was not tired any more. I asked him to come back for follow up in three months, because we had to keep on top of things, in case something showed up, and gave him an appointment. Three months came and went, but Tom was a no show. My secretary tried to call him, but his phone was disconnected. I did not know what happened to him.

Five years later I saw his name in the office appointments book, for that day. I was wondering whether he was still alive. That question was answered. He was alive but did he make the appointment because the cancer came back?

That question was answered soon enough when he was called in my consultation room.

"Tom what happened to you? I was looking for you. How are you doing, and what brings you back"?

"I could not be better doctor except that my hemorrhoids are killing me!"

I did a complete physical examination. There was no sign of cancer. The only finding was a very swollen hemorrhoid with a large blood clot inside it! I opened it under local anesthesia and removed the clot. I gave him an appointment to came back in a week, but he never showed up, so I thought to myself: "No news, good news! He must be doing fine!"

This patient's cancer had infiltrated beyond the boundaries of the organ where it first developed to the liver and involved a large portion of the right lobe, but it did not spread to any distal location. In this instance the radical dissection of all the visible tumor of the organs involved resulted in the cure of the patient.

Another patient who presented with a similar problem was James. He was 61 years old and presented with the clinical picture of bowel obstruction, a blockage of the intestine. He was admitted through the ER with abdominal pain, distension, vomiting and weight loss. Complete work up revealed a malignant tumor of the colon next to the stomach.

James had symptoms for several months but did not want to see a doctor, until he reached a point when he could not eat and was very weak. I reviewed the results of all the tests and explained to the patient that he had cancer of the colon that closed up the lumen. He understood that the only solution was to have an operation to remove the malignant tumor and restore the bowel function.

During the operation I found a very large cancerous mass of the colon with direct extension to the stomach, the spleen, the diaphragm, the abdominal wall and the tail of the pancreas. This was a very advanced cancer locally, but there was no evidence of any spread to distant organs. The liver, where the colon cancer spreads first, was normal. I knew that if I could remove all the visible tumor, the patient had a good chance at extending his life and even a cure.

I removed a large part of the colon, the part of the stomach that was infiltrated by the cancer, the spleen, the tail of the pancreas, the involved portion of the diaphragm, and the part of the abdominal wall that had tumor by direct extension. Six different organs were partially removed together and sent to pathology as one mass. The diaphragm defect was closed with a piece of goretex graft. The portion of the stomach removed did not effect the continuity of its lumen, and the abdominal wall defect resulting from the removal of the tumor was closed primarily. The colon was full of stool because of the obstruction, precluding the reattachment of its remaining ends. I fashioned a colostomy instead. Post operatively the patient did amazingly well and was discharged home 10 days later. He was offered further treatment with chemotherapy but refused.

He was readmitted three months later and had the colostomy closed and the colon reattached. I saw him every three months for two years, and he remained cancer free. He made another appointment six years later, at which time he informed me that he was found to have a lung tumor and was told he needed an operation. He wanted me to do it, but I informed him that I was not a specialist for lung surgery, but my friend Dr. Zairis could do the operation. I highly recommended Dr. Zairis, and I could help him do the surgery, as we usually worked together, and James agreed to that. The important thing is that this patient, despite the locally advanced cancer, had no distant metastasis, so the radical operation that I performed cured him from the disease, giving him an extension of useful living. The lung cancer was new and had nothing to do with the colon cancer.

If the Lion is the King of the Animal Kingdom, The Whipple Operation is the King of the Surgical Procedures. It involves removal of a part of the stomach, a part of the common bile duct, a part of the pancreas, and a part of the small intestine. Once all these portions of the organs are removed the continuity of the systems involved have to be reconstructed. For the reconstruction it takes a lot of talent, a lot of skill and a lot of patience. The operation is done for cancer of the pancreas, or the bile duct, or the beginning of the small intestine. There are usually a lot of complications associated with this procedure and the long tem survival of the patients is very limited.

I did several Whipple operations, but one patient in particular comes to mind. This was a slim Chinese man who presented with jaundice from a cancer of the end of his bile tube, inside the head of the pancreas. I operated on him in 1990. He recovered well, and I saw him in my office three and then six months after the operation, and then he disappeared. I did not know what happened to him until 2006, when he called the office and talked to Sharon! He asked her for a copy of his operative report, his pathology report and the discharge summary of his admission. He said he needed it for his Medical Doctor, who did not believe that he had a Whipple operation, because people don't survive for so long after that procedure. Sharon prepared the copies of the documents he requested and gave them to him. That answered my question.

Another patient that had a similar problem was Mary B.. She was the mother of a nurse who worked in the ICU. She was 61 years old and needed a cataract Surgery. Blood work done for her preparation, showed an abnormality of the liver tests. Further work up revealed a cancer of the end of the bile duct inside the head of the pancreas. I did a Whipple operation in 1986. I followed her for a year and she was doing very well. Thereafter I would ask her daughter whenever I saw her at the hospital about How Mary B. was doing. The last time I heard that she was doing fine at the age of 90, was in 2015.

Another interesting situation developed on a patient I operated on for cancer of the nasopharynx, the area behind the nose. The cancer had also spread to the lymph nodes of the neck. She got radiation at the primary tumor site, and I did a left radical neck dissection of the muscles and lymph nodes. The patient was the mother of an assistant administrator at the hospital who also chose the medical attending physician in his mother's care. He chose Dr. Danny, someone I thought was an obnoxious man, and I did not particularly like.

"I will be the doctor. You just do the operation," he told to me.

I did not even respond. After the operation, I took the patient to the ICU and she was recovering well. The second day after surgery, I went to see her after finishing my first operation of the day. Outside her room, I saw her son.

"How is your mother?"

He stunned me with his answer. "Not well. They are trying to revive her!"

I rushed in the room and there was Dr. Danny.

"She had a cardiac arrest," he said and looked at his watch. "I will pronounce her dead at 10:26 a.m."

"No, you will not!" I screamed.

I pushed him out of the way and started resuscitation and at the same time asked the nurse in the room what had happened. Dr. Danny walked out of the room and told the son that his mother was not going to make it. The nurse informed me that the patient had some PVCs (extra heart beats, out of rhythm) and Dr. Danny injected a drug intravenously to treat the problem and then the patient went into cardiac arrest, i.e. the heart stopped beating. Based on the nurse's description of the sequence of the events leading to the cardiac arrest, I concluded that Dr. Danny caused the problem by injecting the drug too fast. In that case, continuing resuscitation had a good chance of bringing the heart function back and saving the patient. Sure enough, after five minutes of resuscitation, the patient's heart started beating on its own, and the doctor-induced death was reversed.

I went outside and talked to the son. I informed him that his mother was resuscitated successfully, and she was OK. I also asked him to request that Dr. Danny be removed from the patient's care before he does something stupid again. The son went a step further and proceeded to fire Dr. Danny. He asked a cardiologist, whom I trusted, to assist with his mother's care. The patient's recovery from then on was smooth and uneventful, and she was discharged home in good condition a few days later. Even now when I remember that patient, I get upset thinking that had I not walked in when I did, she would have died at the hands of Dr. Danny.

Another event that almost took a patient's life had to do with a misdiagnosis. A female patient in her 50s was admitted with fever and abdominal pain. She was started on intravenous fluids, but no other action was taken. The next morning, she spiked a fever of 103 degrees, which triggered convulsions. Her physician reacted to that by asking a cardiologist to evaluate her. The cardiologist saw her and performed a spinal tap, which is a procedure that involves inserting a needle in the back, into the spinal canal to get some fluid for examination.

This was a totally unnecessary procedure that would be of no benefit for the patient's condition. I was consulted next, because the patient had complained of abdominal pain when she first came to the hospital. I had been making my morning rounds when I received the call, so I was at the patient's bedside within a few minutes after having checked her laboratory test results first. The patient appeared to have had a stroke by the time I saw her. Examination of the abdomen revealed all the findings of acute appendicitis. I discussed my diagnosis with her family and recommended an appendectomy, thinking that her sepsis (severe infection) caused by the appendicitis had something to do with the stroke, in which case the only way she could improve would be by treating the cause of the sepsis.

The family consented to the operation and I promptly proceeded to operate on the patient. The findings were impressive. The appendix had ruptured, and the abdomen was full of pus. I removed the appendix and washed the abdomen with large amounts of warm saline. I placed a drain in the pelvis, closed the wound and transferred the patient to the ICU. She was unresponsive and unable to breath on her own, so she remained on the respirator. I started her on TPN the next day. She was stable, though her mental function was still compromised due to the stroke.

Again, I made sure I kept ahead of any more complications and spent a lot of time at her bedside. The nurses seemed convinced that the patient had no chance of recovery but did not know how to tell me, that whatever I was doing was futile. A brave nurse found the courage to ask me, the million-dollar question.

"Dr. Christoudias, do you think it's worth it? Do you really think there is a chance she can get better?"

My answer was very simple. "I've heard that question before. The truth is, if we give up on her, she will definitely not pull through. Taking into consideration that she was in excellent health before this event happened, she has a good chance of recovery if we give her the treatment she deserves. I noticed some movement of her extremities and that is a very good sign."

This patient was a supervisor at a large company, and I was hoping that she would respond to some good, old-fashioned medical and nursing care. I performed a tracheostomy about a week after the operation to prevent damage to her voice box, something that could happen from prolonged pressure by the breathing tube. In a few more days, she was responding to verbal commands and moving all her extremities. She was soon able to breath on her own without the help of the respirator and was transferred out of the ICU to a regular bed. She got intensive physical therapy, which she continued after she was discharged home. A full recovery was expected and achieved.

I was delighted to receive a post card of the Parthenon and the Acropolis of Athens from her, a year later. She thanked me for making her dream of visiting Greece possible. I did not tell anybody then, but that postcard brought tears of joy to my eyes, realizing the immense impact my actions could have on some people's lives.

While all these things were going on with my practice, we had a new family member, a baby girl born on Feb. 27, 1982. We named her Maritsa after my mother. She was a beautiful girl, like her mother, and was the perfect addition to our two boys, who were demonstrating their ingenuity with their activities. My only regret was that I was not able to spend as much time as I would have liked with my children due to my very demanding and busy practice.

That year I made sure that we took a vacation together, in August 1982. My niece Maria, Stavros's daughter, came from Cyprus to spend a month with us so we all drove down the jersey shore to Wildwood, where we stayed for a week. On the way there, 6-month old Maritsa vomited in Sharon's handbag, freaking everybody out. The baby turned out to be fine and we had a nice time, with daily visits to the boardwalk. We spent a lot of time on the rides and playing games, enjoying every minute. Stavros was fixated on the bam-bam girls, a bunch of mermaids carved on the side of a model ship on the promenade. Christos developed a tendency to wander around and get lost, so we had to keep an eye on him.

Sharon was always busy taking care of everybody else, which made me wonder whether she ever had a chance to relax, taking into consideration that she also worked hard as my office manager, nurse, secretary and accountant. We always enjoyed the opportunity to travel and be together without the demands of my practice. My professional life was demanding but I knew what I was getting into when I became a Doctor. I never regretted it and never complained about it.

Wildwood became our favorite vacation spot and we always spent at least one week every year, in the area. The trip was long and traveled almost the entire span of the Garden State Parkway. It became nearly impossible when we happened to hit traffic. Whenever that happened it triggered intense questioning by the kids. "Are we there yet?" they asked over and over until we reached "there." The best part of the Wildwood vacation was the boardwalk, with the endless rides and games, which led to collecting countless stuffed animals. The worst part of the vacation was our trip back home. The kids wanted the vacation to last forever, but everything, good or bad, comes to an end sooner or later.

Another patient I took care of, early in my practice, was a 35-year-old construction worker who had a horrific accident at work. He was working on a ladder at a construction site when he slipped and fell, and landed on an exposed iron rod that projected out of the cement floor. The iron rod penetrated his left buttock, causing excruciating pain and bleeding. He was brought to HNH-ER where I was called to see him and take care of him. On physical examination the abdomen was rigid, indicating penetration of the iron rod through the tissues and into the abdominal cavity, with probable injury to the colon. The patient's description of the incident was very revealing.

"Doctor, I felt such a pain, I thought I was dead!"

It did not take any effort to convince Jay that he needed an operation. I called the operating room and alerted them that I had a critically ill patient who needed emergency, life-saving surgery. One of the rooms was already being prepared for another operation, which was pushed back to accommodate the emergency patient. Yielding your scheduled time to another surgeon—called bumping—was a common practice in any operating room. Sooner or later every surgeon finds himself in a situation when he has to rush a patient to the operating room, for a life-saving emergency operation. Some surgeons try to abuse this privilege, but when they do, they pay dearly for it—surgeons would not trust them anymore and will stop yielding to them.

Jay was taken to the operating room within 15 minutes and placed under general anesthesia. Though the wound was on the buttock, the life-threatening injuries were in the abdomen. After packing the buttock wound with sterile gauze to control the local bleeding, I opened the abdomen and exposed the pelvis. There were free stool in the abdomen, indicating a laceration of the rectal wall. Careful exploration revealed the injured area of the rectum. I placed a clamp proximal to the injury and stopped the stool from spilling into the abdomen. The iron rod had gone through the skin and the rectum and its path went by the large pelvic vessels, lacerating some of the secondary branches and causing significant blood loss. Had the rod injured the large pelvic artery and vein, the patient would have not survived the trip to the hospital. The bleeding vessels were identified, clamped and tied closed, which fully controlled the bleeding.

The abdomen was then cleared of the stool and vigorously irrigated with warm saline solution to decrease the concentration of the contaminants in the abdominal cavity. The area of the colon laceration was also vigorously washed, and the injured edges debrided and repaired. The intestinal clamp was then taken off the rectum and the colon mobilized and brought out of the abdomen through a different incision and sutured to the skin. The abdomen was then sutured closed, leaving the exteriorized colon exposed. The exposed colon was then opened and a colostomy bag attached to the skin around it to collect the stool. This is what we call a colostomy, which in this case was diverting the flow of the stool away from the repaired injury until the wound completely healed. The patient had a transfusion of two units of blood at the beginning of the operation because he lost a significant amount of blood since the injury happened.

The patient was transferred to the ICU for close observation and monitoring. All possible measures to prevent infection and other complications were taken, and thankfully he pulled through, without any major issues. He was transferred out of the ICU to a regular bed two days after surgery. His colostomy started working on the fifth post-operative day, at which time we started him on solid food. The colostomy care lessons were started, but the patient was too apprehensive about taking care of the colostomy bag. The nurse who was teaching him volunteered to make home visits until he was comfortable with handling his colostomy. The patient was discharged in good condition. The plan was that I would see him in my office in four weeks and two months thereafter, at which time we would determine the timing for closure of the colostomy so he could return to normal bowel function.

At four weeks he came to my office with Cathy, the nurse, and he did so again two months later. I thought he had a problem taking care of his colostomy, leading to the need of a protracted period of nursing visits. He was admitted back to the hospital three months after the first surgery, for closure of the colostomy and restoration of the colon integrity. Everything went well and Jay recovered without any complication. His story had an even happier ending. Jay and Cathy got romantically involved and got married. As far as I know, they lived happily ever after.

Everything else regarding my practice was routine, save for some patients who came my way with weird, unusual and challenging conditions. One of these weird situations was a 58-year-old gentleman that came to the HNH-ER with a large abdominal hernia, associated with a bad infection with a large abscess. I saw the patient at the request of his internist, reviewed his history, the chart, the lab and x-ray reports. The physical exam revealed a terrible infection at the area of the abdominal hernia, with a collection of pus commonly called abscess. I scheduled the patient for surgery, and as it was the time that the morning shift was finishing and the only team scheduled for the evening shifts were already booked, I asked Mary R., the surgical tech, whether she could stay to help out with the operation. She volunteered to oblige, but Lilly, the OR nursing supervisor, objected to that because she did not want to pay overtime wages.

I waited for the other team to finish before I could proceed with the operation. The findings were a big surprise. The patient's abdominal wall at the site of the hernia was completely obliterated. Skin and underlying thin layer of fat were the only tissues separating the intestines from the outside. The muscles and other tissues, which normally hold the abdominal wall together, were completely disrupted, showing visible intestinal peristalsis (moving) under the skin. Under general anesthesia I opened the skin and entered the abdomen at the area of the abscess, and there it was, the surprise cause of the small intestinal perforation causing the infection. A standard-sized ordinary toothpick went through the wall of the bowel, was at the center of the abscess cavity.

I clamped the bowel proximal and distal to the perforation to stop the contamination. I removed the toothpick and washed out the area with copious amounts of saline. I resected the area of the small intestine and reconnected the bowel, restoring the integrity of the gastrointestinal system. The patient did well but my differences with Lilly were only exacerbated.

Not long after this incident, I booked three emergency operations before the shift changed—acute appendicitis, strangulated hernia (a hernia that could not be reduced, possibly containing dead bowel), and incarcerated (not reducible) hernia. Lilly pulled the same BS again. Instead of keeping a second team and running a second room on the evening shift, she sent everyone home except for one team. She was the type of person who brown-nosed the chief of surgery but could not care less about the other surgeons. She acted as if the chief of surgery's patients were more special than the rest of the patient population. She also treated her staff with total disrespect, causing moral to plummet. And to top it all, Lilly lacked any modicum of professionalism.

That night, I didn't start operating until midnight. The patient with the appendicitis had a perforation of the appendix with peritonitis, possibly due to the delay imposed by the OR supervisor. The second patient had dead bowel, which I had to resect before repairing his hernia. I managed to reduce and repair the third patient's hernia, before any complications developed. The patients became sicker because the operations were delayed and that infuriated me.

I finished operating at 6 a.m. but stayed in the OR and waited for Lilly to come in. I went to her office and told her off, asking her why in the world did she not keep a second team to start my emergency cases in the afternoon. I told her she caused the patients to get worse while waiting for an OR team.

She had the audacity to come back at me, with "You did not say they were emergencies; they were just add-ons."

I lost it and screamed at the top of my lungs. "Where the hell did they get you from? The flea market or something? If you don't know that acute appendicitis, an incarcerated hernia and a strangulated hernia are surgical emergencies, you don't belong in the OR, never mind run it as the supervisor!"

As I walked out, I saw Dr. George Keyes, an orthopedic surgeon and a good friend. He was surprised to hear me screaming like a madman. He had never heard me raise my voice over the years we knew each other, never mind being totally flustered and yelling at the top of my lungs.

He came over to me and grabbed me by the arm. "George. Are you all right? I never knew you could get this angry!"

I explained to him that the only thing that makes me angry and infuriated is when the incompetence and stupidity of people in power affect my patients' wellbeing. I wrote a long letter to the director of surgery, Dr. Eugene, who in turn concluded that it was my fault since I did not stress clearly enough that my cases were emergencies. Of course, that was a lot of BS. He had Lilly brown nosing him and take care of all his Operating Room needs as if she was his personal servant. I also knew that he was not thrilled that I got so busy so fast and wanted to make sure I didn't think I was as important as he was, which explained why he sided with Lilly.

Ultimately, Lilly was too incompetent for the administration to overlook. They got flooded with complaints by many surgeons and within a couple of months she was given her walking papers.

Visiting Taiwan and Meeting Sharon's Family

On the family side, life was going well. In February of 1983 Sharon went back to Taiwan with her mother and our three children. Her brother Teddy was getting married to LianPei, so Sharon flew there ahead of me and I followed two weeks later. This was my first visit to the place Sharon grew up, and it was an eye opener for me. In Cyprus, the rain is considered precious. In Taiwan, the only weather I saw in the two weeks I spent there, was nonstop rain. At best there was one day with a two-hour window of sunshine when we traveled by train from Taichung to Taipei. On the way, Stavros, who was three and a half years old, had an asthma attack. As soon as we reached Taipei, Sharon called a nursing school classmate of hers who referred us to a clinic headed by a pediatrician from Philadelphia, Pennsylvania. When he saw Stavros, in a shirt with the "Wildwood" logo on the front, he started describing his fond childhood memories of the Jersey shore. The doctor prescribed medications that rapidly improved Stavros's condition.

One of the most impressive places I have visited in my lifetime was the National Palace Museum in Taipei. The Chinese artifacts, real national treasures of the museum, were brought to Taiwan by Chiang Kai-Shek when he fled there, from mainland China in 1949. There were countless pieces of art that blew my mind. The translucent jade-ite cabbage from the Ching Dynasty looked so real I felt I could take a crunchy bite out of it. An ivory miniature carving of a room with a bed, curtains, and tiny people inside was so small, I needed a magnifying glass to appreciate the extraordinary details. I was truly impressed.

Teddy and Liang Pei's wedding was a beautiful and elegant ceremony attended by many friends and relatives. Following the precious exchange of the vows there was a feast with a rich variety of delicious dishes.

The 13 days of my stay went by fast and were full of activities. There was the wedding, the never-ending rain, pond fishing, and the trip to Taipei with Stavros for his asthma attack. And of course, the unforgettable museum experience. We had also visited some wood carving places where I bought a carving of tigers on a rocky landscape, which appealed to me for its masterful execution.

It was time to return home, back to work. We went to the airport where we said our goodbyes and headed for the check in counter with our suitcases. We handed over our passports and tickets thinking we were going to breeze through nice and easy, but the airline representative who examined the passports had other ideas.

"The three children overstayed their visas by one day and that poses a security problem," he said. "They cannot travel. You need to get security clearance and a visa extension from the ministry of interior before they can get on the plane."

Three children, ages six, three and one, "pose a security threat to the country." That was a ridiculous assertion. I tried to reason with the guy, but it was clear that there was nothing he could do to help. He said we had to cancel the trip and go to a ministry in Taipei to get clearance. I had to return to New Jersey because I had scheduled operations to perform. At the same time, I did not want to leave Sharon behind and have her travel alone with three small children. I checked in, but Sharon and the kids waited to see if I could resolve the problem.

I went to a security officer who was nearby and told him I wanted to talk to his superior. The officer was taken aback, thinking that I wanted to complain to his boss about him. I told him I had to resolve a problem with my family's travel. I reached the airport manager and explained the situation, assuring him that my small kids are too young to even comprehend what a security threat means, never mind posing such a threat themselves. At the same time Sharon called her brother, who was an active Air Force officer, to see if he could help.

Sharon actually thought that any attempt to resolve this matter would prove fruitless, because "it's impossible for them to change their minds."

We managed to get the ball start rolling with calls to the ministry from both the airport and Sharon's brother's unit. The airplane departure time was fast approaching. When the last call for boarding came, the matter was still not resolved. I had no choice but to kiss Sharon and the children goodbye and board the plane, hoping they would ultimately be allowed to join me before it took off. The airplane doors were closed, and the engines were running but the scheduled departure time came and went, and we didn't move off the tarmac.

An announcement came over the speaker. "We apologize for the delay, but we were waiting for security clearance of three passengers. The clearance is completed, and we will be departing momentarily."

"They are coming!" I thought to myself.

The plane door opened and one after another Stavros, Christos, and Sharon with Maritsa in her arms, walked onto the plane. I heard the words so many times that "you can't succeed unless you try." It is so true, but I would add that even if you don't succeed, at least you feel content that you have given it your best. Sharon told me how they were quickly processed once the approval for the kids' departure came. Little six-year-old Christos had to drag the suitcase, which was bigger than him and all of them ran to get to the plane.

We flew to Chicago and then, after a couple of hours, continued the flight to JFK. Our suitcases did not arrive with our flight, but were delivered the next day, about 3 a.m. It was another interesting trip, especially the part of the departure from Taiwan.

The home-office combination had served me well. The dentist who was renting the office moved to his own building and I demolished the walls I had built in my house with my brother John. Sharon reclaimed her living and dining rooms, and the Florida sunroom. I was much happier too, occupying the space that was designed specifically to be a doctor's office. There was a spacious waiting room, two examining rooms, an operating room, a receptionist area and a consultation room. The great advantage of the office was its central location across the street from New Milford High School on River Road, which was a county Road. All of that made the office accessible and easy to find.

The characteristics that made the building advantageous for an office, also made it a disadvantage for a family home. The road was busy and when Christos was 3 years old, he tried to run into the street. I grabbed him and brought him back to the house as he cried and tried to free himself from my firm grip.

A more serious thing happened with Maritsa when she was 18 months old. Sharon was busy with the office when she realized that the River Road traffic came to a screeching halt. She looked outside and saw Maritsa standing in the middle of the road. Thankfully all the cars stopped. She ran and picked Maritsa up, bringing her in to safety, but that was a wake-up call for us.

We started looking for a house with a lot of land so our kids would have a place to safely play. We found a house in Saddle River that had 2.9 acres of land and bought it. We then expanded the house and moved there on July 4, 1986. It was a great relief having a property that provided ample space for our children to play in a secure and safe environment. That same year I opened a second office on Teaneck Road across the street from Holy Name Hospital, in an office building I bought with my colleague and friend, Dr. Ignatios Zairis.

A New Era in the Art and Science of Surgery

The 1990s presented new, earthshaking advances in the surgical field, which in turn brought about big challenges and great opportunities in the brand-new field of laparoscopic surgery, or minimally invasive surgery (MIS). This was made possible by the development of visual technology, which was applicable to the Operating Room.

Laparoscopy—from the ancient Greek word lapara, meaning abdomen, and skopo, meaning look)—meant we could look inside the abdomen. It had been used in the past with basic, antiquated, anachronistic equipment that consisted of a solid tube with a light and a lens at its end that was inserted into the abdomen. The operator could see the intra-abdominal organs by looking through the other end of the tube (scope). The person holding the scope was the only one who could view the different organs, albeit in a limited fashion. There were different scopes available, which were intended to inspect different body cavities, or tubular and hollow organs. Laryngoscope (scope for the voice box), bronchoscope (windpipe scope), colonoscope (scope for the large intestine), gastroscope (scope for the stomach), and cystoscope (scope for the urinary bladder).

The number of the laparoscopic procedures performed before 1990 were few and had relatively little value. All these changed dramatically by advances in visual technology, which allowed the entire picture of the internal organs to be projected on a large TV screen. In addition to the visual revolution, new instruments were designed which could be inserted to the surgical field area through a surgical port—a special tubular structure—inserted into the abdomen through a tiny cut. Two or more surgical ports were inserted into the abdomen, which was inflated with carbon dioxide through a needle. The scope was connected to a TV monitor and inserted in the abdomen exposing the internal organs in a spectacular fashion for everyone in the operating room to see on the large TV screen. In the past, open surgery allowed only the surgeons to have full visual access to the surgical field. The other OR personnel were not aware of the exact work the surgeon was doing.

The new era of laparoscopic surgery showed up in earnest in 1990. When I first heard about it, I was not very enthused. In actuality, I had big doubts about the credibility of the "great revolution" in surgical technique. Nonetheless, I signed up for a special course offered by the New Jersey Laser Institute. I wanted to see it and experience the technique myself. It was a "two-day symposium concerning the principles and general surgical applications of contact laser surgery and operative endoscopic techniques for laparoscopic cholecystectomy, appendectomy and adhesiolysis." I sighed up with an open mind, but kept my expectations low, so I would not get disappointed. The course was scheduled for Sept. 22-23, 1990. The night before the symposium, I attended a function at the Glen Point Hotel in Teaneck, which did not finish until midnight, so I went to bed at 1 a.m. and got up at 5 a.m. so I could make it to the course in New Brunswick, New Jersey, scheduled for 7 a.m.

The theoretical portion of the course dealt primarily with the physics and practical applications of laser energy. Although I did not get enough sleep, I was so fascinated and stimulated by the new technology that I felt fully alert and full of energy. The course got exponentially more exciting when we got to the practical application of performing a cholecystectomy on a pig using the laparoscopic technique with laser energy. I felt that I had just walked through a majestic gate, and entered into the realm of a new world, filled with fascination, excitement and infinite possibilities and opportunities. I was mesmerized by the process, which allowed me to remove the pig's gallbladder in a significantly less traumatic fashion, more efficiently and faster than the method I was accustomed to and had used my entire professional life. I realized that great changes were happening in the science and art of my profession and would have a big impact on patient care and my own life. As I was performing the gallbladder operation on the pig, I realized that there was a need for laparoscopic instrumentation, that was comparable to what was being used in open surgery. I thought I could design instruments that could make laparoscopic surgery easier. There was a need for further developments that would make laparoscopic operations easier and safer.

The two day course was concluded, and I headed home to get some rest. As I was driving, I could not suppress the ideas for new instruments, which were popping furiously, in my head.

I arrived home and spent some time with my family. We played some games, told a lot of jokes, and went to bed, exhausted from the emotional intensity of the Laser course in laparoscopic surgery.

Normally I have no problem falling asleep. Once my head hits the pillow, I am out. But this day was anything but normal. I wrote some notes that night at 1 a.m. and a few weeks later I woke up at 4 a.m. to take more notes.

"On Sept. 22-23, 1990, I took the Laser Endoscopic course in New Brunswick, New Jersey. I saw the great potential for performing other endoscopic surgical procedures such as bowel resection, and the need for new instrumentation. Ideas for new instruments started popping into in my mind and I could not fall asleep. I got up at 1 a.m., and started writing things down.

- *Technique for bowel resection.*

- *How to get a long suture into the abdomen by using a straight needle for continuous suturing. The "needle-stitch" was designed.*

- *Trocar with inflatable balloon, to prevent slipping of the trocar outside the abdomen.*

- *Endoscopic scissors with constant sharpness, and disposable blades.*

- *Endoscopic scalpel with a retractable sheath, for protection against inadvertent injury.*

- *"Suture assistant" endoscopic forceps with a gap in the center.*

- *Blunt balloon dissector-sponge stick with inflatable balloon.*

- *Bowel resection atraumatic forceps with double grasping system.*

- *Cholangiocath guide.*

- *Atraumatic cholangiocath guide with funnel shape head.*

- *Liver Biopsy clips.*

I developed some of these instruments for the market, while some more were developed by other surgeons who evidently had the same ideas.

I was eager to start using the new method of laparoscopic laser surgery, but before that happened, I needed to do three things. First, I had to practice my hand-eye coordination skills with a pelvitrainer, a special contraption that mimics the conditions of laparoscopic surgery in the operating room. Second, I had to observe an actual gallbladder operation in the operating room by someone who is already experienced in the procedure. Third, and just as important, I needed to find a patient who was willing to be the first to have the new operation by me.

I ordered a pelvitrainer on Sept. 26 and it arrived on Oct. 5. With the help of my son Christos, 13 years old at the time, I set up the pelvitrainer in the basement. I made some modifications to the contraption to meet my needs, using a video camera connected to a TV set, which allowed me to practice the laparoscopic skills of manipulating, cutting and suturing the tissues. I practiced using chicken meat and spent every free chance I had, perfecting my skills. After about 60 hours of practice, I felt confident about my abilities and proficiency to perform my first laparoscopic cholecystectomy. I was ready to do it!

My second objective was met when I made arrangements to visit Dr. Lee, a surgeon in Cincinnati, Ohio who had three laparoscopic chole-cystectomies scheduled for Nov. 17, 1990. I observed the procedures and found it all quite interesting. I was fascinated by how smooth the operations went. It was an instructional and professionally reward-ing day.

The First Laser Laparoscopic Cholecystectomy at Holy Name Hospital

The third objective, finding a patient who would be the first to undergo a laparoscopic removal of the gallbladder, was relatively easy. On Nov. 9 I saw Margaret in my office. Margaret had symptoms of a gallbladder attack a few days earlier. The attack had subsided spontaneously, so she had no pain when I saw her, but she needed a laparoscopic cholecys-tectomy. I had operated on Margaret in the past for acute appendicitis, so we were familiar with each other. I explained to her that she had the option of an open or laparoscopic operation.

She had heard about the laser surgery and wanted to know more about it. I explained the whole procedure and told her that I had learned how to do it in a special course and practiced my skills with a special contraption. I let her know that if she agreed to have a laparoscopic operation by me, she was going to be my first patient, since I had not as yet used the technique on a human. I also told her that she wiould also be the first patient that had a laparoscopic Gall Bladder removal at HNH. I explained to her that if I had any difficulty, I would convert the operation to the open method, with which I have extensive experience. In addition to that, since she had no insurance, I informed her that I was not going to charge anything for my services. She did not hesitate to consent. She trusted me based on her previous experience with the appendectomy, so I proceeded to schedule her operation for Nov. 29.

At the time, scheduling a laparoscopic operation was complicated because the hospital did not have the necessary Laparoscopic instruments and equipment to setup the OR. In addition to the laser machine, laparoscopic scopes, monitors, and instruments were needed. The demand was so great for the new equipment, that vendors of the instrument companies struggled to keep up. To accommodate everyone, vendors carried a complete instrument setup and loaned it out, rotating hospitals until the individual purchase orders could be filled.

Margaret L. was going to be the first patient to undergo laser laparoscopic gallbladder removal at Holy Name Hospital and I was going to be the one to do it. I could not wait. I had spent a tremendous amount of time practicing on the pelvitrainer and I felt totally prepared to carry out the operation in an efficient and safe manner. I wanted the operation to be a success, otherwise it would not look good for me or the hospital. I had no doubts that the patient would be fine, regardless of how the operation was done. But I really wanted to use the new method, without the large cut. I was concerned that if Margaret developed an acute gallbladder attack, I would have to operate on her using the old method, since the availability of the equipment was on a scheduled basis and not provided for emergencies. Thankfully, Margaret did not have any serious acute gallbladder problem before the scheduled surgery.

The day finally arrived. I was at the hospital before 7 a.m. and I watched as the OR got ready for the operation. The laparoscopic instruments and scope were sterilized, the laser-generator and monitors were set up, and the patient was already in the pre-op holding area. The surgical team was comprised of myself, my assistant surgeons Dr. Poole and Dr. Forcina, the anesthesiologist, the OR nurse and the scrub technician. The patient was brought in and positioned on the operating table. The room appeared more crowded and congested because of the additional equipment—two large TV monitors, the laser generator, and the irrigation set. The patient was draped leaving only the abdomen exposed. In the meantime, the anesthesiologist, Dr. Melba Vittal, administered general anesthesia so the patient was already asleep.

"Scalpel," I instructed the surgical tech. She handed me the scalpel and I made a 10 mm cut, at the lower border of the umbilicus, down to the dense tissue called fascia, and inserted a 6 inch needle inside the belly through the cut. "Verres needle". I connected the needle to the CO_2 source and inflated the abdomen. The needle was removed and replaced with a 10 mm port, and the scope with the camera inserted into the abdomen.

The insufflation of the abdomen with gas lifts the abdominal wall off the abdominal organs and creates a space in which the scope and the surgical instruments can function. Upon insertion of the scope inside, I proceeded to do a visual exploration of the entire abdomen, which was a real treat for me and the entire team. The exploration showed some scar tissue in the right lower abdomen from the appendectomy surgery I had performed a few years earlier. No other abnormalities were seen, save for the gallbladder, which appeared thickened, a sign of chronic infection and inflammation. The findings were expected taking into consideration the history of repeated gallbladder attacks that Margaret had reported.

Another 10mm and two 5mm ports were inserted in the abdomen. The table was manipulated for optimal visualization of the Gallbladder area. The gallbladder was engaged with two graspers and lifted towards the head, exposing the area of the bile duct and the artery of the gallbladder. Both of these structures, had to be dissected free and identified before they were closed up with special clips and cut, allowing the gallbladder to be peeled off the liver and removed.

This was my first laparoscopic removal of a gallbladder, but I had seen well over 1,000 gallbladder operations to know that this operation was not going to be easy, because of the chronic infection of the gallbladder.

I used the laser beam to score the area of dissection. As soon as I started, all of a sudden everything went red, evidently from blood that spurted on the scope. Though it was not a good thing to happen right at the beginning of the operation, it did not concern me too much, because I knew that it must be coming from a tiny branch of the cystic artery, which does not pose any problem with blood loss and can be easily controlled. I removed the scope, cleaned it and the port, and reinserted it, directing it about 30 degrees away from the gallbladder so the spurting blood would not obliterate the vision again. Sure enough, I saw a fine spurt of blood at the area I had used the laser beam earlier. This tiny amount of bleeding caused a huge problem by completely obliterating the surgical field and bringing the operation to a sudden halt. This kind of thing happens all the time, but the blood does not wind up in the "surgeon's eyes," which appeared to be the case when the blood landed on the scope. With clear visualization of the bleeding point, the situation was easily corrected with the laser beam, which coagulated the area and stopped the bleeding instantly.

From then on it was smooth sailing with no other unforeseen complications or problems, though it became clear that better instrumentation was necessary to render the operation faster and safer. There was a need for a cloth dissector, which we call a surgical peanut, used in traditional surgery. The "peanut" consists of a tiny ball made of surgical gauze, which is engaged by a clump and used to separate the tissue planes by dissecting between them. I saw the need for a similar instrument from the first time I performed laparoscopic surgery in the animal lab, and I was in the process of developing one.

The other problem that I saw with laparoscopic surgery was the intense surgical smoke plume, which was generated with the use of the laser beam. The plume presented two issues. The first issue was that when present it compromised visibility, giving the surgeon the feeling of working in a "smoke house." The second issue was the potential toxicity of the plume to the patient and the surgical team. The surgical smoke plume is created not only by the laser beam, but by the electrocoagulation too, which had been in use for decades before laser energy became available. In the open surgery however, we aspirated the smoke with a suction tube, which if used in laparoscopic surgery, would evacuate the carbon dioxide and obliterate the surgical field. I knew I had to come up with a solution to this problem, and I did, a few years later.

The operation on Margaret took about two hours, which was three to four times longer than it would have taken me if I had done an open operation. The important thing was that it went well without any serious problems. This was not a typical type of elective surgery, with a pliable, easily engaged and manipulated gallbladder, but one with a remarkably thickened wall, which made its manipulation a problematic challenge, causing a longer operating time. Other than that, there was no adverse effect on the success of the operation and her uneventful recovery. Margaret recovered fast and was sent home the next day, much faster than with a traditional open operation. That made me extremely happy.

My surgical experience, coupled with the intense preparation for this day with due diligence, had paid off. The first Laser Laparoscopic cholecystectomy at Holy Name Hospital was now in the books.

Fine tuning Laparoscopic Surgery with Instrumentation

As time went by everybody adopted the new technique of laparoscopic surgery, but some of us were better than others. Certain things became evident with time. One of them was that electrocoagulation was more effective and safer to use than laser, and less expensive too. Electrocoagulation was in use for many decades before the laser beam was made available and practically every surgeon was familiar with its use. It did not take long before the laser beam was replaced with the familiar electrocoagulation for laparoscopic surgery.

The second realization I discovered was the desperate need for a surgical, laparoscopic gauze "peanut" to facilitate the peeling of the gallbladder from the liver where it was attached. In open surgery, we usually used our finger, or the surgical gauze "peanut" held by a clamp to peel the gallbladder from the liver, like we peel the skin of an orange or a tangerine. There is a plane between the gallbladder and the liver and once found and exposed, the removal of the GB is straight forward, fast and safe. There was no similar instrument at the time that could accomplish this laparoscopically, and I was determined to produce one. It took me about a year to develop a workable instrument.

First, I started with an instrument that could engage tightly, securely and safely with the standard gauze ball peanut we were using in the open surgery. That did not come out as well as I hoped. The standard gauze ball was too big to go through the laparoscopic port smoothly and securely, posing the danger of falling off in the peritoneal cavity, which could lead to a disaster since it would be practically impossible to retrieve it from the abdomen. I then changed my direction into developing a new gauze dissector altogether. There was a surgical grade tube gauze, which was used as a finger dressing with a splint. The tube gauze was mounted over a tube and then the tube was placed over the finger and the gauze unloaded over it. The tightness of the gauze was controlled by the amount of torsion applied on the tube, as it was moved towards and/or away from the finger. That illuminated my way towards the creation of the "laparoscopic peanut." I needed to develop a frame onto which I could mount the gauze, a way to secure the gauze on the frame, and another long instrument onto which the new peanut could be threaded and delivered through the port into the abdomen to be used on the target organ.

I looked through the Yellow Pages and visited several machine shops before I found the right ones to manufacture the frames and the instruments from surgical steel. There was a problem that needed to be solved before I could develop a functioning prototype. The tube gauze available was too wide to allow the formation of the tight gauze ball I needed. I used several sizes of tube gauze in my practice, so I looked at the package to find the manufacturer and see if they were willing to make some custom-made sizes of tube gauze for me. The manufacturer was located in Tenafly, New Jersey, only 15 minutes from my office. I called them and went there for a meeting. They were very helpful. They custom-made several sizes of tube gauze and found the most suitable ones that could be used for the manufacturing of the 5mm and 10mm instruments.

Now I had the frames for the "peanuts," the surgical steel instruments onto which the frames could be attached, the appropriate dimensions of the surgical grade cotton gauze, and the shorter "manufacturing instruments" to receive the frames for the "peanuts." The only thing missing was the tube with the right dimensions onto which the gauze could be mounted. For that, I could use the laparoscopic ports, which would also ensure that the manufactured peanuts fit the lumen of the ports, since they go through them during the manufacturing process. I manufactured several "peanuts," sterilized them and the instruments, and used them in the actual operations. They worked like a dream. In the meantime, I got FDA approval, and also applied for a patent, which I secured after a very expensive and time consuming process.

In a few more years, I managed to combine the laparoscopic peanut with an irrigation set and electrode to develop a multi-functional instrument, which could do dissection, suction and/or irrigation and electrocoagulation with simultaneous smoke evacuation. I got FDA approval for the instrument and had custom-made instruments and electrodes for my use. The importance of this instrument was that it provided all the functions needed for a gallbladder operation, avoiding the need for repeated instrument exchanges. This rendered the operation faster, safer and more efficient. An additional advantage was the fact that whenever I was using the electrocautery for dissection or bleeding control, I could easily evacuate the smoke plume produced by activating the suction.

This provided a clear picture on the TV monitor and practically eliminated the danger from the smoke plume.

The number of the laparoscopic gallbladder procedures performed increased significantly in comparison with open conventional operations, which were totally replaced by the new techniques and technology. The use of the laser beam as an energy source fell by the wayside, completely replaced by the electrocautery, with which every surgeon was already familiar.

In the beginning, since this was a completely new surgical modality and technology, it was impossible to find any reasonable amount of information in the medical literature. The only way to learn more about this branch of the surgical art was to follow it as it developed at various conferences that were specifically created for this purpose. Personally, I joined the Society of Laparoscopic Surgeons, which included practicing surgeons who, initially at least, were generally not associated with academia. One of the advantages of the new laparoscopic technology was that you could record the entire operation and review, edit and present the operative findings to your colleagues, rendering it a precious teaching tool. I used this valuable tool myself, presenting my techniques and innovations as video presentations in several international meetings in the United States, London and Cyprus over the years.

There were so many new things to learn before one could become a savvy laparoscopic surgeon. Things like knowing the right direction of the camera in relation to the TV monitor. The camera had to be pointed at the monitor, otherwise when the instrument was moved it would end up going in the opposite direction than the intended target. Another element of importance was the use of carbon dioxide in the abdomen to lift the abdominal wall off the abdominal organs, to create the space necessary for the visualization of the structures and the manipulation of the instruments.

During laparoscopic surgery, a lot of the gas is absorbed by the body and enters the blood stream but is normally expelled when it reaches the lungs. If the lung function is not normal then the carbon dioxide (CO_2) stays in the body and can cause a condition called CO_2 narcosis, during which the patient becomes unresponsive. I learned about this condition in medical school and heard about it at the conferences and SLS (Society of Laparoscopic Surgeons) meetings but never saw one until the time I did a laparoscopic cholecystectomy on an elderly patient with chronic lung problems. The operation went smooth, the anesthesia was reversed, and the patient woke up. He had no pain and was happy that his surgery was over. I walked to the Post Anesthesia Care Unit (PACU), also known as recovery room, and sat down to write the postoperative notes, postoperative orders and instructions for patient care. The patient was wheeled into the PACU just a few seconds later and connected to the monitors. By the time I finished my post op orders and notes a few minutes later, the PACU nurse run to me alarmed.

"The patient is unresponsive and not breathing," she said. She was very distraught.

I rushed to the patient's bedside just a few feet away from where I was sitting writing the past operative orders. He was completely out, eyes wide open, gazing into infinity, not breathing. I asked the nurse to call the anesthesiologist over and call the lab to draw blood gases on the patient, as I grabbed the Ambu bag, which is a handheld device connected to oxygen to provide positive pressure ventilation. I placed the mask of the Ambu bag over the patient's mouth and nose and started ventilating the patient. The anesthesiologist came over and placed a tube into the patient's breathing tube and connected it to a breathing machine. In my mind what I just saw was a textbook case of CO_2 narcosis. I just had to verify and document it by checking the blood gases, which would tell us the concentration of oxygen and carbon dioxide in his blood. Had the patient not been treated for his breathing problem, he would have not survived. It was just a matter of placing the patient on a breathing machine for long enough, to get rid of the excess CO_2 in his system. The arterial blood gas analysis confirmed the diagnosis, with CO_2 levels three times higher than normal. About an hour later the patient was taken off the respirator and did not present any other problems. He went home the next day in a good condition.

As the evolution of laparoscopic surgery progressed, the surgical community developed the standards or indication and contraindications for the new techniques and technology. Initially, we were told that an acute gallbladder attack was a contraindication for laparoscopic surgery, but that did not last for long. As more experience was gained, it became clear to me, and the laparoscopic surgery community in general, that the new technique was very appropriate for the thickened, swollen and even gangrenous gallbladder. For me, by using the peanut I developed, the gallbladder could be peeled off the liver and removed with the same ease or difficulty as with conventional open surgery.

With time, more general surgery operations were performed laparoscopically—appendix removal; groin, abdominal and hiatal hernia repair; colon removal; removal of adhesive bands (scar tissue) causing small bowel obstruction; and splenectomy. Other specialties also adopted the minimally invasive surgery in their practice, rendering the patient recovery easier, faster and less painful.

Life on Life's Terms

In December of 1992, our very athletic daughter Maritsa developed severe hip pain after playing basketball. There was something strange about that pain. It was nonspecific and it came after rigorous activity, such as playing basketball. The pain persisted so we took her to Holy Name Hospital, and I asked a pediatric surgeon to evaluate her. A comprehensive evaluation, lab tests and x-rays, did not show any abnormality. The symptoms continued, however, and Maritsa looked pale and felt tired. I called her pediatrician, Dr. George Ioannou, and took her there for evaluation. He gave me a prescription for blood tests, though he did not find any obvious abnormality. On our way home, I drove to Holy Name Hospital and had the lab draw the blood specimens requested by Dr. Ioannou. Later, I went back to the Hospital to see my patients and planned to check the blood results.

As soon as I arrived at the hospital, the pathologist, Dr. Evelyn Braun, paged me and wanted to discuss Maritsa's results. I rushed to her office. She told me that the blood smear evaluation showed acute lymphocytic leukemia. I thanked her and walked out. Initially, it just did not register in my mind that she had a malignancy.

Acute Lymphocytic Leukemia (ALL) was a term I was familiar with. I had come across it, seen it, and saw the terrible outcomes it could have from the time I was a medical student. I saw a little angel lose her life from it when I was rotating in pediatrics as a medical student in Athens. I was shaken from that experience, but it still did not register when I first heard Dr. Braun tell me those horrible words. That lasted only a few seconds. As I walked down the hallway it hit me. What did she say? I questioned myself. Did she say ALL? Did she say leukemia? It was like I was hit by a ton of bricks. Was it true? Maybe I did not hear it right.

I rushed back to Dr. Braun's office. "Evelyn, did you say ALL?"

She looked at me and said apologetically, "Yes, that is what I saw in the blood smear. A bone marrow is needed to confirm the diagnosis."

I was petrified. I thanked her for her help and headed out. My little girl's life was in jeopardy, though there was a better chance than not, that she could be cured with chemotherapy. Regardless, I was devastated.

I drove home trying to figure out how to tell Sharon and how to explain that to Maritsa. It was something that I did every day—telling people bad news. It was part of the routine activity in my practice. Being a bearer of bad news came with the territory of my job. I had developed special ways of breaking such news with compassion and discretion, with total respect for the patient's and family's feelings. Talking to my wife and my daughter, however, was totally different. I was a part of the suffering party and I felt the pain that came with the scary news, in a different way.

I went home and talked to my wife. I explained that Maritsa had Acute Lymphocytic Leukemia and that she needed to have a bone marrow biopsy to confirm the diagnosis, followed by chemotherapy. I called the medical oncologist I usually worked with, Dr. Mark Pascal, and asked him, whom did he recommend for Maritsa's treatment.

He did not hesitate. "Dr. Harris is a great pediatric oncologist and has an excellent group of associates working with him. I recommend him and his group without any reservations. I will find their information and call you back"

He called them for me, found who was on call, and made arrangements for Maritsa's evaluation and treatment. "Dr. Frances Flug is on duty today. She will see Maritsa as soon as you take her to the Tomorrow's Children Institute at Pediatric Oncology Department at Hackensack University Medical Center."

I talked to Maritsa and told her that we found the reason she had those hip pains, and the reason she was feeling tired. There was a problem with her blood, and we had to take her to the hospital for more tests and definitive treatment. She was brave, just saying OK. It was Dec. 19th, right before Christmas, and also it was two days before Sharon's birthday. We usually had a big celebration for Christmas and Sharon's birthday, but that year, 1992, everything was put on hold.

Me, Sharon and Maritsa got in the car and headed for the pediatric oncology department at Hackensack Hospital. On the way, Maritsa expressed her feelings about the situation.

"Why me? And why this time of the year?" These were the only words of complaint she uttered, and the only time she complained during her two-plus years of chemotherapy.

Dr. Frances Flug was a kind, gentle, thoughtful and compassionate Doctor but she was also straight forward. "Children with ALL have a better chance of complete remission if they are 10 years old or younger," she informed us.

Maritsa was admitted to the hospital for a bone marrow biopsy, which confirmed the diagnosis. The next step was to decide what treatment she would receive. Dr. Flug presented our options, and we chose the study protocol suggested by her. Maritsa would undergo intravenous chemotherapy for two years as per protocol. The medication had to be given through a central venous access, meaning it had to be instilled in the central vein close to the heart.

A special device called a portacath was inserted under general anesthesia in the operating room. The device consisted of a metal "drum" with a plastic "roof" and an outlet connected to a silastic tube. The "drum" was placed under the skin through an incision and the silastic tubing inserted in the vein by the collarbone and advanced to the desired position into the superior vena cava, close to the heart. The "drum" was visible and palpable, like a "bump," pushing the overlying skin higher than the surrounding area. It could be accessed any time with a needle and acted like an extension of the venous system. Blood could be drawn from it for testing, and chemotherapy treatments or other drugs and fluids could be administered through it.

Maritsa behaved bravely and never complained about having to endure all the hardships that go alone with such an intensive treatment—nausea, vomiting, loss of appetite, malaise and exhaustion and hair loss were included in the package of trying to beat the disease. She was connected to an intravenous setup and received the chemotherapy patiently and bravely. She needed blood and platelet transfusions, and our friends and relatives were happy to donate. Sharon's sister Joy, offered and gave Sharon a large check, to help for Maritsa's care. Everybody around us was supportive and kind. They provided encouragement and tried to soothe our pain in any way they could.

Family and friends provided food and others sent letters and cards with good wishes and prayers. All her classmates sent her their wishes in writing. All this love, kindness and concern gave Maritsa and our whole family the strength to endure and became part of our healing process. It was so difficult for Sharon and me to see our daughter suffer, but we had to endure and be strong. Strangely enough, most of our strength came from Maritsa herself. She was stoic and never said much when she was getting the treatment. She appeared to be enveloped in a cocoon, isolated and untouched by her surroundings and the hospital environment.

After the first course of chemotherapy was completed, a repeat bone marrow biopsy showed encouraging results—the leukemia was in remission! She was discharged from the Hospital on New Year's Eve. We were invited to join Dr. Ignatios Zairis, his wife Ellie and other guests at their house to ring in 1993. We were not planning to attend, but Maritsa wanted very much to go. She enjoyed playing Blackjack and did not want to miss the opportunity to celebrate and welcome the New Year.

As soon as we left the hospital, Maritsa was back to her normal self again, cheerful, talkative and active, and I was not about to deny her the request to attend the party. We had concerns about her strength, but we bypassed that with the rational that if she did not feel good at any time, we could always get in the car and go home, five minutes away. The other concern was her ability to fight infection, which was alleviated by the fact that her white cell blood count was normal the day she left the hospital. The whole family—Maritsa, Christos, Stavros, me and Sharon—went to Ignatios' and Ellie's house and had a nice time welcoming 1993. Everybody was happy to see Maritsa on her feet again, cheerful, happy and acting like her normal self as if nothing had happened. We went home at 1 a.m. feeling content and hopeful that 1993 would bring better things than 1992.

The treatments lasted two years, with repeated hospital admissions for chemotherapy infusions. Maritsa put herself into her special world of isolation and insulation from her surroundings every time she was admitted, and then returned to her normal self upon leaving the hospital. That was her way of coping with a bad situation. I did not know where she found all the strength she demonstrated.

Sharon's reaction was quite different. She stayed at Maritsa's bedside during the treatments, going home a couple of hours here and there to wash up whenever I was able to relieve her. She was a basket case. It took her weeks before she recovered from the trauma of each of Maritsa's treatments, and by then the next treatment was coming up. It was a time of continuous trial and suffering, because we had to deal with the effects of the treatments and the uncertainty of the future. I continued to work, but my mind never left my little girl. I was at her bedside with every opportunity I had, to be with her and also give some well-deserved relief to Sharon. The two boys were also affected. With all the attention directed to Maritsa's problem, they felt neglected and showed an aggressive behavior towards each other. We took it a day at a time, which was the only way to cope.

Maritsa did not go to school for months at the beginning of her treatments, but she was able to keep up with her education, courtesy of her teachers, who volunteered and tutored her privately while she was confined at home. Maritsa had her ups and downs during her treatments, with the onset of various complications during chemotherapy. At one time she became extremely nauseous, developed diarrhea and repeatedly vomited gastric juices mixed with blood. She was on antibiotics, but I immediately recognized that she had an infection with clostridium difficile, a spore-forming bacterium. There was a specific treatment for that, so I asked Sharon to let the doctor who came for morning rounds know about it, so he can administer the appropriate treatment.

The pediatric oncologist Dr. W. made rounds that morning and Sharon was there. She told him that I thought Maritsa had clostridium difficile—also known as C diff—and needed treatment with vancomy-cin. His response was as stunning as it was infuriating.

"You have to forget that you a doctor or nurse. Here, you are just the patient's family," he said. He was implying that we could not use our medical or nursing knowledge to suggest treatment!

Sharon's answer was brilliant. "Just because we are the patient's family doesn't mean that we all of a sudden become stupid."

That did not help, however. The only thing they did was to send a stool specimen for cultures. They refused to treat her before the culture provided proof of the infection. I was not about to get into a fight with the pediatric oncologist, though I was certain that I was correct about the diagnosis based on Maritsa's symptoms. C Diff infection, usually happens when a person takes antibiotics that kill the normal, good bacteria of the intestine, allowing the c. difficile bacteria to grow and cause the serious condition called clostridium difficile enterocolitis. This condition is associated with fever, high wide count, nausea, vomiting, abdominal distension and diarrhea, all of which were present with Maritsa. The infection can be treated with another antibiotic, called vancomycin, or by the ingestion of another microorganism, called lactobacillus, which replenishes the normal bacteria of the intestine and stops/prevents the growth of the harmful c. difficile germs. Lactobacillus is found in yogurt and also is available in a pill form. The earlier the treatment is started, the faster the recovery, and I was not about to sit back and do nothing.

I decided to treat my daughter with an alternative method by using yogurt. She had to take a tablespoon of plain yogurt three times a day. By the next day, her symptoms improved and within three days, her symptoms subsided. By then the chemotherapy infusion cycle was completed and Maritsa was ready to go home. The pediatric oncologists were happy that she got better without the treatment I had requested, until the stool specimen culture report came back. The results were reported before she went home and were positive for C. Diff, confirming my diagnosis and condemning their reluctance to treat her.

They gave us a prescription for vancomycin, so that Maritsa could get the treatment for C Diff at home. Other than this instance of negligence, in my mind, the treatment she received at the pediatric oncology service at Hackensack University Medical Center was stellar, and we are grateful for that. I am thankful that I had the knowledge and ability to circumvent their reluctance to treat her effectively by providing the alternative treatment with yogurt, and without antagonizing her pediatric oncologists.

The treatments were completed according to protocol, two years after the diagnosis was made and the participation in the study was initiated. A bone marrow biopsy confirmed that Maritsa had remained in remission throughout that period. The biggest hurdle was over. We then had to wait for a period of another 10 years before we could be sure that she was cured, but there were no more hospital admissions and no more chemotherapy. Her hair, which was completely gone during the treatments, gradually grew back. Even after beautiful hair had grown back, she had difficulty removing her baseball hat, which she had been wearing day and night while she called herself "Mr. Clean," a reference to the trademark bold guy on the liquid soap with that name. Eventually her Aunt Joy, Sharon's sister, took her to a New York City hair salon, and had her beautiful new hair trimmed and styled, a move that detached her from the baseball cap.

Life was normal again. There was a scare in 2001 when we were in Cyprus and Maritsa developed a high fever. We did a blood test, which thankfully did not show any abnormality. The 10 years went by, and Maritsa remained in perfect health and was considered cured. In high school she was an exceptional athlete, breaking school records in track and field, and scoring over 1000 points for her basketball team.

Our Wonderful Children

Sharon an George with Maritsa Christos and Stavros

All three of our children participated in sports. Christos was a star football player, voted all county during his senior year when his Ramsey High School football team won its division. He was also voted "all New England Small Colleges" when he played football at Tufts University. Stavros also played football in high school, but he excelled in girls more than athletics. For him girls were more appealing than the football field!

With the completion of Maritsa's treatments, Sharon returned to the office regularly, running it in a way that only she knew how, since she was the one who had set it up at the beginning of my practice. Sometimes I wondered how she did it. She took care of three children and the house while running the office, all at the same time. She proved herself a person of extraordinary skills and abilities.

Our secretary Pat filled in, during the critical period that Sharon was attending to Maritsa.

Having gotten over the critical period of Maritsa's health problem, we returned to a status of normalcy again. I continued to work hard, attending to my established and very busy practice, while also trying to make it to the athletic events of my children. We traveled to Boston to see Christos's football games at Tufts or Maritsa's basketball games, also at Tufts. We also visited Stavros at Boston University, but he had no interest in sports and continued to specialize in girls. He joined the ambulance corps and that is when he realized his calling to enter the field of medicine. He actually had volunteered as a high school student and worked at Holy Name Hospital's OR, which he seemed to enjoy. He followed in my footsteps and became a surgeon. Christos became a computer engineer and Maritsa studied psychology, although she appeared to enjoy the basketball games more than her studies.

Stavros, our second child, graduated from Ramsey High School in 1997 and secured a spot in Boston University to study human physiology. He joined the ambulance corps there and he appeared to enjoy the human aspect of it. It prompted him to make the decision to study medicine and follow in my footsteps. He later secured admission to UMDNJ, to study Medicine.

Maritsa was the last child to leave for college after graduating from Ramsey High School in 2000. She was accepted at Tufts University School of Engineering, but she kept changing subjects, eventually deciding on psychology. The only constant subject that she did not drop was basketball. She was a smart and intensive player and had great success, which made me happy, especially after what she had gone through.

Instrumentation Development

With the trying times behind us, I again concentrated on the field I loved: laparoscopic surgery. The laparoscopic repair of groin hernias called for an instrument that facilitated the approximation of the two edges of the peritoneum. I came up with such an instrument and named it the Maritsa Tissue Approximator, in honor of her bravery and toughness during her trying times.

The instrument was a simple and straightforward solution to a very specific need. We needed an instrument that would grasp and secure one side of the peritoneum and bring it to the opposing side, and with a second jaw grasp and secure the opposing side, bringing both sides of the peritoneum together so they can be sutured or stapled. I designed an instrument with two jaws, independently operated by two controls. The jaws were comprised of a central plate and two mobile jaws, one on each of its sides. Each of the two jaws, was controlled by a corresponding trigger, and was connected to it by a control wire. I made drawings of the instrument and applied for a patent. I also talked to an instrument maker, who had a display of his tools at one of the surgical meetings I attended. I asked whether he could manufacture the instrument for me, and he said he could make two prototypes for $4,000. The instruments were ready a few months later.

I tried them in the operating room, and they did exactly what they were supposed to. I was thrilled. I had helped create the only instrument in existence that had two jaws and two controls. The patent was issued after some objections from the patent office were overcome.

In the meantime, I had another patent issued for the "endosponge-stick probe", which consisted of an inflatable balloon at the end of a rod covered by a gauze or mesh. The instrument could be inserted in the abdomen and when the balloon was inflated, a large surface instrument was formed, which could be used for manipulating and/or retracting the different organs. I had showed the design to an instrument company representative for his opinion. A couple of months later, he came to me and told me that he saw my instrument at another vendor's set up at a surgical meeting he attended. He gave me the brochure they were using to advertise it.

The manufacturer was an instrument company called "Cabot Medical" headquartered in Pennsylvania. I called them and asked to talk to somebody about their new instrument, which they called "Soft Wand." My call was forwarded to Mr. Glen Stahl, Director of Marketing

"I am Dr. Christoudias and I am calling about the soft wand," I said.

"How can I help you?" he replied.

"I want to know if you have a patent for that instrument," I asked.

"Not yet but we have applied for one," he said.

"Well, you are not going to get it, because I already have a patent for the exact instrument with the same details."

I faxed him a copy of my patent so he could evaluate it. They initially tried to deny that my patent was a detailed description of their instrument, but they eventually conceded that I was the owner of their instrument's patent.

I had a meeting with them at their headquarters, a couple of hours-drive from Bergen County. We reached and signed a royalty agreement in a friendly atmosphere. Glen told me years later they had developed the instrument in cooperation with a surgeon from Illinois, Dr. Frantzides, who also happened to be from Cyprus, just like me. We had the same idea, at about the same time, and we both came from the same tiny part of the world. Cyprus is an Island in the Mediterranean Sea, 3,572 square miles. We never knew each other and have never met. I just happened to apply for a patent before he did and had the patent issued over a year before the new surgical instrument "Soft Wand" was launched by Cabot Medical instrument company.

In 1996 my double grasper, the "Maritsa Tissue Approximator" patent was issued and shortly thereafter I received a call from Marlow Surgical Instruments Company, who expressed an interest in licensing the instrument. Mr. Marlow came to my office from Ohio with his machinist and we reached an agreement. They redesigned the instrument, produced it, and launched it, but only had limited success. I guess it was too complicated for some people to use but it definitely helped me immensely, especially in a laparoscopic groin hernia repair.

A few years later Marlow Instruments Co, was sold and I got control of the Double Grasper again. I formed an instrument company, Apollo Surgical Industries, and marketed the Double Grasper. I also finalized the development of the gauze dissector-peanut and received approval for marketing by the FDA. I designed and patented the machine for the manufacturing of the "peanut" and found a machinist in Bergen County, NJ, to build it for immediate use.

I did not do much marketing, because operating was my first priority, and I was always very busy.

After my daughter graduated from Tufts, she studied as a surgical technician for a year and took charge of the company. She made arrangements with a big instrument company, Symmetry Surgical, to acquire the Double Grasper and the Dissector. That was the end of marketing my instruments for me and Maritsa

Maritsa got married to her high school sweetheart Timothy and they have two amazing girls, Abigail and Madeline. Maritsa pursued a career in real estate, opening her own brokerage, Hera Realty Group LLC.

As time went by, I developed advanced laparoscopic skills, which allowed me to perform more complicated operations with the laparoscopic method, such as colon resections, hiatal hernia repairs, appendectomies, lymph node removal, splenectomies, lysis of adhesions (scar tissue removal) for small bowel blockage and the removal of abdominal tumors.

One such patient was a man in his 60s with abdominal pain. His CAT scan showed tumor in the pelvis. He was referred to me, to determine whether I could remove the tumor laparoscopically. After evaluation and examination of the CAT scan images, it appeared that I could most likely remove the tumor using the minimally invasive technique. The tumor was about two inches in diameter. I explained to the patient that despite my confidence that I could remove the mass with the laparoscopic method, there was a possibility that I might have to convert to the open surgical technique if any difficulties developed during the procedure. The patient consented and we proceeded with the operation a few days later.

During the operation I found that the pelvis was completely covered with scar tissue, which "glued" the intestines to each other making the operation more dangerous and difficult. Nevertheless, I still thought that with persistence and patience, and using my tools, I could reach the tumor and remove it without opening the abdomen. The patient had an appendectomy when he was a teenager, and that was likely the cause of the scar tissue.

I worked diligently and carefully, using my laparoscopic "peanut" to peel the scar tissue from the intestine, or the intestine off the scar tissue, until the tumor was reached. I continued to peel it off, avoiding any injury to the intestine, until it was completely separated from all the surrounding structures. Thankfully, the tumor did not appear to have a lot of circulation, and that made the dissection easier, with minimal bleeding. The minimal bleeding was a little strange, since the tumors usually have a rich blood supply, causing a good amount of bleeding during the operation.

The tumor was totally separated from the normal structures of the pelvis and placed in a "retrieval bag." The 10 mm incision, through which the bag was inserted in the abdomen, was slightly enlarged and dilated, allowing removal of the tumor. The tumor was then immediately sent to the pathologist for examination under the microscope. The process is called a "frozen section" biopsy, during which the specimen, or a small portion of it, depending on its size, is frozen and sliced in extremely thin portions, and colored with special dyes on a slide. The whole process usually takes about 20-30 minutes, so I started closing the incisions without delay, since there was nothing else that needed to be done.

Within three minutes, Dr. Braun, the pathologist called through the intercom, "George, I have the diagnosis."

"Already?" I responded surprised. "Did you do a frozen section?"

"No, I did not have to. When I transected the specimen, I found out it was a 4 by 4-inch gauze, so that gave me the diagnosis. I don't see a true tumor, so I don't need a frozen section," she stated.

The diagnosis explained the lack of circulation of the "mass", the only blood supply was limited to the scar tissue that enveloped the gauze. Evidently the gauze was left behind during the appendectomy operation the patient had over 40 years earlier. The body recognized it as foreign material and isolated it by forming a layer of scar tissue around it. With time the scar tissue started interfering with the normal function of the intestine, causing an intermittent partial blockage associated with pain.

I saw the patient the next morning to send him home and told him the good news—that he had no cancer—or the bad news that the surgeon who had operated on him before, left behind a souvenir, which he carried with him since his last operation.

He shook his head. "Now I get it! That's why it took me forever to get better after that operation. I was sick for months," he said.

At the time of his appendectomy in the 1950s, the gauze used during the operation did not have any radiopaque markers, which could be identified by x-ray. The CAT scan and MRI were not invented yet.

In the modern era, every item used in the operative field is either radiopaque or has a radiopaque marker. If any item is inadvertently left behind inside the abdomen during the operation, it will show up on an x-ray of the abdomen. This sounds very simple and it usually is, but at times it can be much more complicated than this, as I found out in two occasions during my practice.

A retired, elderly doctor with history of kidney failure presented with gastrointestinal bleeding. A plain x-ray of the abdomen was done and was reported as normal by the radiologist who read it. I was asked to evaluate the patient, because he did not like the first surgeon who saw him. The examination did not show any major problems, other than the normal changes that are associated with renal failure, such as anemia. There was some blood in the stool but no evidence of significant active bleeding.

I reviewed the x-rays and the reports and noticed two metal frames in the pelvis, measuring about two inches wide and four inches long, which were not mentioned on the radiologist's report. I thought that maybe they were part of the stretcher the patient was on when the x-ray was taken, or some kind of device outside the body. I was intrigued by the possibilities, so I reviewed the x-rays from the previous admissions. Sure enough, the metal frames were present at the same location in the pelvis, which prompted me to examine the frames more carefully. I recognized them as the detachable components of an abdominal Balfour Retractor used in open surgery. The patient had abdominal surgery several years earlier at another hospital in central New Jersey. I figured that the two components of the Balfour got detached and fell inside the abdomen at the end of his last operation, and the surgeon did not even realize it. The renal doctors and the radiologists were embarrassed that they missed the retractor components clearly demonstrated for several years on the films.

I discussed the findings with the patient and the family. I thought that the bleeding was not serious enough to need surgical treatment and would probably subside spontaneously. As far as the retractor components were concerned, I recommended that they be removed with laparoscopy at a later time, once the GI bleeding episode was definitely cleared.

When the GI bleeding stopped, the patient was discharged home. He said he was going to think about removing the retractor components and let me know. I never heard from him after that. So, this was a case involving retained foreign bodies during an operation, which showed up on x-rays at later times, but were repeatedly and totally missed for many years by the radiologists and the kidney specialists taking care of the patient.

Another strange incident occurred in 2014, just a couple of years before I retired. An obstetrician tried to circumvent the normal protocol of counting all the instruments and other items used, before the operation started and again after it was completed. This protocol was to make sure the counts were correct, and nothing was left in the abdomen. This doctor eliminated the before and after counts and instead did an abdominal x-ray after the operation to demonstrate that there were no surgical items left behind.

One day, as I was finishing my patient rounds, rushing to get to my office, I received an urgent call by the nurse in obstetrics, asking me if I could help the obstetrician retrieve a 4-inch gauze from the abdomen laparoscopically. He had just completed a delivery with a c-section, and the x-ray taken after the operation showed that there was a 4X 4-inch gauze inside the abdomen that had to be retrieved. The patient was scheduled to go to the OR in 30 minutes, she said.

"Hold on," I replied. "Wait until I come and evaluate the patient."

I went there and asked why this obstetrician used 4X4 gauzes inside the abdomen, which we normally never use. I was told that he did not use any, but the post-surgical x-ray taken showed the gauze in the abdomen and "they have no idea how it got there."

"This does not make any sense whatsoever," I told them.

As we were discussing that, there was a call from the OR asking the nurse to transport the patient to the OR for the operation.

"Just hold on," I insisted. "The patient is not ready to go to the OR. I have to finish my evaluation." Then it dawned on me. "What kind of anesthesia did the patient have?" I asked.

"Epidural," the nurse replied.

Epidural anesthesia is administered through the spine with a large needle in the back. I then looked at the nurse and asked her.

"Come with me. I think I know what happened."

We went to the patient's bedside. She was a short and chubby young lady lying on her back. I pictured myself struggling to find a piece of gauze in her belly for hours without success. I asked the nurse to help me turn the patient on her side, so I could check her back, and there it was, a 4 by 4-inch gauze with the x-ray marker taped to the middle of her back, over the spot where the needle was inserted for the epidural anesthesia.

The anesthesiologist put the wrong gauze with the x-ray marker on the puncture wound and taped it there. He was supposed to use a plain gauze, since the ones with the marker are used only in the surgical field.

The x-ray plate was placed under the back of the patient while she was still on the operating table and the x-ray was taken. This resulted in the appearance of the 4X4-inch gauze, giving the false impression that it was in the abdomen.

I removed the gauze and replaced it with a bandaid and requested another abdominal x-ray. Sure enough, the gauze disappeared, and the new x-ray was clear. This was a perfect example of a bad situation created by the obstetrician who tried to circumvent the OR protocol of a complete count before and after surgery, an action that sharply deviates from "standard practice." It was then aggravated by the anesthesiologist who taped the surgical x-ray marked gauze on the spinal puncture side, causing the deceptive appearance of a surgical gauze in the abdomen. To top it off, there was the unbelievable decision to take the patient to the operating room to remove a surgical gauze from the abdomen, which could not have been there, since no such gauze was used in the abdomen during the operation.

The obstetrician involved was embarrassed for scheduling the patient for surgery, which made him look stupid. Lucky for him and luckier for the patient, the nurses got me involved because of my advanced laparoscopic skills. If the patient was taken to the OR for the gauze retrieval, we could have been looking for the nonexistent gauze for hours and we would have never found it. The obstetrician did not even say thank you, but that did not bother me. I was content that I saved the patient from serious pain and suffering and the hospital and the obstetrician from severe embarrassment and probable lawsuits. I was more upset that my involvement in this situation made me quite late for my office hours, and had my patients waiting, something I hated to do. I rushed back to my patients and apologized for the wait.

Our oldest child, Christos, graduated from Ramsey High School in 1995, and started going through the routine college selection process. His participation in football and the distinction of been selected All County, helped him secure a position at the School of Engineering at Tufts University, studying computer science. Sharon drove him to the Tufts campus in Massachusetts, as I stayed behind attending to my practice. He did well, despite the fact that he appeared to spend more time on the football field that the study room. He taught me how to use email, which was relatively new, and at one time he appeared to be entertaining the idea of studying medicine.

"What do you think about me studying medicine?" he asked me by email.

"I think you would make a very good doctor. You are smart, compassionate and kind."

It took him a few days to make his decision. "I don't like your hours! I'll choose computer science," he wrote.

This emanated from the countless times that we planned something, and I had to cancel because I had to run to the hospital for an emergency. I also worked seven days a week, and I was on call 24 hours a day, totally dedicated to my profession, which in general prevented me from spending enough time with my children and family. Christos's decision resulted from his experience as the son of a surgeon. Besides that, I always stressed to my children that they should do what they love, so they will love what they do, because they are going to be doing it for the rest of their lives.

After graduating from Tufts University with a degree in computer science he founded a web page company, with another Tuft's graduate. They named it Digital Bangalow and met with success. He bought his partner out and then sold the company.

Christos eventually relocated to San Francisco, and was employed by "Instacart", a company that deals with online orders and deliveries of groceries, throughout the United States.

My practice was successful, and I was extremely busy. My reputation as a minimally invasive surgeon received a big boost in 1996 when the Bergen Record newspaper published in their health section, an article about me entitled "On the Cutting Edge." It enumerated my accomplishments on the professional level and my inventions and innovations in the field of laparoscopic surgery, having made several scientific presentations on the subject in surgical meetings nationwide and internationally. At the time of the publication, I was actually in Cyprus at an international conference presenting my experience in laparoscopic hernia repair.

I was also selected as a "Top Doctor", by the Castle Connelly Guide year after year, and on January 14th, 2002 I was recognized in a report by the New Yorker Magazine as one of 32 top minimally invasive general surgeons in the New York Metropolitan Area.

All the accolades were great and a perfect boost to my ego, but nothing pleased me more than having a positive impact on people's lives. Every time I saw a patient I had operated on or cared for as part of a team, and it saved that person's life, I felt very happy and content. It was as if I had managed to fulfill my purpose in this world. I came across many challenging situations, which demanded the use of all of the skills I had acquired during my training and from the extensive experience I had from my many years in private practice.

Dr. Ignatios Zairis, a colleague and friend who also trained at KCH-DMC, specialized in cardiothoracic surgery and started his Bergen County practice in 1984. We operated together many times, but Dr. Zairis worked at several area hospitals, so at times it was difficult to reach him. One such time was around 2010, when Holy Name hospital needed him to evaluate a patient with a very high fever and markedly elevated White Blood Count, which was indicative of a severe, acute bacterial infection. The patient had stated that he had "stuck a pencil in his heart."

His medical attending wanted to have Dr. Zairis evaluate him, but since he was not available at that moment, they paged me to see the patient until Dr. Zairis was finished with the surgery he was doing at another hospital. I reviewed the patient's history and examined him. I then checked all his labs and vital signs, and examined his chest x-ray with the radiologist, looking for the pencil he said that he stuck in his heart. But no such pencil showed up on the film. I carefully checked his chest for a wound that would have been created by a penetrating foreign body, and I could not locate any such indication. Clinically the patient had a severe infection, but he kept insisting that he stuck a pencil in his heart. Although that appeared too farfetched, I was not ready to dismiss his claims as a psychotic reaction and label him as "crazy."

I recalled the situation at KCHC during my training when a patient complained that he had a "nail in the head," which had actually turned out to be true. I was determined to further investigate the pencil claim to ensure that I was not missing anything. I ordered a CAT scan, which takes an x-ray of the body in thin slices at different depths. If there had been a pencil in the heart hidden by the heart's shadow on the plain x-ray, it would be revealed in the slices of the CAT scan. I ordered the CAT scan as an emergency, and upon examination of the films with the radiologist, we distinctly and clearly saw that there was a pencil, in the area of the heart! Unbelievable(!), Impossible(!), but True!!!!

I was flabbergasted because, to be honest, I did not expect to find anything from the tests I ordered, but nonetheless, my previous experience with the "nail in the head" guided me to the right decision. I prepared and scheduled the patient for surgery so by the time Dr. Zairis finished and came to Holy Name Hospital everything would be ready to proceed with the operation.

Dr. Zairis operated on the patient and I assisted him. The procedure was done thoracoscopically, a minimally invasive technique using three tiny cuts in the chest. As soon as we inserted the scope inside the chest cavity and directed it towards the heart, there it was! A pencil was sticking out of the pericardium (the sac that covers the heart) with a distinct "No. 2" clearly visible under the eraser. Don't ask me how he managed to stick it there, because I have no idea how he did it! What mattered was that the pencil was there and had to be removed if the patient was going to get any better.

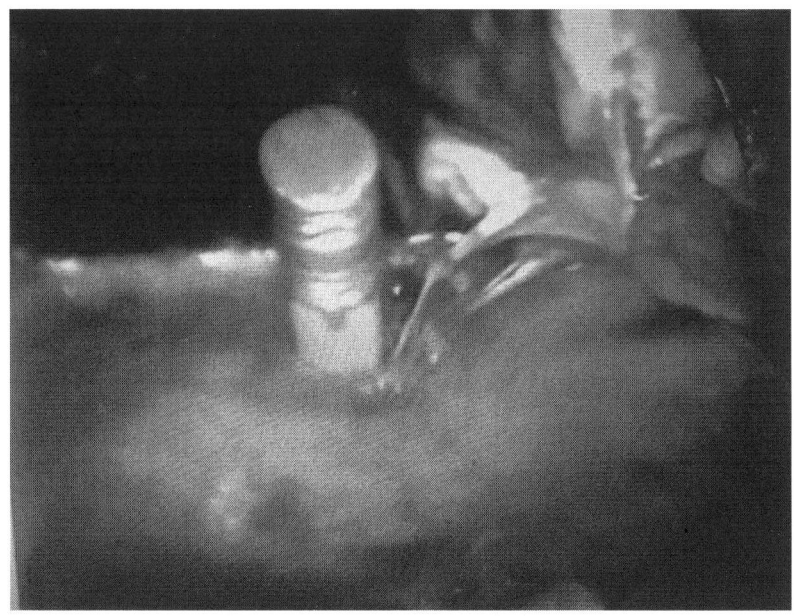

Pencil in the Heart

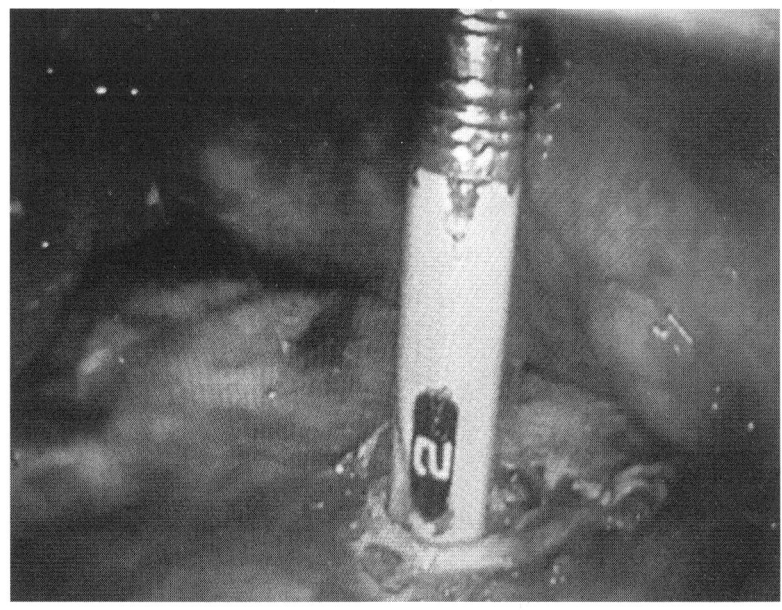

Pencil in the Heart

The pencil was retrieved and removed through one of the ports. The infected fluid in the sac around the heart was suctioned out and sent for culture and sensitivity to identify the germs responsible for the infection and the proper antibiotic needed to treat it. The sac around the heart was then washed out and the area drained.

The patient fully recovered physically, and was referred for psychiatric evaluation and treatment. I was happy that I did not discount the patient's words, and in so doing, I helped avert a total disaster. Pericarditis (infection of the space around the heart), secondary to a foreign body, and from a number two pencil of all things, is not something you are going to read in any medical textbook or journal. I don't think there was ever another case like that, nor do I expect that there will ever be another one!

While in private practice, I had two traumatic experiences, both involving children. I always had special feelings for the children. Not only are they adorable, they are pure, which renders them loving and trusting. They amaze me with their unadulterated way of thinking, and the answers they sometimes come up with, crack me up. There is always a soft spot in my heart for them, and I feel terrible when I see them hurting.

It was winter and there was a lot of fresh snow on the ground. A six-year-old boy asked his parents to allow him to go snow sledding. He was an only child and there was no way they were going to deny him the opportunity to have some fun. They made their way to a gentle hill near the county road, which appeared to be a perfect spot for snow sledding. The boy had a good time sledding down the hill, and then climbing back to the top for another go, time after time.

It didn't end well. The sled overshot the hill's boundaries and landed on the county road in the path of an oncoming car. He was hit and sustained severe head injuries. He was brought to the Holy Name Hospital ER. On evaluation the boy was comatose, unresponsive and restless. His major injuries were limited to the head. He had difficulty breathing, so he was intubated and connected to a respirator. A call was placed to the neurosurgeon and the boy was transferred to the ICU, but his condition continued to deteriorate rapidly. I felt so sad, and totally powerless to help him. He died before the neurosurgeon arrived at the hospital. I was devastated that he died at this tender age, before he even experienced what life was all about. I had difficulty accepting what happened, but I had to be strong, as I was the one who had to go to the boy's parents and deliver the bad news.

I consider myself tough when dealing with difficult situations, but my toughness evaporated, and my mental strength melted out when facing the death of a child. I went to the parents, who were anxiously waiting in the ICU waiting room. I informed them that their child did not make it. I mentioned that the injuries were too severe, and nothing could be done to save him. Tears ran profusely down my face, as I could see the pain in their eyes. I could feel their devastation as they sobbed endlessly and hugged each other in despair. It was God's will I said, though I did not really believe that. I just said it, as a way to indicate that there are situations that are beyond our control. Nobody could convince me that God did not have enough Angels and wanted to take another one by ending this kid's life. I could not fathom the agony the parents would have to endure, with the thought that they may have been partly responsible for their son's death by allowing him the opportunity to have some fun. It is always like that. When you lose somebody you love so much, you always find a way to blame yourself for it. I was afraid that such a thought might possibly haunt them for the rest of their life. This traumatic experience stuck in my mind, just as another instance involving a nine-year-old boy.

When I moved to New Milford, New Jersey, I accepted an appointment to serve as the town's police surgeon. My duties mainly involved making the death pronouncements of people that died at home. My compensation consisted of a small nominal fee per case. I accepted the appointment to help out the police officers, because they were not allowed to remove the body of the diseased, until the death was certified, by a qualified person.

We had a small family gathering on Saturday, Nov. 20, 1982 and stayed up late. Winter was already making its presence known, with a cold wave blanketing the area. Everybody went to bed around midnight, tired from the long day with the guests. Suddenly, I was awakened by the telephone. It was a New Milford Police Officer.

"Doc, we need you for a pronouncement," he said in a stern voice.

I got up, washed my face and went to the location under police escort to do the pronouncement. I saw a charred house and there was a distinct smell of burned wood in the air. A fire destroyed the house just hours ago. There were several people inside, and everybody managed to get out except for the nine-year old boy, Kevin. He was found dead after the fire was extinguished and I was called to certify his death. It was dark and cold in the wee hours of Sunday, Nov. 21, 1982, as the police escorted me through the burned, dark, charred ruins of the house, to the lifeless body of this child. I did the necessary evaluation and proceeded to verify his death. I was shaken by the experience.

When the fire started there were many members of the family in the house. They were all on the second floor and jumped out of the windows, escaping the fire and suffering some injuries in the process. The question was, why was Kevin found on the first floor? The story I got at the time was that the eldest sister was not accounted for after everybody, including Kevin, got out of the house. Kevin then ran back into the burning house to save his sister and never came out alive. I am not sure that's exactly what happened, but I went home with a heavy heart. I could not get this child hero out of my mind. His young life ended abruptly and prematurely, and I was so sorry for him and his surviving family. Losing your house is bad enough but losing a member of the family at that tender age is unfathomable. To make things worse, it turned out that the fire was set on purpose by the eldest sister of seven children, who was 18 years old. She was arrested and charged with killing her nine-year-old brother, a real Greek Tragedy that I will carry with me for the rest of my life.

The deaths of those two children were the saddest part of my professional life, but there is nothing I could do about that. It comes with the territory, and despite the hurt I felt, I had to go on and bury the pain deep inside me.

Living the Good Life

Trip to the Islands of the Aegean Sea

I remember reading in a medical economics journal the response to a question posed to a large number of doctors: "Is there a specific thing in your professional life, that you do not regret doing?"

The unanimous answer was: "The time I spent with my family!" I took that seriously and tried to spend as much time with my wife and kids as possible, though at times it became problematic because of the demands of my profession.

As a family we took our first vacation at the end of August 1980, 3 years after starting my practice in 1977. We traveled to Cyprus with 3-year-old Christos, and one-year-old Stavros.

We stayed in Nicosia and spent some time with family and friends. We then traveled to Polis, on the westernmost part of Cyprus and stayed at the Marion Hotel, which was known to us from the time we spent there during our honeymoon, in 1976. We traveled around and explored the area. We saw a sign "Takkas Beach" so we drove to it, discovering an Idyllic pebble- beach about 2 miles from the hotel, on the way to the Baths of Aphrodite. It was about 10 am, and there was nobody minding the shop, a hut with a restaurant, located about ten feet above the water level and thirty feet away from it.

Takkas Beach

1985, Christos, Stavros, Maritsa, Takkas Beach

We opened the refrigerator, got some soft drinks and descended to the pebble beach. We were already in our Bathing suits. A little while later, the owner, Takkas himself, showed up, with the groceries for the restaurant and freshly caught fish. I climbed up to the restaurant and after the introductions I told him what we took from the fridge. I picked the fish I wanted him to cook for us and walked back down to the pebble beach. We went in the water with the kids and then played with them using the pebbles.

The waters were crystal clear. We could see everything at the bottom of the sea very clearly. More people came to the beach, but it was still very quiet because in September the schools were open and vacation period was over, leaving the beach to the very few people that were vacationing.

At about noon, I heard Takkas shouting: "Doctor your meals are ready". We walked up to the restaurant and enjoyed a delicious meal with full view of the sea and the soothing sound of the waves. Takkas' daughter, a cute 6 year/old girl was helping him serve the customers, while his wife Maroulla was the chef!

We stayed at the Marion Hotel for several days but spend most of our time at the Takkas Beach.

We traveled to Cyprus almost every year, and we always visited The Marion Hotel and Takkas Beach, Sharon Christos, Stavros, Maritsa and me and enjoyed every minute of it, every time we went.

Takkas' Daughter Married a Greek American man from Long Island New York, whom she met when she came to study in America. Her father gave a party at his beach restaurant for her wedding, with over 1000 guests!

We still visit Takkas beach, which is ran by his wife Maroulla. Takkas died at a terrible accident, when the tractor he was riding flipped and killed him, several years ago.

I just needed to concentrate on the good things that came my way, like the cruise to the Greek Islands of the Aegean Sea in August of 1986. The cruise was associated with several seminars and lectures of medical interest as the boat hopped from one island to another. All the Doctors brought their spouses with them. I had spent six years in Athens attending medical school, and I had heard a lot about the charm of the Greek Islands and their beauty and 3,000-year history. I had always wanted to visit the islands, but I never got the chance. I spent all of my time studying, something that rendered me short of time, but more importantly, I was also short on "drachmas." My desire to tour the Greek Islands never left me, and this was my opportunity to fulfill my wish. Sharon and I signed up for the cruise. We first flew to the Athens International Airport, where we met our guide Alex, a happy go lucky person who was fluent in French, German and Italian, but not in English, so I often found myself translating the words he did not know. We all got on the bus, which took us to a boat in Piraeus, chartered for our group of over 30 people.

The set-up of the boat was good, despite the fact that it was quite old. The captain, a man in his late 30s, was familiar with the Aegean Sea, and was polite, confident and competent. We had our own chef, and the members of the crew were cordial and attentive. The boat sailed for the Cyclades, a group of Islands in the Aegean Sea, which include Delos, Naxos, Paros Mykonos and Santorini and the Dodecanese, another group of Islands in the Eastern Aegean Sea, which include Rhodes, Patmos, Symi, Kos, Kalymnos and Astypalaia.

When the boat took off Sharon became nauseous, despite the scopolamine patch she placed behind her ear. She could not enjoy the trip, could not eat anything and could not walk around the boat. Her misery was worsened by the mouth dryness caused by the scopolamine patch. A couple of days later her nausea was cured with the help of our friend Dr. George Keyes, an orthopedic surgeon practicing at Holy Name Hospital. He had Sharon stand on the deck and told her to look straight at the horizon and nowhere else, for a while. A few minutes later the nausea was gone, and Sharon could enjoy the boat trip as much as everybody else. She could appreciate the delicious Greek food prepared on boat without the stomach upset she had felt before, every time she stepped into the dining room.

At the time of our Aegean cruise, in August of 1986, there was an intense heat wave in Greece that caused the death of many people in Athens. We felt the heat wave, but it was lass severe and more tolerable on the Aegean Sea than in the continental area of Greece. Every island we visited offered its own charm and long, rich History. Delos, a small Island with no water, in the ancient times, was known as the "Holy Island" and had a history dating back three millennia. It is uninhabited, since it does not offer the resources to sustain life. There are innumerable antiquities on the island, and according to mythology, Delos is the place where Leto, the Goddess of motherhood, gave birth to the twin Gods, Apollo and Artemis (Diana in Latin).

The largest Island of the Cyclades group is Naxos. It had fertile soil, beautiful beaches and a rich history. In ancient times, it was a wealthy "city-state" and had plenty of monuments. The churches were actually built on the foundation of ancient temples. Naxos has a population of over 10,000 and its capital of the same name is a large town with modern amenities. It spreads inland from the sea, with beautiful, picturesque white houses with blue doors and window shutters dominating the landscape. We walked around the town, admiring the beauty and doing some shopping. The boat was anchored at the port all day, which gave us the opportunity to visit many sites of interest.

The advantage of going on a cruise with a chartered boat, is that we went from island to Island carrying our hotel with us, or to be more accurate, having our hotel move us to the next destination while we were asleep at night. No need to pack and unpack our things. When we went to sleep, the boat was anchored at one island and by the time we woke up, we were at a different port. We visited many islands in the Cyclades and Dodecanese groups, the bigger being the island of Rhodes. The most inspiring from a religious point of view was the island of Patmos where Saint John the Evangelist wrote the Book of Revelation, also known as "Apocalypse" which is the Greek word for Revelation. Syme was the most idyllic and tranquil island. The most relevant for our medical profession was the island of Kos.

The island of Rhodes, at the most southeastern border of the Aegean Sea, had a rich history and plenty of archaeological monuments. One of the Seven Wonders of the ancient world, The Colossus of Rhodes was built there. There was plenty to see and do, from archaeological and historical sites, to arts and crafts shopping, to natural wonders like the valley of butterflies. There was even a golf course. There were fortifications from the time of the crusaders of St. John, who were the masters of the island at the time. The shops were full of local artifacts and crafts. While at a store specializing in handmade tablecloths with elaborate hand-sewn decorations, and witnessed an interesting bargaining process between Mary, another passenger of our boat, and a pushy salesman. Mary was presented with a beautiful, large tablecloth, and was asking a lot of questions, something that led the salesman conclude that she was ready to purchase the merchandise. He pushed hard for the sale, making Mary feel trapped.

"Listen, I like it very much, but I don't know if it fits my dining table. I will go home and measure my table and if it fits, I will come back to buy it," she said.

She completely disarmed the salesman, who ran out of arguments to convince her to purchase the tablecloth. Of course, she never returned for the tablecloth since her dining table was a few thousand miles away.

A few people went to the golf course, while the rest of us took a chartered bus to the valley of the butterflies, which was on a mountain, at a higher altitude. It was an extremely hot day, one that demanded air conditioning. We got on the bus and as we headed for the valley of the butterflies the heat was unbearable.

Alex, our guide, addressed the passengers: "Don't worry! We will turn on the air condition." He asked the driver to do it, only to find out that the air condition was not working. "The air condition is not working, but no worry! We shall open the windows." It turned out the windows were not made to open. I felt sorry for the passengers, and even more sorry for Alex. This was just one of several times he was humiliated by his ignorance and lack of preparation.

We got to the valley of the butterflies, but the whole trip was overshadowed by the bus fiasco. The next stop was the island of Patmos, where St. John the Theologian lived and died. He was the only Apostle who died of natural causes and not by violence. He lived in a cave on the island, which we got to visit. We saw the rock on which St. John rested his head inside the cave and where he wrote the book of revelations.

John Keys, the brother of Dr. George Keys, had a question. "Is St. John of the Greek Orthodox Religion the same as the Catholic St. John"?

The answer was yes. The split between Orthodox Christianity and Catholicism did not happen until the year 1054, about 1,000 years after St. John's life. We also visited the Monastery of St. John the Theologian, which was founded in 1088. It was located on the top of a hill in Chora, the capital of Patmos. There was a room where religious treasures were safeguarded, and where only Orthodox Christians were allowed to enter. We walked up the hill to the gate of the monastery, where we had to be dressed appropriately in order to enter the monastery grounds. Appropriate clothes were provided at the entrance to the monastery for those that did not meet the dress code. The borrowed clothes could be worn over their shorts while inside the monastery and were returned at the end of the visit. A panoramic view of Chora and its white houses awaited the visitors at the top of the Monastery. It was an uplifting experience.

The next island, Syme, was impressive with the smooth, tranquil, elegant beauty of its shoreline and the whitewash houses. We experienced a calming effect from the visit.

On the island of Kos, we had a special local guide who had spent some time in the United States. We were happy that we were going to have a "real guide" show us the island where the Father of Medicine, Hippocrates, was born, lived and practiced the art and science of our profession.

Instead we were faced with a conspiracy theorist, who claimed that he was persecuted by the CIA and other dark forces. It was clear to any medical professional with basic psychiatric knowledge that the guide should have been in a psychiatric clinic. He did at least have knowledge about the island of Kos. We were guided to the area where Hippocrates was born in 460 BC, lived and studied the art and science of medicine. This was the place where he practiced and taught, recording and leaving the foundations of medicine for posterity. We visited the grounds of the "Asklepoeon," the hospital where Hippocrates learned, practiced and taught medicine. It was located on a hill with a gentle inclination.

We sailed from Kos for Mykonos, a famed island of the Cyclades group. We were approaching the end of our cruise, and Mykonos was going to be our last island to visit. That was where the Captain's Dinner was going to be served; the last dinner on the boat was with the Captain. It was the third week of August, and that is the time known for the "Meltemia,"—strong winds coming from the north that caused rough seas. The sea was so rough, that I was afraid we may not make it to Mykonos. Sharon was in the cabin, nauseous, unable to get up. Of the 30-plus passengers only a handful of us made it to the dining room. Even some members of the crew were incapacitated. I had my dinner and went up to my cabin. Sharon was unable to stand up, not only from the nausea, but also because of the great swings of the boat, which climbed up the huge waves and then dropped down to the void between the waves.

I was not going to stay in my cabin waiting for something bad to happen. I stood outside and held firmly onto a metal pole, which was a part of the boat structure. I went up and down for what seemed like endless hours. I could hear the angry, deafening roar of the Aegean Sea, a scary sound, interrupted occasionally by the breaking plates that fell out of their cabinets in the kitchen. All the while, I was holding onto the metal pole for dear life. I planned what to do in case the boat went down. I was not optimistic that anyone would survive if that happened, but I surely was going to try. The plan was to run back to the cabin a few feet away, grab Sharon and two life jackets, and try to swim away from the boat pulling Sharon with me since she did not know how to swim. I knew that this was probably not going to work, but at least I could be hopeful that it might. After all, life without hope is finished, and the boat had not capsized as yet. The boat was going up and down, but it had not gone under. I remembered one of the first Latin sentences I learn in high school: "Dum spiro, spero," meaning "as long as I breath, I hope." I kept breathing and hoping, but it seemed like time had stopped moving. The rough seas lasted for hours, but to me it seemed like never-ending centuries before the boat arrived safely at the port of Mykonos Island. It felt so good to walk off the boat and onto solid ground.

That evening, the Captain's Dinner had to be modified because there were not enough plates for a three-course meal. All three courses had to be compounded onto one plate, but everybody was happy to be alive and dry. We enjoyed the dinner and complemented the captain for keeping us safe. All and all, this was a precious experience, educational, enjoyable, relaxing and adventurous. My dream and desire of cruising the Greek Islands had been fulfilled. The only thing missing to make our experience complete was the presence of our children, Christos, Stavros and Maritsa, something we corrected three years later, when we took a cruise to the Greek Islands of the Ionian Sea, West of Continental Greece.

Cruise to the Ionian Sea Islands

In 1989 we signed up for a catamaran cruise on the Ionian Sea. The trip with the catamaran was arranged by our friend Harry Nafpliotis, a physical therapist. Our group included a total of 25 passengers, a smaller group than the one we had in 1986. This time we took our three children with us: 12 year-old Christos, 10 year-old Stavros, and 7 year-old Maritsa. We flew to Athens and from there we were bused to Piraeus, where the catamaran was anchored. Stella was our guide, but unfortunately, she was not any better than Alex, our 1986 cruise guide. Despite the guide, we managed to get the necessary information about each island we visited from written documents. Stella, realizing that we expected much more from her than what she had to offer, bailed out in the middle of the cruise.

The boat took off from Piraeus and headed towards the Isthmus of Corinth. We arrived there early the next morning. The isthmus was a narrow part of land joining the peninsula of Peloponnese to the continental Greece. A four-mile long canal was built in 1893, connecting the Aegean Sea with the Ionian Sea and shortening the voyage between the two by 440 miles. We passed through the canal, and proceeded to the Ionian Sea, our destination. We visited the Islands of Zakynthos, Lefkada, Kefallonia, Ithaca and Corfu. The islands as a group had a striking difference from the Aegean Islands in that they were covered by greenery. The islands of the Aegean Sea appeared drier, with the brown color of the rocks dominating the landscape. Again, we observed that each island had its own character, magic and beauty, which had a calming effect on our soul. The boat crew was fantastic, and the entire trip was a continuous party.

The best part was the presence of our kids. They really enjoyed the new experience and we enjoyed it with them. We usually had breakfast on board, and either lunch or supper we ate on land. On Aug. 24 we were in Kefallonia. The boat was anchored at the Port of Argostoli, the capital of the Island, and in the evening, Sharon, me, and our children explored the town on foot. We saw a nice restaurant with outside seating under a grapevine and sat down for supper. We ordered some delicious Greek food and some wine. There was another table of European customers seated near us. As we started eating, we noticed that the the the grapes hanging on the vine had started swinging. At the same time, it felt as if someone was shaking our chairs. It took a few seconds to realize that we were experiencing an earthquake.

There were no solid structures that could collapse and hurt us, so we stayed right where we were sitting. The people at the next table, however, started shouting "earthquake" as they jumped out of their chairs and went running from the outside to the outside! We started laughing at the panic-stricken customers. The shaking went on for a while and when it stopped, the other customers came back to their table, and we all went on to enjoy our meals. It was the first time that our kids had experienced an earthquake.

The other experience that I will never forget is the time that the catamaran anchored at the most beautiful beach I had ever seen. It was a beach in the Island of Ithaca known as the island of the Trojan War hero Ulysses, who led the Greeks in defeating the Trojans by building and using the Trojan Horse some 3,000 years ago. This beach was blessed with crystal clear turquoise waters and bright white sand. It was accessible only by boat, as it was surrounded by these huge, majestic white rocks, which appeared to be elevated about 100 feet, straight up from the beach. The boat had to anchor about 100 plus feet away from the beach, because the depth of the waters closer to the beach could not sustain the weight of the boat without hitting the bottom. From there we were going to swim to the shore, or, for the people who could not swim, they would be ferried to the beach with a dinghy, a small boat, which could safely be maneuvered in shallow waters. We were all looking forward to getting to the beach, but unfortunately the dinghy's motor broke down. Since Sharon did not know how to swim, she had to stay on the catamaran. Christos and Stavros were good swimmers, but Maritsa was just seven years old, not yet an experienced swimmer. I wanted to take her with me to shore but Sharon had serious doubts about the wisdom of having her swim that far without a lifejacket.

"Maritsa, do you want to come with us?" I asked.

She didn't hesitate for a second. "Yes, I do," she declared.

"OK! We will swim together, and I will always be by your side. When you get tired, you grab my shoulder and rest, while I continue to swim and carry you towards the shore. If you feel rested and want to swim again, just let me know. We will do that until we reach the shore."

She got it and she was ready for it. The sea was very calm and the swim comfortable. Maritsa was doing well. She was calm and determined, and though she had to take a few breathers, she swam all the way, without much ado, right next to me and with Christos and Stavros nearby. It was worth the effort. The beach was magnificent, with crystal clear, velvet waters and the clean, bright white sand and the rock formation towering in the background. It was too bad that Sharon was left behind. She watched us from the time we left the boat until we reached land. Then she relaxed with a sigh of relief. We waved at her before we lay down on the sand. We stayed there for about an hour, swimming or resting on the sand and enjoying the beautiful surroundings. We swam back to the boat and joined Sharon before the boat sailed for the next Island.

The last island we visited was Corfu, one of the northernmost and westernmost Greek Islands. We spent a day there, mostly in the capital, also named Corfu. We went around the town, doing more looking than shopping. When we got tired, we sat down in one of the many coffee shops and enjoyed a soft drink and a sweet. We came across a hub for horse and buggies, so we stopped and let the kids ride away to their full entertainment. While the kids were riding around, Sharon and myself, sat at a coffee shop at an outside table. Suddenly I heard somebody calling my name.

"Dr. and Mrs. Christoudias, nice to see you here!"

We turned around and were amazed to see Mrs. Dina Mouzakitis. Dina and her whole family were my patients and they owned Rudy's Restaurant, in Hackensack New Jersey, which we visited often. I knew the family was from Corfu but I did not expect to see them there. That was a pleasant surprise, which led to a nice conversation about the island.

Back at the boat later that evening after resting in the afternoon, we sat down for the Captain's Dinner. We were treated with a variety of Greek specialties, which we enjoyed under the sounds of delightful and stimulating Greek music. Everybody was on deck dancing to the Greek tunes, as wine flowed for the adults and soft drinks for the children. Christos, Stavros and Maritsa joined in and kept dancing. It was clear that they were enjoying every second of it. We joined in with our kids and danced as a group, though Sharon was kind of shy to participate for too long. The music kept going and so did we until after midnight when the party finally came to an end. Maritsa, however, was not ready to accept, that the party ended. When I told her that the party was over, she surprised me with a scream.

Dancing on Deck Ionian Sea Cruise

"Keep the music going! I want to dance more!" Not only did she say it, she meant it too!

I knew my little girl as being determined and tough, but she was never so demanding and bossy. For a moment I wondered whether she was drinking wine instead of lemonade, but I knew that it was not true. It was just the wild streak in her, and the good time she was having, that made her want to keep it going. I gave her a hug and woke her up to reality.

"Maritsa, it's over. Time to go to sleep! We can continue tomorrow."

When the night was over, so was the cruise. The next day we disembarked with our luggage and bussed to the airport. We had a beautiful time, and in addition to the souvenirs we carried home some fond memories.

Trip to Cyprus with Family and friends

In September 1996, I was invited to participate in an international convention relating to health sciences in Nicosia Cyprus organized by the Greek Diaspora. The subject of my presentation was laparoscopic repair of a groin hernia and included a video demonstration of the technique I used. The children were not able to come with us, since Christos was already at Tufts University studying computer science, and Maritsa and Stavros had to attend Ramsey High School. Our friend Harry Nafpliotis, a physical therapist, was also going to participate in the conference and his wife Gloria and her brother Ivan came along. Since we were also planning to tour the Island of Cyprus, we invited our good friends, Peter and Joyce Cosmas, to join the group. Peter, a funny guy, was our accountant, and like the rest of the group, aside than me and Sharon, he had never been to Cyprus. We thought we were going to have a nice time together but had no idea what was about to transpire during our stay and travel in The Island of Love.

We arrived in Cyprus and had our convention. My presentation went well. During the convention the rest of the group visited the old section of Nicosia within the walls, built by the Venetians and Ottomans, centuries earlier. After the meeting it was time to tour the island. My nephew's wife had recommended a car lease company, so we rented a stick shift SUV that could accommodate eight people, though the last two seats could only be accessed through the door at the rear of the car.

I drove and Harry sat in the front passenger seat, while Sharon, Joyce and Gloria sat in the second row. Peter and Ivan sat in the back. Ivan was tall and every time he got in or out of the SUV, he banged his head on the car ceiling. Everyone joked that we should try to secure a helmet for Ivan, otherwise he may not survive the journey.

We headed for Paphos, a city with rich history, impressive archaeological sites and plenty of beautiful beaches and five-star hotels. Paphos is the city where Saint Paul received the "40 lashes minus one" while preaching Christianity in Cyprus. There is also a catacomb in Paphos, which was constructed during the earlyRoman times.

We arrived at our hotel, which appeared to be brand new with generous use of marble and granite and other top-shelf building material. The decorations of the common areas, restaurants and rooms were well planned and executed. The landscape was also beautifully done, with plenty of lovely trees, bushes and flowers, and a meandering walkway that defined the elaborate design. An Olympic-sized swimming pool was further away from the main building and extending towards the natural sandy beach. We made good use of our time in Paphos and visited the impressive sights of the Archaeological Park. We sunbathed by the pool or the natural sandy beach and we indulged in the delicious food offered by the myriad restaurants.

The Archaeological Park of Paphos had a history that expanded from prehistoric times to the Middle Ages and modern times. It included several Roman villas with exquisite mosaic depictions of scenes from Greek Mythology. The mosaics dated to the third and fourth centuries AD and it was amazing to see the mastery with which the mosaic scenes were put together, having survived in a condition that still stuns visitors.

We also toured the agora and the Odeon, a Greco-Roman theater in the same area. In 1980, the Odeon was inscribed on the UNESCO World Heritage List of outstanding ancient remains. We visited the local archaeological museum, and I was amazed to see a display of a 2,500-year-old surgical scalpel, not much different than the scalpels used in the operating rooms of our times.

The most memorable time was experienced in Paphos, during the last two days of our stay and on the trip back to Nicosia. We were heading for the pool and beach after a nice lunch. The whole group walked together through the beautiful landscape when Peter Cosmas, the accountant, came up with a profound observation.

"Cyprus is very, very boring. It's 86 degrees with sunshine every single day."

Peter Cosmas must have been on good terms with God, because the Lord was listening, and decided to take care of his boredom. We reached the pool area and settled down. Sharon and I took two sunbeds on the sandy beach by the sea, while everyone else went to relax by the pool. At one point, I decided to go to my room to get something to read. As I passed by the pool, I noticed that the water was forming strange waves, as if it was dancing to the rhythm of the Greek music playing in the background. As I tried to climb a step on the walkway, I started tilting to one side and backwards.

"I must be having I stroke," I thought to myself.

Then I heard Ivan's voice. "It's an earthquake," he stated calmly.

He would know; he lived in California and the San Andreas Fault passed by his backyard. He was quite familiar with any and all earthquake activities.

I ran back to Sharon, who was screaming at me, thinking that I was the one shaking her sunbed. She suddenly realized that it was an earthquake. We stayed by the pool until later in the afternoon. When we went back in, I heard the clerk at the reception desk telling everyone that there was not going to be any more earthquake activity. That did not sound right to me, so I approached her and asked how she could be sure about that.

"I am not sure," she said, "but I just say that to calm the people down."

Our hotel was a brand-new structure, but it had suffered some damage from the "shake-up." There were some cracks along the walls but no major structural damage. Overnight, we felt a few aftershocks until the morning and that kept us on our toes. We thought the earthquake was enough of a break for Peter's boredom, but there was more excitement to come.

After a rich breakfast we spent the morning packing and after sign-ing out we went by the old castle near the small port of Paphos, where there was a plethora of seafood restaurants. We had our lunch and walked around by the castle. The sky suddenly got invaded by a swarm of dark clouds, which appeared to be fast approaching from the west. We got in the car and we were ready to head back to Nicosia, hoping to get ahead of the impending storm, but first we had to pass by the jewelry store to pick up a custom-made necklace that Ivan had ordered the day before.

By the time we all got in the SUV, with Ivan hitting his head on the ceiling again, the sky was completely occupied by black clouds. I drove to the jewelry store as it started raining hard. When Ivan jumped out and run to the store, lightning and thunder came upon the surround-ings, and our car was assaulted by a barrage of intense, walnut-sized hail. The deafening noise lasted for more than 20 minutes, covering the entire area with a white coating of ice balls. Ivan wisely stayed in the jewelry shop because had he come out, his battered head would have not been able to withstand the hail assault.

The hail was followed by torrential rain and Ivan braved a run to the SUV, opening the rear door and hitting his head on the ceiling again as he entered the car. Finally, we were good to go. Paphos is not a big city and at that time did not have an elaborate maze of roads. There was one main road coming from Limassol that passed through the center of town and continued towards the town of Polis. There were several narrow offshoots of streets heading towards the sea and several towards the mountains. The streets were designed and built by people who trav-eled by donkeys, mules and horses.

I headed for the main road. Cyprus does not typically have much rain, so it was not prepared for heavy downpours. It did not take but a few seconds before I realized that all the side streets had become small rivers that made traveling difficult if not impossible. Some streets became too dangerous to cross. Suddenly it was like I was driving a car in Venice and not the usually "bone-dry" town of Paphos. I turned back and tried a different route, only to be faced with the same situation. I realized that we were not going anywhere until the waters receded.

When the intensity of the rain diminished, it took about an hour before all the water ran down to the sea, rendering the roads passable again. By then it was late afternoon and there was still a light, steady rain coming down. I found my way to the main road and continued unimpeded towards Limassol and from there back to Nicosia. Limassol was about a 60-minute drive away with good weather conditions. I figured it was going to take us 90 minutes traveling in rain on a hilly road with suboptimal visibility.

We were halfway to Limassol when the windshield became foggy. I turned on the defrost system, but it did not work. It was rainy and dark, and I could not see the road. We needed something to clean the condensation off the windshield, so Joyce Cosmas took her socks off and gave them to Harry, who was sitting on the passengers side. Harry used the socks to continuously sweep the condensation off the windshield so I could see the road. I called over to Peter Cosmas.

"Hey, Peter! Do you still think that Cyprus is a Boring place?"

Everybody broke into laughter.

"It's been a long time since I had such excitement," Peter said.

As we got closer to Limassol, Sharon said something that reflected what appeared to be on everybody's mind.

"What kind of car is this! How can the defrost system not work?"

My response was simple. "Sharon, it usually does not rain in Cyprus. Cyprus is very dry and hardly ever do you need the defrost. Let's be grateful that at least the windshield wiper is functioning well."

By the time I finished my words, as if God was listening again and wanted to make things even more interesting and exciting, the windshield wiper on my side flew off its metal frame into the wet darkness of the night. Joyce's socks were no longer able to provide the visual clarity necessary for safe driving.

I opened the window and followed the road by moving my head out of my side window. Fortunately, the rain stopped a few minutes later, just as we reached Limassol. I left the window half open to prevent windshield condensation.

There were no more problems for the remainder of our trip, and we arrived safely in Nicosia. The next day I took the SUV back to the people I leased it from.

"Were you trying to kill me with this car?" I asked the lady in charge of the car rentals.

"Why?"

I told her the story and she couldn't stop laughing.

We flew home the next day. I was glad that the Lord cured Peter Cosmas's boredom and gave everyone a nice time and a memorable experience.

I returned to my practice and I was as busy as ever, especially after an article written about me in the health section of the New Jersey newspaper the Bergen Record on Aug. 19, 1996. The article's title was "On The Cutting Edge, Teaneck Surgeon Develops the Tools of the Laparoscopic Trade." It told the story of my contribution to the new surgical laparoscopic techniques and the development of some new instrumentation.

The responsibilities were heavy and the hours long, but my love for the art of surgery and my fellow human beings was greater, giving me unbelievable energy, joy and great satisfaction in the process. Throughout the period of my practice I always saw the person inside the patient and developed a bond with each and every one, promising to do my part in caring for them, and asking them to get involved in their care.

"It takes a lot of work and a lot of effort to get over your problem. Fifty percent is up to me and the other 50 percent is up to you," I used to tell my patients. "I promise I will do my 50 percent and I want you to do your half." I was very happy to see that all my patients did their part, as I did mine

Class Reunion and a home in Cyprus

In 2001 a 40-year High School class reunion was organized by a bunch of classmates. There were several hundred students in the class of 1961, at the Pancyprian Gymnasium High School. I made arrangements to travel to Cyprus that Summer of 2001 for the reunion, which was held at a Nicosia Hotel Grand Ballroom.

Sharon did not want to travel that year, but my son Christos, did accompany me.

It was nice to meet with my old classmates, most of whom I had not seen since graduation. Many of them changed very little, while for some time was not so kind, shaping them to completely different looks and shapes, so we had to reintroduce ourselves, and have a laugh about the changes that happened to the appearance of so many of us over the last 40 years It was a joyous event and it was good to see so many old friends, in the same place.

Feeling the affinity for my old country I felt the need to buy a house, where I could escape to, every year for relaxation, in friendly surroundings. My property in Karavas was under occupation of the Turkish Invaders, so I needed something in the free part of Cyprus.

I was vacationing with my son Christos at Ayia Napa, a tourist destination, with beautiful beaches. Christos statement when we were there, was clear

"Baba, this is the place to buy!" I agreed. I bought a house about 3 blocks from the water, which was still under construction, It was completed by the next summer. Since then we visited Cyprus every year. In 2004 I had a second house custom built, just one block from the sea., and sold the first one

Help Is On The Way

Stavros graduated from Boston University and was accepted to medical School at UMDNJ, where he met his future wife Moira, also a Medical student. After graduation they both secured surgical Residency positions at Morristown Memorial Hospital. They got Married in 2009, while they were still residents, and had their first child, a boy, in 2011. He was our first grandchild, and was named Georgos after me, keeping the ages old tradition of naming the first boy after the paternal grandfather, a move that made me very proud and happy!

Moira did a subspecialty and became a Breast Surgeon, and Stavros specialized in General Surgery, with special interest in Laparoscopic Surgery. They both joined my practice in 2012 and then created their own professional entity, Heritage Surgical Group, a move with which I was in full agreement.

Operating with my son and daughter in law was an experience I was looking forward to. I wanted to see their surgical skills and bedside manners since they were going to be trusted with the care of my patients. I also wanted to pass on what my surgical experience of 42 years had taught me.

I was not disappointed. They both had already advanced surgical skills and were able to work in a deliberate, precise and elegant manner. I knew then that my patients were going to be in good hands! I stopped seeing breast patients and diverted them to Moira.

I continued to perform some general surgical and cancer surgery procedures, and had Stavros assist me. I also assisted Stavros with his operations, and though he had very refined advanced skills, I still wanted to show him some "tricks" that would refine his skills even further. He always resisted my suggestions, but I know that he adopted most of them, because I saw him using them later, when we operated together. In the process I also learned a few things from him

There was one operation however that he learned exclusively from me. That was the operation for laparoscopic repair of incisional hernia, a procedure that he could not learn anywhere else, because I was the one who designed it, invented it and used it. Before my retirement I published a study, which examined the results of my procedure for repair of the incisional hernia. The study demonstrated superior outcomes, in comparison with the other methods of hernia repair.

I worked with Stavros for four years before retiring in 2016 at the age of 73. I enjoyed operating with him in multiple procedures. His skills and bedside manners made me proud. He is recognized as a Top Doctor by his peers, carrying on the legacy of his old man, and Moira also accomplished the same distinction of a top doctor, as a Breast surgeon.

Moira and Stavros had two girls after Georgos, Maeve and Teagan, that made us feel blessed with five grandchildren!

Essentials for a Successful Operation

My successful career was coming to an end. I felt very content with my accomplishments over the 46 years I worked, doing surgery, but I knew that I could not take all the credit for the very good outcomes of my operations. It takes a lot of work, by many people to accomplish good outcomes of any and all the procedures.

First, I had an outstanding office staff run by the best office Manager, my wife Sharon. She was always on top of things, making sure that all the necessary lab work and tests were carried out before the patient was admitted for surgery and all the paperwork was completed. She was assisted by our secretary for thirty years, Pat Stagno. All the patients were given the appropriate instructions before their operations, and my office staff was always available to guide them and answer any questions.

Then, the nursing and ancillary personnel of the Hospital, that prepared the patient for the operation, had an important role in following the protocol so the patient was ready for the Operating Room in a timely fashion.

In the Operating Room, the nurses and the OR technicians are of paramount importance. Everything the surgeon needs for a specific operation has to be brought to the room before the operation starts. This takes a lot of organization, knowledge and preparation by both the OR nurse and technician, who would hand the surgical instruments over to the surgeon, during the operation. The technician will perform better if she/he knows the steps of the operation and the instruments used by the specific surgeon she/he is scrubbing with. For example the technician who worked with me most of the times, Gina Cottrell, was exceptionally good, because she knew what instruments I used and when. I could do any operation with her and I always had the instrument I needed in my hand before I even asked for it, though the first time she scrubbed with me she got me upset. She had just graduated and was assigned to my room. I asked for an instrument and she gave me an argument! I yelled at her and she cried. After that, we never argued again for the 25 plus years we worked together, and I was delighted every time I had her as my scrub technician. I have to say that all the OR nurses and technicians were very good at Holy Name Medical Center, and some of them were exceptional.

After an operation the patient is moved to the Recovery Room, AKA (PACU) Post Anesthesia Care Unit, where the patients are monitored very closely until the anesthesia effects ware out. Once the patient is fully awake gets transferred to a regular floor, until they are discharged home.

I feel grateful to so many health professionals, nurses, OR technicians and ancillary personnel, for their very important role in taking care of my patients with me. God Bless them!

Life After Retirement

On December 28th, 2015, I performed the last operation of my career, with my son Stavros.Aris, was an 87 years old man, with a tumor of the stomach. He was also from Karavas, Cyprus, a family friend and distant relative. He is now 90 and doing well, in 2020. On Dec. 31, 2015, 16 days shy of my 73rd birthday, I retired from the practice of surgery. I pondered many times over what life will be like, when all of a sudden, I would not have to answer any calls, or run to the hospital to take care of patients. I had been working since I was six years old, and very rarely did I have the luxury of using my time for myself. I always had a duty to perform, a job to do or somebody to help or save, so I was wondering what life would be like, when I don't have to attend to anybody, but my family and myself.

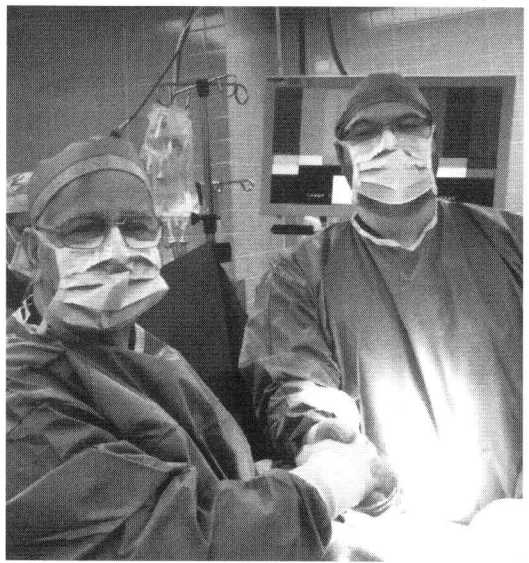

Last Operation with Stavros

It did not take long to find out. Life is beautiful.

Uwe Hagen, a friend from Germany, had described to me several years earlier, what his friends do when they retire: "The first year they travel. The second year they fix their house and from the third year on they sit home and wait to die!" That was funny and yet a grim proposition, so I stayed away from that example.

I did travel to several destinations in Europe and stayed at least for 3-4 weeks in Cyprus every year. I had a house by the sea in the free part of Cyprus which I had custom built in 2004. I had a big lot, so I planted 18 olive trees, two pomegranate trees, three Palm trees, a carob tree, a fig tree, three buganvilias, many lantanas and a rose garden. I also planted lemon and orange trees to remind me of Karavas, but they did not survive the strong winds coming from the sea. There is nothing better for breakfast than freshly peeled pomegranate just cut from the tree, cracked green olives from my trees cured and prepared with cilantro, garlic, olive oil and lemon, as per my mother's recipe, served with halloumi cheese, fresh tomato and cucumber and sesame bread toast.

I always meet with my high school friends every year when I go to Cyprus. Our dear friend George Drakos passed in 2014, so Nikos, Stelios and occasionally another friend and classmate, Dr. John Christodoulides from Buffalo N.Y. if he happens to be in Cyprus, get together at a restaurant, usually a fish tavern by the sea. We remember the good old times and catch up with the events that came our way, since our previous meeting.

The DNA Family

In May 2017, I received a message through the "23 and me" DNA company. The sender was George Portoukalian, who informed me that he was born out of wedlock in 1933. DNA results showed that he has a lot of Greek "cousins," most of their families were from Karavas, Cyprus, and I am one of them, second or third cousin. He was a retired member of the US Air Force, and he was residing in North Carolina. He has been trying to find out his father's identity for over 25 years, without any success, and he was wondering whether I was willing to help him out. I thought about it and it appeared a very intriguing proposition, so I responded that I will do my best to help him in his quest.

His wife, Shelah, a 21st century "Sherlock Holmes", was doing a lot of research and was passing to me all the information they could find, to see if I knew any of his online DNA cousins, or if I was familiar with their families. In the process I learned a lot about my family, since I had to do my own research on the names and families they were forwarding to me. I interviewed all the people from Karavas that live in Bergen County, NJ and Virginia, and I found more relatives than I knew I had. The exhaustive research went on for fourteen months, and we were not any closer to finding George's father than when we started this quest, though we had frequent communications through email, including all the cousins that participated in the quest, from London to Turkey to New Zealand and the USA, among them cousins Nick Loucas and Nancy Loucas, Uncle Christ's grandchildren.

In July of 2018, I was informed by George Portoukalian that he had exciting news. He received a message by another relative named Tommy Michaelides who told George that his DNA indicated that George was his first cousin. Tommy said that George was his closest relative in the entire DNA database and he wanted to talk with him to share information. They talked on the phone immediately and Tommy gave George some information about his father and grandfather. George then contacted me and wanted to know if I knew them? I asked him to give me Tommy's number, so that I could call him and ask him more about his immediate relatives.

I called Tommy and found that he was from Cyprus. He came to study engineering in the US and was subsequently offered a job and settled in Tennessee. He is married and has two kids. He told me his last name was Michaelides and that his grandfather, Christakis, worked for Kallis Bus Company in Karavas. I told him I knew his family and I think that his father has a first cousin who lives in New Jersey, Maro Zampas. Her husband, Stavros, was my second cousin. When he told me that his grandfather was the son of "Hedgehog" (a nickname for Maro Zampas' grandmother), I became certain I knew his family. He did not know of Maro, but I knew that finally we were getting very close to figuring out the puzzle of George's father.

I talked to Maro, who confirmed that Tommy's Grandfather Christakis was her uncle. After investigating further we reached the conclusion, that George Portoukalian was the son of Mihalas, the brother of Maro's father John. At that time I had to make another phone call. George answered the phone.

"George, I have news for you. Not only do I know who your father is, but I also had met him and knew him. He was my father's friend"! George was stunned! He then broke his silence.

"Was he a gentle man"? he asked.

"Yes, George. He was a very good man"

Mihalas Michaelides, George's father, married in the States and had a daughter, Cleopatra (Cleo). He returned to Cyprus in the 1940's after a divorce. He got remarried before returning to America. I met him while he was in Cyprus, as my father's friend. He owned the movie theater in Karavas, so every Saturday when we went to the village, we used to go to the movies. Mihalas was there and he would always strike a long conversation with my father.

I told George everything I knew about his father. I also told him that a good family friend who lives in New Jersey, Maro Zampas, was his first cousin. I suggested that he send her a DNA kit, to shed more light on their relationship. He sent her a DNA kit, and the results confirmed that they were indeed first cousins.

He connected with his first cousin Maro, and they continue communicating often. In the process of my research I found out that Maro is also my third cousin, just like George. Their great grandfather, Papaporphyris, a priest, and my great grandfather, Loukas Economou, were brothers. George also found out from Maro that he had a sister,

Cleopatra, who also happened to live in North Carolina, his State, and three brothers in New York. He also had two more brothers, but they had already died.

There was a happy ending with the siblings and their families, meeting for the first time of their lives at Cleo's house in North Carolina on October 28, 2018. They have been in frequent contact since then. Unfortunately, Cleo passed away 14 months later.

George Portoukalian Meets Sister Cleo for the First Time

The Christoudias Family

Looking back, our family kept together despite some transient differences.

Stavros, the oldest brother, born on May 23, 1934 continued to expand his business in running duty free shops in Cyprus and Greece, real estate developments and management in Cyprus and Greece, and marketing several products. He lost his wife to a stroke in 2007, and a couple of years later he was diagnosed with lung cancer with spread. He was treated with chemotherapy and died on February 3, 2011. His older daughter Maria with her husband Marios and children Panayiotis and daughter Constantina, live in Cyprus. Stavros' second daughter Charis moved to Athens, Greece. She has a son named Stavros after his Grandfather and a daughter named Aliki. Stavros always wanted a son, but he thought that he was not blessed with one.

In August of 2018, just as we confirmed the identity of George Portoukalian's father, I received a message via Ancestry. "My name is Kevin and I just found out that we are first cousins. Did you have any uncles in London in 1956? I was adopted when I was 3 weeks old, but I don't know my blood relatives."

I responded to him but did not hear back until the beginning of October 2018, six weeks later. "Do you want to explore our relation or not?"

At the time I had just arrived in Cyprus for vacation. Kevin did not receive my first reply, so I answered again that I had no uncles in London in 1956, but my older brother Stavros was there. In all probability, he was my nephew! He wanted to know more about Stavros, so I told him I was going to be in Cyprus until the end of October and if he happened to come to Cyprus we could meet. I was amazed to see his next e-mail. He had planned to travel to Cyprus and stay with a friend, from Oct. 21-28, so we could meet on Oct. 27. I informed him that he had two sisters, and I was going to ask them if they wanted to meet him.

I called Stavros' daughter Maria: "Hi Maria, how are you?"

"OK Uncle George. Let me put it on speaker! I am in Athens with Charis and we were just getting ready to sit down for a coffee."

I asked: "Are you sitting down?"

Charis Jumped in: "Good or bad?"

I told them the story, and that there was a high probability that they have a brother they never knew, and that I was going to meet him on Oct. 27, at my Cyprus house by the sea. I asked them if they were interested in meeting him.

"You don't have to decide now. Have your coffee, think about it and when you make your mind up, you let me know." I suggested.

Charis' answer: "What coffee Uncle George? What coffee! After what you just told us, we need at least a double scotch!"

Kevin and his wife came to my house with their friends on Oct. 27, 2018 for the meeting. Maria had already joined Sharon and myself earlier. Charis was too busy, so she could not make it.

Maria had contacted Kevin before the meeting, and they talked on the phone. Her first question was; "Did you have a nice life?" to which Kevin responded "yes!"

We introduced ourselves and talked about Stavros, and our families. Kevin's appearance and mannerism were stunningly similar to those of my brother.

Kevin was wondering, why "Stavros did not want him!" I assured him that Stavros had no idea about his existence, and there was nothing that he wanted more than a son.

Maria gave him a lot of their father's pictures and the meeting turned out to be a joyous occasion. We finished the day with a rich, delicious meal at a fish tavern by the sea, near my house.

We kept in touch, as Kevin met with Maria and Charis in Athens a couple of more times since then. He also went to Cyprus and met his uncle Costas and cousins Christos, Evgenia and Christina, Dora's daughter. I received an email from Kevin recently, stating how happy he was that he found his beautiful family.

Irene's two daughters studied in the United States. Mary married John Cantonides whose roots are from the same area of Cyprus and settled in Maryland. They have two sons and a daughter. Cleo, the younger daughter married George Neophytou from Karavas and settled in Liverpool, U.K.. They have three daughters.

Irene, born on Jan. 28, 1937, developed Alzheimer's disease, and is in a chronic care facility in Cyprus.

Costas, born on Oct. 28, 1938, inherited the Steve's Super Store, which over time faltered, and closed down. He worked for Stavros for a while and then he opened his own logistics company with Stavros' help. With hard work, "Christoudias Logistics" became the biggest logistics entity in Cyprus with close to one hundred employees. He retired and passed the company to his son Christos and daughter Evgenia and the enterprise continues to flourish under their leadership.

Anastasia, born on Jan. 29, 1941, came to the United States after the Turkish invasion of Cyprus, with her husband Angelos and their two sons, Christos and Kyriakos. They live in New Milford, Bergen County, New Jersey.

John (Captain Trouble), born on Sept. 7, 1945, graduated with a doctorate in structural Engineering from Milan Polytechnic and started a land development company with Stavros. At the time of the Turkish invasion he was in England, and since the Cyprus airport was closed, he came to the United States and stayed with me. He passed a special test and was licensed as an engineer in the United States. He worked at a pipe support company for nuclear plants, and also did some successful building projects on the side. He retired at the age of 67 but was called back to work when his company got a contract to review the plans of a nuclear plant in the Far East, because there was a serious shortage of p eople with his expertise. In 2015 he suffered a stroke and had to work very hard to recover enough to gain sufficient function of his right extremities. He lives in Point Pleasant Beach with his wife Aphrodite. They also travel to their house in Cyprus for several months every winter, and spend some time with their daughter Tina, who settled there with her husband Spiros.

Their son Marios has a doctorate in computer science from MIT, and also lives in Point Pleasant Beach, with his wife Julia.

Theodora, the youngest of the family, was born on April 2, 1949. She had four children, Christina, Ioanna, Artemis and Nicolas.

She had a massive stroke from which she died a few days later, on March 3, 2015.

The four of us that are still alive and able, communicate often, and get together whenever we can. We talk about our kids and grandkids and go back in time, talk about our parents and relive our childhood and all the mischiefs we perpetrated! We enjoy talking about the good old times, as our generation is fading away.

Back to the Future

I enjoy talking about the old times and shedding the light on our memories, but what I enjoy immensely though, is the time I spend with my grandchildren, Georgos, Abigail, Maeve, Madeline and Teagan. It is wonderful to be able to spend time with them and spoil them as much as possible, something I was not able to do as much as I wanted to, with my own kids. Sometimes I take them or pick them up from school and other times I babysit them with Sharon at our house.

When I am with them I imagine them going through all the experiences that life has in store for them, so I turn the focus away from the past and try to shine the bright light on the future, their future. I ponder how they are going to push through all the storms, to reach a dry land and a sunny day. My purpose in life now is to instill in them our family values of honesty, integrity, hard work, love and care for our families and our fellow human beings, the values that I am so grateful I received from my own parents.

We see our children and grand children often, except for Christos who lives in California. I talk to Christos often though, so we are always in touch. During one of those conversations, a few months ago he asked me a question: "Do you have any regrets about your life?" "Not that I can think of" I replied. "But let me think about it, and I will let you know next time we talk". So I tried to think what, if anything, I might have done differently in my life. A couple of weeks later I called my son:

"Christos, after thinking about your question, I realized that there is something I do regret!"

"What is it?" he asked.

"I never told my parents, how much I love them while they were alive", and a tear ran down my cheeks!